Gardening with GUSTO

A Handbook & Cookbook for Canadian Gardeners

CARLOTTA HACKER

Doubleday Canada Limited

Canadian Cataloguing in Publication Data
Hacker, Carlotta, 1931–
　　Gardening with gusto

Includes Index.
ISBN 0-385-25409-1

1. Vegetable gardening.　2. Cookery (Vegetables).
I. Title.

SB323.H32　1993　635　C92-095313-1

Designed by Tania Craan
Illustrations by Maria Sanchez
Printed on ∞ acid-free paper
Printed and bound in the USA

Published in Canada by
Doubleday Canada Limited
105 Bond Street
Toronto, Ontario
M5B 1Y3

Contents

Acknowledgements

I wish to thank all friends and relations who have offered me recipes, and I am particularly grateful to my sister-in-law Jean for her perfect Pumpkin Pie and my sister-in-law June for her delicious Garlic Boursin.

I am grateful to Canadian Organic Growers for permitting me to reprint their recipes for dog and squirrel repellants. Above all, I wish to express my thanks to Maggie Reeves of Doubleday Canada Limited for her wonderful enthusiasm and many creative suggestions.

Introduction

There are said to be two things that money can't buy: love and homegrown tomatoes. You could add homegrown raspberries. Firm, juicy raspberries picked straight from your own berry bushes are a world away from the sad, mushy things normally found in the supermarkets. In any case, there's something rather magical about eating food you have grown yourself – wandering out into the garden on a hot summer's evening and plucking a few sprigs of parsley and thyme to flavour an omelette, or a handful of strawberries to decorate a dessert. Even a few tubs of herbs and tomatoes on an apartment balcony can give pleasure that is out of all proportion to the time and effort involved.

Vegetable gardening need not in fact take up much time. The trick is to begin small. Don't suddenly decide to be a farmer and plough up half your lot for vegetables. I have friends who have done this, and it has always been a disaster. They start off with grandiose plans, revelling in "at last having the space to grow all that we want," and before the first summer is over, the gardening is already a chore. They can't keep up with the weeding, let alone finding time to thin the carrots. I visit the same people a few years later, and they're not even growing lettuce. They have been turned off the whole idea of vegetable gardening.

So if you haven't grown vegetables before, start small, with just a few of your favourites and a selection of herbs. You can always add more as space and time permit. But even at the beginning you can be adventurous without adding to your workload. If you have a back deck or a wire fence, you can grow a trellis of runner beans, such as scarlet runners. They require no special care, and their prolific red flowers attract hummingbirds, which hover in the air beside them as they feed on the nectar. That this pretty vine also produces delicious beans seems almost super-fluous. Melons also can be grown on a deck, climbing up the steps or planted in a tub in a sunny corner; even on a tiny patio you can have the luxury of watching the fruit ripen and then treating your friends to a fruit salad piled high in melon halves.

The main purpose of growing fruit and vegetables is to eat them, but most gardening books don't take you on to that all-important stage. Every gardener welcomes ideas on different ways of serving the fresh produce, especially when there is a glut. Lettuces, for instance, have a way of coming into season all at once – and then going to seed before you can eat them. Some can be given to non-gardening neighbours, but what do you do with the rest? The answer is to make bolted-lettuce soup. It's remark-ably tasty, because bolted lettuce loses its bitterness when cooked. Zucchini also can be made into a wonderful soup. Both soups freeze well, as do soups made from leeks, carrots, and almost every other vegetable. Similarly, surplus fruit can be processed in various forms and then stored in the freezer. In this way, the fruit season can be made to last all year so that in the depths of winter you can enjoy the taste of fresh berries or juicy peach pies.

The aim of this book is thus to encourage non-gardeners to experiment with "grow your own" – a most satisfying hobby – and to share some of my favourite recipes with other home gar-deners. The gardening advice covers the main facts that the average backyard or balcony gardener will find useful, as well as offering numerous handy tips and a variety of background infor-mation. The approach is straightforward and practical, avoiding the type of scientific detail that is more likely to confuse than help. Gardening is not at all difficult and should not be made to seem so. You certainly don't need to become a specialist in order to get successful results. Even fruit trees are not as complicated to grow as many people think.

Simplicity was also a guiding factor in my choice of recipes: they had to be not only delicious, but comparatively easy. For this reason, I did not include jam making and pickling. Although both are excellent ways of preserving homegrown produce, they are specialized processes and there is no lack of books about them. It seemed more to the point to concentrate on recipes that are not so readily available, especially those that I have developed over the years in response to the output of my garden. To help those who don't do much cooking, I have included a section describing how to make a few basics, such as chicken stock and pastry, so that all the recipes can be followed easily, whatever one's expertise as a cook.

Although the recipes are primarily based on fruit and vegetables, it seemed worth including some of my favourite ways of using garden produce in meat dishes, as with Herbed Chicken Breasts – a particularly easy and tasty way of cooking chicken that relies on fresh herbs for its succulent flavour. Like most of the recipes, this dish has the advantage of being low-fat and low-cholesterol. However, when I feel that something really must have butter or cream, I add it, on the theory that if you keep a sensible diet most of the time, you can indulge occasionally for the sake of taste. For instance, you simply cannot make a good vichyssoise without using real cream, and the thicker it is, the better.

The gardening advice takes a similarly commonsense approach, trying to be as "organic" as possible, but not fanatically so. My general policy is to share the garden with the insects, using what preventive methods I can, but not worrying too much about the occasional beetle or caterpillar. Only if there is an infestation destroying the crop do I resort to spraying, and then only for perennials, such as strawberries, which can carry on the infestation to the following year. For the most part, homegrown produce should have the advantage of being as nature made it, full of goodness as well as flavour.

Both gardening and cooking are activities that should be enjoyed, not endured. As someone who loves to do both, I dedicate this book to fellow enthusiasts, hoping that it will increase their enjoyment, as well as serving as a helpful know-how guide on how to grow and cook a wide range of fruit and vegetables.

Asparagus

If I had so little space and time that I could grow only a few crops, one of them would be asparagus. This may seem perverse, but in fact asparagus requires very little attention and it can be accommodated in even the smallest lot. Friends of mine who live in a semi grow asparagus alongside their chain-link fence. Each spring the asparagus gives them a succulent crop, and each summer it grows into a thick hedge of feathery ferns which provides privacy from the neighbours. With limited space, it seems far more sensible to grow a luxury crop such as asparagus, rather than something less adventurous such as lettuce, which is likely to be cheap and plentiful in the stores just when your own lettuces also are at their peak.

Asparagus is not difficult to grow. The only important thing to know is that you must not cut down the ferns. Leave them untrimmed until the frost kills them in the fall, for they provide the nourishment that produces the next year's crop. Years ago, when I was a novice at gardening, we moved into a house that had a large and mature asparagus bush in the garden. Since it looked as if it was going to seed (which indeed it was) we decided to cut it back. We killed it. The following spring not one single asparagus spear poked up through the soil. Nothing at all. Fortunately, the experience did not put me off trying again.

If you have never grown asparagus, it's well worth a try. Establishing the bed may take you one or two days, but from then on there is virtually nothing to do, and you will be able to feast on the crop for a month or more each spring, year after year. An asparagus plant can live for twenty years or more, so a couple of day's work getting things started brings a pretty good return for one's labour.

 How to Grow
Planting

Asparagus can be grown in all provinces and in most types of soil. It does least well in heavy clay; a clay soil will need some topsoil and peat moss mixed into the bed.

For a single row of asparagus, dig a trench about 30 centimetres deep by 45 centimetres wide (12 inches x 18 inches). If you don't like digging, you can always hire a neighbour's teenager to do it, or hire someone through the gardening ads in your local newspaper. Flood the trench with water to make a muddy environment that the roots will take to quickly. After the water has sunk in, build small mounds in the trench about 30 centimetres (12 inches) apart. The mounds should be a rich mixture of well-rotted manure and topsoil, and you will need one mound for each asparagus crown. Water the mounds.

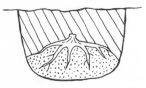

When planting asparagus, drape each crown over a mound of well-rotted manure and topsoil.

The asparagus crowns (roots) can be bought at local garden centres. They usually come in packets of eight. The crown looks rather like an octopus, with a central knob surrounded by tentacles. Place one on each mound, with the knob facing up, and gently spread out the roots (tentacles) around the mound. Since this is your best chance to give the bed a really thorough fertilizing, add more manure or compost and then fill up the trench with earth, making sure that all the crowns are at least 8 centimetres (3 inches) below the surface.

✏ Ongoing Care

The first year, a few very thin spears (stalks) will appear. Leave them alone. As they grow taller, they will branch and become

feathery ferns. During the year you may have to weed the bed occasionally and, of course, water it if the weather is dry, but there is nothing else to do except perhaps add a little manure in the fall.

The second year, cut away the dead ferns in early spring. (They can be cut any time after the frost has killed them, but I prefer to leave this job until spring because the ferns help hold the moisture in the bed over winter.) Weed the bed thoroughly so that once again it looks like virgin soil. Before long, the new spears will begin to poke up through the earth. There will be more of them this year, and some may be temptingly thick. You can harvest a few of these stalks, but you will get a better crop the following year if you hold off completely and don't cut any, leaving all the spears to grow into ferns that will build a strong and healthy plant.

The third year. . . . Ah, this is the year you've been waiting for! After you have cleared away last year's dead ferns and weeded the bed, you can start thinking about recipes, for you may be eating asparagus every day. Using a sharp knife, cut the spears just below the surface of the soil when they are about 20 centimetres (8 inches) high. You can continue to cut spears for a full month, though there's no harm in leaving the thinnest ones to grow to become ferns. After the month is up, let all the remaining shoots grow into ferns. By this stage, they should be numerous enough to form a bushy hedge a couple of metres high.

In the following years, you may be able to harvest for as long as six weeks, but make sure that you always stop in time to let a thick hedge grow. From now on, there is virtually no work to be done on the bed, except the occasional weeding and fertilizing. Manure or bone meal can be worked into the soil as a fertilizer during spring or fall, but be careful when doing so, since it is easy to tear the roots if you dig at all deeply.

Pests

Every asparagus bed inevitably attracts asparagus beetles. There are two types. Some beetles look rather like ladybirds – red with black spots – but are slightly more elongated and more orange in colour. The other type is blue-black with six yellow spots. Asparagus beetles are not very agile, and it is easy to pick them off with your fingers. One quick squeeze, and they're dead (wear rubber gloves if you don't want to get your hands messy). Alternatively, you can give them a squirt of insecticidal soap or other organic insecticide. Or you can just leave them be. They don't appear in any numbers until after the harvesting stage when the spears are feathering out into ferns, and I haven't noticed that they do the plants much harm.

Asparagus Recipes

The great advantage of growing your own asparagus is that you don't have to treat it as a luxury. Instead of being an expensive delicacy, it is just something that grows in the garden – and in great abundance during the season – so you can serve asparagus in lunchtime sandwiches or make asparagus soup, as well as experimenting with new recipes. All the same, you will probably want to enjoy the first cuttings the traditional way: plain with melted butter.

How to Prepare and Cook

Wash the stalks, scrubbing them gently with a soft brush to remove any particles of earth. Cut off the lower ends and set them aside to be boiled up later as part of a soup stock (page 7). The remaining stalks will be about 15 centimetres (6 inches) long.

The most common way of cooking asparagus is to tie the stalks together in bundles (about eight stalks per bundle), stand them upright in a double boiler, pour boiling water about halfway up the pan, and cover with the inverted top of the double boiler. Return the pan to the heat for 8 to 10 minutes so that the tips of the asparagus are steamed and the lower parts are boiled. Then remove the asparagus from the pan, cut off the string, and dry the stalks on paper towels, sprinkling lightly with salt.

I find this a rather messy and involved procedure, and it is not necessary with fresh-picked asparagus; the spears are so tender that they cook in a few minutes and are just as good boiled as steamed. After various experiments, I have found that the following recipe gives the best results. It is both quick and easy. What's more, you can see what you are doing, since no saucepan lid is needed.

QUICK BOILED ASPARAGUS

Bring to the boil a pan of chicken stock (just enough to cover the asparagus you are going to cook). If you have no stock, use a chicken cube or chicken powder and water. When the stock is at a rolling boil, lay the asparagus stalks in the pan according to size, the larger ones first. The larger will be cooked in 4 minutes; the smaller in 3 minutes. They will be firm and still slightly crunchy. Remove them from the pan and lay them on paper towels to drain. Serve immediately, pouring a little melted butter over each serving.

Keep the broth in which you have boiled the asparagus. It can be used for boiling up your next batch of asparagus and can also serve as the stock for asparagus soup (see below). However, if you are not planning to reboil the broth within the next day or two, store it in the freezer in the meantime.

ASPARAGUS VINAIGRETTE

It is all too easy to overindulge on high-fat dressings during the asparagus season, since most of the popular sauces and mayonnaises use butter, eggs, or sour cream. A delicious alternative, which is both low-cholesterol and low-fat, is an appetizer of asparagus vinaigrette. The vinaigrette should be a very light one so that it does not overwhelm the taste of the asparagus. My favourite is the one I devised for avocado pears. It is unusual in that it contains twice as much vinegar as oil, rather than the other way round.

2 Tbsp	white vinegar	30 mL
1 Tbsp	canola or corn oil	15 mL
½ tsp	Russian mustard	2 mL
	salt and pepper to taste	
18	asparagus stalks	18

Combine the first four ingredients, stirring with a fork. Cook the asparagus as described above and drain it on paper towels. Sprinkle lightly with salt if desired and place in the refrigerator in a bowl covered with plastic wrap. About 10 minutes before the meal, portion the asparagus into individual bowls, three or four stalks per person. Pour a little vinaigrette on each serving and return to the refrigerator until needed. *Makes 4 to 6 servings.*

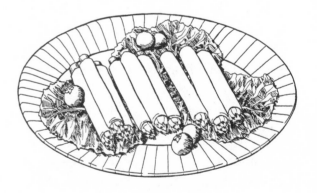

ASPARAGUS ROLLED SANDWICHES

I associate these scrumptious rolls with formal receptions and cocktail parties, but they also make excellent lunchtime sandwiches – all the more delightful because one doesn't expect such delicacies for an ordinary weekday lunch. They are particularly good made with freshly baked rye bread, but any type of bread can be used.

3	asparagus stalks (per person)	3
3	bread slices (per person)	3
	salt (optional)	
	margarine or butter	

Cook the asparagus as described for Quick Boiled Asparagus (page 6). Cool it and sprinkle with a little salt if desired. Cut the crusts off the bread and flatten each slice by rolling with a rolling pin. Spread each slice very thinly with margarine (or butter). Wrap each slice around an asparagus stalk, letting it overlap a little and cutting off any bread that is left over. The asparagus stalk should poke out slightly at each end of the roll. Cut each roll in half crosswise. Pack the rolls tightly in a dish, cover with plastic wrap to keep moist, and place in the refrigerator. *Makes 6 small rolls per person.*

CREAM OF ASPARAGUS SOUP

This soup is best made with homemade chicken stock (page 249) or with stock in which asparagus has been boiled, but you can also use stock made from chicken cubes or powdered chicken mix. Most recipes for asparagus soup tell you to use leftover pieces – the tougher, lower ends of the stalks – but this produces a mediocre soup that can easily be both tasteless and stringy. For a really savoury soup, use everything except the lower ends. They can be boiled up later as the base for your next batch of stock (boil them for

half an hour or more and then discard them, keeping only the liquid).

3 cups	chopped asparagus	750 mL
3 cups	chicken stock	750 mL
	(or chicken and	
	asparagus stock)	
1 Tbsp	butter	15 mL
2 Tbsp	flour	30 mL
2 cups	milk	500 mL
	whipping cream (optional)	

Boil the asparagus in the stock for 15 minutes. Strain, reserving the stock. Return the asparagus to the saucepan, together with the butter. Heat gently and stir in the flour. Then gradually add the milk and stock, stirring constantly. Boil gently over a medium heat for 5 minutes. Pour into a blender and blend for a few minutes until smooth. Return to the saucepan and reheat, adjusting the seasoning if necessary.

For a dinner party, add a dollop of whipped cream to each serving and sprinkle it with a garnish of chopped asparagus. You can use the very thin spears of asparagus for this garnish, boiling them for a couple of minutes in the stock when you start making the soup. *Makes 4 to 6 servings.*

ASPARAGUS VICHYSSOISE

This is my favourite of all cold soups – utterly delicious – yet I have never seen a recipe for it. I stumbled on it by chance when tasting a batch of asparagus soup to see if it needed any seasoning when being reheated for lunch. The soup tasted so good cold that I decided to serve it for dinner as a vichyssoise.

	Cream of Asparagus Soup (page 7)	
⅓ cup	whipping cream	83 mL
	a few thin asparagus spears for garnish	

Make the soup as described for Cream of Asparagus Soup (page 7). Cool it and place in the refrigerator. About half an hour before the meal, stir in the cream and adjust the seasoning, adding a little salt if necessary. This soup tastes best very cold, so it can be moved to the freezing compartment of the refrigerator about 15 minutes before serving. Ladle into cold bowls and decorate each serving with a garnish of chopped asparagus stalks, which have been cooked for no more than 3 minutes.

An asparagus vichyssoise makes a marvellous surprise dish to serve to guests on a scorching summer evening. You can make the basic soup during the asparagus season and store it in the freezer (page 250). On the morning of the dinner party, place the frozen block of soup in a saucepan with a little water and gently bring it to the boil, stirring constantly. Boil for a few minutes, cool, and then proceed as above. The garnish can be provided fresh from your asparagus bed. The plants continue to push up a few new shoots throughout the summer, and it does no harm to cut one or two occasionally. *Makes 4 to 6 servings.*

ASPARAGUS AND HAM AU GRATIN

Here is a quick and easy supper dish, which can be cooked and served in individual ramekins or in any other ovenproof dish.

24	asparagus stalks	24
4	cooked ham slices	4
1 Tbsp	grated parmesan cheese	15 mL
	SAUCE	
1 Tbsp	butter	15 mL
3 Tbsp	flour	45 mL
2 cups	milk	500 mL
	salt	
3 Tbsp	grated parmesan cheese	45 mL

Cook the asparagus as described for Quick Boiled Asparagus (page 6). Cut each slice of ham in half and roll it around three asparagus stalks. Tuck two of these rolls into each ramekin.

Combine the butter, flour, and milk to make a white sauce. (For instructions on making a white sauce, see page 248.) Season with salt, stir in the cheese, and continue to stir as the sauce comes to the boil. Let it cook gently for a few minutes and then pour it over the ham rolls. Sprinkle with grated cheese and place under the grill until brown and bubbling. *Makes 4 servings.*

 **Freezing**

Asparagus tends to be stringy when frozen. It freezes best in the form of soup.

Beans

Young green beans, when freshly picked, are one of the delights of summer. They have a crispness and flavour that you never find in bought beans. Even homegrown beans will lose their quality if they are allowed to lie around for any length of time before cooking. They are best picked within an hour of the meal and then kept in the refrigerator if they are not being cooked immediately. The ideal for the home gardener is to pick the beans while actually preparing the meal. Since tender young beans simply need their tops snipped off (and sometimes not even that), the picking, washing, and snipping takes only a few minutes and can easily be done at the last moment. Shell beans do not need such careful treatment, though they too are best eaten soon after picking.

Since most supermarkets and garden stores sell only a few popular varieties of bean, it is best to order your packets by mail from a seed catalogue company (pages 238–39). You will then be able to take your pick of bush beans, pole beans, snap beans, yellow wax beans, red kidney beans, limas, broad beans, and many other varieties. All varieties are planted the same way, with the eye facing downward, since the root will emerge from the eye. All except broad beans are "tender plants" and should be planted after all danger of frost is past. Broad beans, being more

How to Grow
Planting

hardy, can be planted early in spring, as soon as the ground can be worked.

To plant the beans, mix some peat moss and well-rotted manure into the soil, pat the earth flat, and then push in the beans with your finger, spacing them about 5 centimetres apart and 2.5 centimetres deep (2 inches by 1 inch). Cover with earth and give the row a light watering. With the exception of broad beans, it is best to do the planting after warm weather has set in. Most beans need warm soil temperatures for germination, and they may rot rather than germinating if they are allowed to lie in cold, wet earth.

Pole Beans and Runners

These climbing beans need a support which they can wind around as they grow. It can be the railings of a deck, or netting hung over a fence, or strings hung taut from a horizontal wire – anything that will allow them to climb. A popular trick is to make a tripod of poles, planting a number of seeds round the base of each. Fixed firmly in the ground, the poles are tied together at the top to form a tepee-like structure, which is pleasantly attractive when covered in bean vines.

Pole beans can be grown up a tripod of wooden stakes.

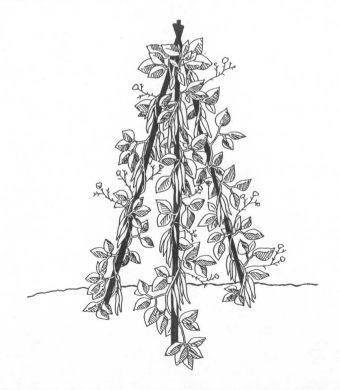

Most pole beans can stand a lot of heat and do well in full sun, but scarlet runners prefer cooler conditions with some shade for their feet. They do admirably when planted just under the overhang of a deck, or any place where the roots are in moist shady earth while the leaves get plenty of sunlight. These vigorous climbers remind me of Jack and the Beanstalk, because once they start growing, it seems they will go on forever. As long as you keep picking the beans, the plants will go on sending out more tendrils, which in turn produce more flowers whose pods will grow to become beans. The flowers are a delight in themselves – a glory of red blossoms which attract quick-darting hummingbirds and pollen-laden bumblebees.

If the weather turns very hot and dry, the flowers sometimes wither and drop off without producing beans. If you notice this happening, spray the flowers with a little water each evening. If the beans are not growing with much vigour or if they pause in their production, this may mean that they need more fertilizer, in which case it is easy to add some around the roots.

Bush Beans

To get a crop of bush beans all summer long, you will need to make several plantings at intervals of two or three weeks, since these beans do not continue to produce to the extent that climbers do. Most varieties will grow into a bush about 30 centimetres (12 inches) wide. Although the beans can be planted within 5 to 8 centimetres (2 to 3 inches) of each other, a reasonable space should be allowed between the rows.

Broad Beans

I find that broad beans grow best when planted in a clump, preferably with something to lean against and be tied to – for instance, wire netting or a chain-link fence. Plant the beans about 5 centimetres (2 inches) apart in a clump about 30 centimetres (12 inches) wide and as long as you like. As the beans grow, encircle groups of them with string and tie firmly to the netting. Without such support, broad beans are too easily blown over by the wind and do not produce well. They will also not produce in hot, dry conditions. On scorching summer evenings, it is particularly important to spray the flowers with water so that they do not wither and drop off. Otherwise, despite plenty of flowers, you may get no bean pods until the weather turns cool in the fall.

 Pests

Some years, you may get aphids on your broad beans, but they can easily be controlled with organic insecticides. Slugs, cutworms, and snails can be a more serious threat, especially to young climbing beans and bush beans; they can kill the young plants by eating the leaves and even the stalks.

One way to avoid this problem is to start the beans indoors and transfer them to the garden when they are about 20 centimetres (8 inches) high and fairly sturdy. This has the double benefit of allowing you to get an early start on the season, since the beans will thrive in a sunny window long before it is warm enough to plant them outside. Grow the beans in flowerpots or flats and transplant them into the garden on a cloudy day, disturbing their roots as little as possible. Dig a small hole for each bean plant, fill it with water to make a mud puddle, and then gently press in the plant, together with a pea stick for it to lean against.

The most effective direct action against slugs is to hunt for them in the dawn, catching them on the underside of the leaves and then squashing them. Although this is an unpleasant way to begin a summer's day, it is by far the most effective way of keeping down the slug population, and it is preferable to laying down slug bait, which can poison birds and other creatures too. Even the biodegradable slug powders that are harmless to birds and animals are fairly indiscriminate. You don't know what insects you may be killing along with the slugs.

The "folk" method for protecting beans from slugs is to plant the beans in a nest of horsehair, which is said to spike the slugs and kill them. A more effective modern method is to tie some tinfoil around the stalks as soon as the first leaves open. Slugs and snails are only a threat to beans when the plants are young. Climbing beans, especially, grow very tough stalks once they get going – far too tough for any slug to chew through. And at this stage, they don't suffer if a few slugs eat some of their lower leaves.

Bean Recipes

Green beans picked young and tender can taste just as good as peas, and this is the great advantage of growing your own – that you can get them far younger than any sold in the stores. Snap beans are at their best when thinner than a pencil and about 10 centimetres (4 inches) long. Scarlet runners, which are flatter in shape, can be picked small too, but they are also excellent almost fully grown, provided they have not yet filled out and become coarse. When the beans are so young, they are marvellously tender and therefore need very little cooking. They are also good raw, tossed in a vinaigrette salad.

How to Prepare and Cook

If the beans are very small, they will need only the top trimmed off. Drop them into boiling unsalted water and cook for no more than 4 minutes. For perfection, they should still be crunchy and only just cooked. Drain immediately and season with salt or lemon juice. Larger beans will need to be cut in two or three lengths and will take a little longer to boil. Sample one after 5 minutes to judge whether they are cooked.

Runner beans that have grown to 18 centimetres (7 inches) or more should be topped and tailed and then sliced diagonally. If they have grown coarse, they will need stringing, in which case use a sharp knife to cut a thin slice off each edge. Cook in unsalted water for 10 minutes, drain immediately, sprinkle with salt, and toss in butter.

Shell beans taste best when boiled in salted water, and they generally require a longer cooking time. They should, of course, be shelled before cooking. Although fresh young broad beans can be boiled for as little as 4 minutes, older and tougher ones may need as much as 20 minutes. Similarly, kidney beans may take between 25 minutes and an hour if they have grown to full size and then dried out a bit in their pods. If dried hard, soak them in water for 2 hours and then boil for about 1½ to 2 hours.

Shell beans go well in a wide variety of dishes, but green beans taste so good on their own that it seems a shame to serve them with a sauce or to incorporate them in any recipe that causes them to be over-cooked. If they are to be added to a stew or hotpot, drop them in during the last few minutes of cooking. In soups, too, they should be cooked very briefly.

SUMMER GARDEN CONSOMMÉ

This light and tasty soup is one of my favourite ways of eating green beans, and it takes only about 10 minutes to prepare (this includes picking, washing, cooking, and serving). The base for the soup is a chicken stock, but in this case it does not need to be homemade. It can be an "instant stock" of chicken powder and water, with perhaps a tablespoon of white wine. You can use any combination of garden vegetables and herbs (for instance, green beans, cherry tomatoes, and chopped basil and parsley), but the selection given below creates a particularly flavourful blend of tastes.

5 cups	chicken stock	1.25 L
6	thyme sprigs	6
	celery, leaves of one young stalk	
8	young green beans	8
8	snow peas	8

The trick in making this soup quickly is to prepare the vegetables at the same time as the stock is boiling. Wash the vegetables while the stock is coming to a boil. Then strip the thyme leaves from their stalks and add them to the stock. Then chop and add the celery leaves. Next, top and tail the beans, cut into bite-sized pieces, and drop them into the stock. Boil for 4 minutes. Finally, trim and add the snow peas. Turn off the heat immediately and ladle into soup bowls. *Makes 4 servings.*

KIDNEY BEAN SALAD

This is a substantial salad that is particularly good when made with fresh kidney beans.

3 cups	kidney beans	750 mL
½ cup	chopped sweet red pepper	125 mL
¼ cup	chopped green onion	62 mL
2 Tbsp	canola or corn oil	30 mL
1 Tbsp	wine vinegar	15 mL
	salt and black pepper	

Boil the beans in salted water or chicken stock until soft. Drain, cool, and combine with the chopped pepper and onion. Mix together the oil and the vinegar. Season with salt and whisk briskly with a fork. Just before serving, toss this dressing into the bean mixture and add a little freshly ground black pepper. *Makes 4 servings.*

BROAD BEANS AND CHICKEN IN PARSLEY SAUCE

Broad beans and parsley sauce seem made for each other. Add some pieces of cooked chicken and serve in a circle of mashed potatoes, and you can transform "chicken leftovers" into an attractive and very appetizing supper dish. Note that this recipe needs two different types of pepper: white for the mashed potatoes and black pepper for the sauce.

2 cups	broad beans, shelled	500 mL
4.4 lbs	about 8 large potatoes	2 kg
2 Tbsp	butter	30 mL
3 Tbsp	flour	45 mL
2 cups	milk	500 mL
	salt and pepper	
2 Tbsp	chopped parsley (about four sprigs)	30 mL
2 cups	cooked chicken	500 mL

Drop the broad beans into boiling salted water, the largest ones first, and cook for no more than 4 minutes. Drain. If the skins of the largest beans are leathery, remove them, keeping only the bright green inner bean. Most beans, however, will be tender enough skin and all.

Peel and boil the potatoes until soft, then drain and mash, adding salt and white pepper to taste. Arrange in a ring in four individual ovenproof serving dishes and place in a preheated 300°F/150°C oven.

Melt the butter in a saucepan and gradually add the flour and milk to make a white sauce (page 248). Season to taste with salt and black pepper. Add the chopped parsley, then the chicken pieces and broad beans. Simmer the sauce gently until heated through. Spoon into the four individual dishes and serve immediately. *Makes 4 servings.*

Storing and Freezing

Green beans, broad beans, and limas all keep their quality very well when frozen. Prepare them as usual, then blanch by dropping them into boiling water. Young green beans can be blanched for only 1 minute. Older green beans, broad beans, and limas will need 2 to 3 minutes. As soon as the time limit is up, cool quickly under running cold water, drain thoroughly, and pack into freezer bags, sucking out the air with a straw. To serve after freezing, remove from the bag and tip into boiling water. Green beans will be cooked in 2 or 3 minutes. Broad beans and limas should be boiled until soft. Like other frozen vegetables, beans will keep for at least a year.

All shell beans can be stored as dried beans. This form of storage is especially suitable for kidney beans and white beans. Let them grow to full size and leave them on the plant until their pods dry out. Then shell them and lay them in the sun to complete the drying process. Store in airtight containers. To serve after drying, soak in water for at least 2 hours, then rinse thoroughly and boil for an hour or more until soft.

Beets

Beets are one of the easiest vegetables to grow. Once they get going, they require virtually no attention. They will even do well surrounded by weeds. Apart from thinning the plants in spring and of course watering them in dry weather, you can forget about them all summer and still pick a magnificent crop of large deep-red beets in the fall.

How to Grow
Planting

Beets do best in a light and rich soil, but the bed should be fertilized the previous fall. If you add fresh manure the year you sow the beets, you risk getting coarse knobbly roots rather than smooth round ones.

Beets can be sown as soon as the ground can be worked in spring. First, dig over the bed, adding black earth and peat moss if the soil seems solid and heavy. Sow the seeds in a row, scattering them by hand and then tamping them down with a trowel so that they won't blow away. Cover with a dusting of light earth and moisten with a sprinkling of water.

Nothing will show for at least a week, but soon after that you can start looking for the first tiny shoots. Keeping the bed damp by watering lightly each evening will help the seeds to germinate.

Ongoing Care

When the seedlings have grown about as high as your thumb, they will need to be thinned. Simply pull up those that are clumped together so that the remaining seedlings have room to grow into full-sized beets. If, like me, you hate to let anything die once it has begun living, you can replant the pulled seedlings.

Water the earth on either side of your row and stir it around to make a sludge of mud. Then, wearing rubber gloves, poke your finger into the sludge at intervals of about 5 centimetres (2 inches) and drop the root of a seedling into each hole. Gently squeeze the holes shut so that the leaves stand up firmly. For the next few days, the transplanted seedlings will probably look very sad, lying flat on the soil as if they are dying, but if you keep them watered they will eventually perk up and grow to become excellent beets. By this method, rather than having a single row of beets, you will have a wide band of them, and you won't be wasting any of the seeds you have sown.

For the rest of the summer, there is nothing much to do except keep the beets watered. Once they are established, they can tolerate weeds nearby without ill effect, provided the weeds are not deep-rooted ones like dandelions. There is no need to harvest the beets until after the first frost, though you can thin the beds a little throughout the summer by pulling up half-grown beets. These tender young beets are delicious lightly boiled.

Pests

As a rule, insects are not a problem with beets, but rabbits and groundhogs can be a nuisance. They like to eat the leaves, and when they chew them right down, they can kill the plant. One form of protection is to place netting over or around the beets. Better still, sprinkle the bed with a light dusting of blood meal. The smell of the blood meal frightens the animals away. (See also the organic, kitchen-made rodent repellant, page 237.)

Beet Recipes

Beets are very versatile vegetables. They can be served hot or cold, cooked or raw, plain or pickled, and the leaves can be eaten as well as the root. The leaves are cooked like spinach and taste much the same, except that they are stronger. I like them best wilted in a saucepan and then drained, chopped, and mixed with nutmeg, salt, and a little butter.

How to Prepare and Cook

Dig up the beets carefully in order to avoid spiking them. Run them under the hose and then twist off the stalks about 5 centimetres (2 inches) above the roots. Do not *cut* off the stalks or the beets will "bleed" and lose their colour during cooking. Any cuts in the roots will also cause bleeding, so when washing the beets in the sink, be careful to scrub them gently and do not cut off the long, thin end of the root.

Boil the beets in salted water, varying the time according to size. Very young small beets need no more than half an hour. Large old ones may need as much as two hours. For an average-sized beet, about an hour is generally right. When the beets are cooked, plunge them into cold water. Drain them and then rub off the skins with your hands.

TO SERVE THE COOKED BEETS HOT, slice them and lay them in an oven-proof dish covered with tinfoil. Place the dish in a preheated 300°F/150°C oven for 15 minutes. To serve, remove the tinfoil, spread with butter (optional), and sprinkle with parsley; or pour a white sauce (page 248) over the beets and sprinkle with parsley.

TO SERVE THE COOKED BEETS COLD, chop them into cubes and cover with a vinegar syrup made by combining two parts of vinegar and two parts of sugar with one part of water, and boiling for a few minutes. There should be enough syrup to cover the beets entirely. If stored in the refrigerator in a plastic or glass container with a lid that is not metal, they will keep safely for at least two weeks. (The type of coated metal used for the lids of pickle jars is all right, but uncoated metal may become corroded by the vinegar.) In winter, when tomatoes tend to be tasteless and expensive, these vinegared beets make an attractive substitute in green salads, adding a splash of colour as well as a spicy tang.

BEET SOUP

Borscht is a favourite soup in many Canadian homes, cooked according to traditions handed down by parents and grandparents. The following recipe makes no attempt to be traditional – it is the result of my own experiments – but it is particularly easy to make and has a rich, full-bodied flavour. This soup is especially good when based on homemade chicken stock (page 249) rather than an "instant stock" of chicken cubes and water.

1	potato	1
1	onion	1
1¼ lbs	about 4 beets	600 g
4 cups	chicken stock	1 L
10	basil leaves, large	10
	(or dried basil, 1 tsp/5 mL)	
2 cups	milk	500 mL
	chopped parsley and	
	basil for garnish	

Peel and chop the potato, onion, and three of the beets. Boil them in the stock for 30 minutes, together with the chopped basil leaves. Meanwhile, in a separate saucepan, boil the fourth beet, unpeeled, in unsalted water.

At the end of 30 minutes, while the unpeeled beet continues to boil, add the milk to the saucepan containing the stock. Bring this mixture back to the boil, simmer for 5 minutes, blend in a blender, and return to the saucepan. Place the unpeeled beet in cold water and slip off its skin. Chop it into bite-sized pieces, and add it to the soup. Add pepper and salt if necessary and serve with a garnish of chopped parsley and basil. Like all beet soups, this is excellent with a spoonful of yogurt or sour cream added to each serving. *Makes 4 to 6 servings.*

RAW BEET SALAD

This attractive-looking salad has the advantage of being both tasty and quick to prepare. It is quite piquant and therefore is best served in small individual dishes or as one of several salads accompanying a main course.

1 lb	about 3 beets	450 g
1 Tbsp	lemon juice	15 mL
1 Tbsp	wine vinegar	15 mL
1 Tbsp	canola or corn oil	15 mL
1 tsp	honey or maple syrup	5 mL
	salt and pepper	

Peel and grate the beets. In a small bowl, mix the remaining ingredients, whisking them briskly with a fork. Stir this dressing into the beets. Place the salad in a covered bowl in the refrigerator, leaving it to marinate for at least 15 minutes before serving. Give the beets a final toss and spoon them into individual dishes. *Makes 4 servings.*

BEETS IN SOUR CREAM

Sour cream is not for people who are watching their diet, but it is remarkably good with beets. Yogurt or cottage cheese can be used as substitutes in this recipe, but neither produces the same rich taste.

1¼ lbs	about 4 beets	600 g
4 Tbsp	sour cream	60 mL
	salt and pepper	
1 Tbsp	chopped chives	15 mL

Boil, peel, and slice the beets. Place the beets and sour cream in a saucepan and heat thoroughly – but be careful not to let the mixture boil or the cream will curdle. Add salt and pepper to taste, and sprinkle with the chives. *Makes 4 servings.*

 Storing and Freezing

If you have grown more beets than you can either eat or pickle, you can store them raw or freeze them cooked. For storage, wash and dry the beets, twist off their stalks, and pack them in boxes of peat moss or sawdust. The perfect storage temperature is 32°F /0°C, so they can be stored in a garage in the milder parts of Canada but will need a cool cellar in the prairies and other regions that have severe winters. An alternative is to keep them in the bottom drawer of a refrigerator, packed in plastic bags with air holes punched in them.

For freezing, cook and peel the beets and then package them in airtight plastic bags, sucking out the air with a straw. To serve after freezing, thaw, remove from the bag, slice, and place in a buttered baking dish. Cover and heat in a 300°F/150°C oven until piping hot. The beets can also be eaten cold in a salad, in which case they should be eaten the same day they are thawed; any leftovers should be discarded.

Belgian Endive Chicory

I f you like Belgian endive, you should certainly try growing some. You then won't have to treat it as a luxury because of its high price. By growing your own, you can add it to salads all winter long – and also experiment with ways of cooking it. Packets of seed may be hard to find, but they can be ordered by mail from a gardening catalogue company such as Dominion Seed House. The endive will probably be listed as Root Chicory or Witloof Chicory, for it goes under two names – both chicory and endive.

How to Grow
Planting

You can sow the seed in an out-of-the-way part of the garden because you won't be picking the endive during the summer. Even a shady spot will do. The plant's role right through until frost is simply to grow strong roots.

Dig over the earth, rake it smooth, lightly water the surface, and scatter the seed sparingly. Cover with about 1 centimetre (⅓ inch) of soil, pressed down firmly.

Ongoing Care

When the green shoots push up through the soil, thin them to about 5 centimetres (2 inches) apart. Besides keeping the bed watered and seeing that it does not get choked with weeds, there is nothing else to do until the fall. Meanwhile, do not expect the plants to look like the tightly packed bullet-shaped heads of endive sold in the stores; at this stage of growth, they look more like lettuce than endive.

Before the first frost, dig up the plants, cut off their leaves, and wash the roots thoroughly under the hose. Take about a dozen of the roots and plant them upright, close together, in two large flowerpots filled with light soil, such as sterile potting soil mixed with vermiculite. Stand the pots in a tray of water, and store them in a dark, cool place, for instance, an unheated basement room, where the temperature is between 8° and 15°C (45° to

By transplanting the roots into flowerpots, you can enjoy fresh Belgian endive during the winter. Keep the plants in a dark place, such as a back basement.

60°F). The roots will soon begin to push up tightly packed shoots, which will be ready to cut for the table when they are about 12 centimetres (5 inches) high. If the shoots look too green, it means that they are getting too much light. Cover them with a large box, which will shut out all light.

The remainder of the roots – those you did not plant in flowerpots – can be stored in boxes of sawdust, sand, or peat moss in a frost-free garage or cool cellar. If you take out a handful every couple of weeks and plant them upright in flowerpots, you can have continuing crops of endive right through until spring.

Pests

The first time I tried this outdoor-indoor gardening trick, I got myself a basement full of aphids. But I made two silly mistakes: I used soil from the garden, and I left some greenery at the top of each root. I don't know whether the aphids came in with the foliage or the soil, but they reproduced phenomenally once they were indoors, and it required persistent efforts with organic vegetable spray before the basement was at last rid of the creatures. Ours must have been the only house in Saskatchewan that was plagued with aphids in December.

Since then, I have been careful to use only sterile soil and to cut off the foliage close to the crown. I then wash the crown under a fierce jet of water strong enough to blast away any aphid eggs. The results have been most successful, and we now enjoy salad greens straight from the basement in midwinter.

Belgian Endive Recipes

The slightly bitter taste of endive adds a delicious bite to salads, and it also makes a good salad on its own, tossed in a vinaigrette flavoured with lemon or lime juice. Cooked endive can be equally good, especially when braised in lemon juice and butter. It is said to be an acquired taste, but most people seem to acquire it the first time they try it.

How to Prepare and Cook

Endive turns brown quickly where it is cut, so you should prepare it immediately before adding it to a saucepan or salad. Being tightly packed, it does not usually require much washing. Simply rinse the heads of endive under a tap, trim the base, and tear off any outer leaves that are discoloured or wilted.

To cook the endive, place a pat of butter in a saucepan, add a pinch of salt, about a cup of water, and the juice of half a lemon. Cover the saucepan, bring to the boil, and simmer gently for 45 minutes. Endive braised in this manner can be served plain in its juices or combined with a sauce, such as a cheese sauce. Endive can also be braised in chicken stock, but I find it less tasty that way.

ENDIVE AND WATERCRESS SALAD

A salad with endive in it usually benefits from having freshly squeezed lime or lemon juice in the dressing. I like to add a sweet mustard such as Russian mustard, since this prevents the salad becoming too tart. This dressing works particularly well in a watercress and endive salad – an unusual combination, but one that is both flavourful and attractive with its contrasting shades of green.

1 Tbsp	vinegar	15 mL
1 Tbsp	canola or corn oil	15 mL
1 tsp	Russian mustard	5 mL
1 Tbsp	lime juice	15 mL
	salt	
7 oz	1 bunch watercress	200 g
4	Belgian endive	4

Make the vinaigrette by combining the vinegar, oil, Russian mustard, and freshly squeezed lime juice, whisking briskly with a fork. Add salt to taste. Wash the watercress and place in a salad bowl. Just before serving, wash and trim the endive, slice it crosswise, and add it to the salad bowl. Add the vinaigrette and toss lightly. *Makes 4 servings.*

BELGIAN ENDIVE IN CHEESE SAUCE

The French (and probably the Belgians too) serve endive in various types of sauce, but I find this simple cheese sauce as savoury as any.

	ENDIVE	
8	Belgian endive	8
2 Tbsp	butter	30 mL
¼ cup	freshly squeezed lemon juice	62 mL
	salt	
	SAUCE	
1 Tbsp	butter	15 mL
½ cup	endive liquid	125 mL
3 Tbsp	flour	45 mL
1½ cups	milk	375 mL
2–3 Tbsp	grated parmesan cheese	30–45 mL
	salt and pepper	

Wash and trim the endive and place it in a large saucepan together with 2 tablespoons (30 mL) of butter, 1 cup (250 mL) of water, ¼ cup (62 mL) of lemon juice, and a pinch of salt. Cover and simmer gently for 45 minutes. Drain, keeping the liquid. Place the endive in an ovenproof serving dish.

To make the sauce, melt 1 tablespoon (15 mL) of butter in a saucepan and gradually add ½ cup of the endive liquid, together with the flour and milk (see White Sauce, page 248). When smooth, season with salt and pepper, and add the grated cheese. Simmer for a few minutes before pouring the sauce over the endive. Top with a little grated parmesan and place under a hot grill until brown and bubbling. *Makes 4 servings.*

This dish can also be served with ham to make a light lunch or supper. Simply place chunks of cooked ham alongside the endive, or wrap each head of endive in a thin slice of ham, before adding the sauce. Then place quickly under the grill as described above.

 **Storing**

Endive does not freeze well. To eat it during winter, follow the procedure described above.

Broccoli

Broccoli takes up a good deal of room, so it is not ideal for a small garden – unless, of course, it is one of your favourites, in which case it will take precedence over other vegetables. Broccoli is not usually much trouble to grow, but, to be on the safe side, you should plant it where no fellow *brassica* crop grew the previous year. *Brassica* is the name of the cabbage family of vegetables, such as Brussels sprouts, cauliflower, kale, and, of course, cabbage. All are subject to a host of insects and diseases that can lurk in the soil and infect the next year's crop. But don't let this put you off growing broccoli. It is not likely that your plants will be struck by all possible enemies, and you may have no problems at all.

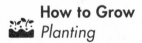
How to Grow
Planting

Broccoli does best in a rich, fertile soil that will not dry out easily. It can be sown directly in the garden, or started indoors in peat pots in March or April, but the easiest way is to buy it as seedlings. Set out the plants after all danger of frost is past. First, dig shallow holes about 45 centimetres (18 inches) apart. Mix a handful of well-rotted manure into each hole, add water to make a mud puddle, let it soak in, and then add the broccoli seedling, pressing down the earth around it.

If you want a fall crop, you can sow one or two broccoli seeds between the plants. Simply press the seed firmly on the soil and add a light sprinkling of earth. On the West Coast and other very

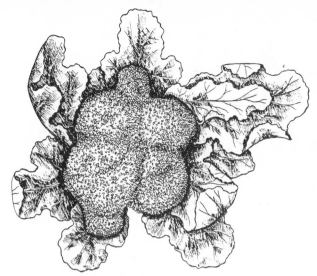

mild regions, it is also possible to grow winter broccoli, sowing in fall for harvesting in spring.

Ongoing Care

There is nothing much to do to broccoli except keep the plants well watered. You will not get a good crop if the soil dries out. Also, watch for signs of insects and pick off any caterpillars you see.

Broccoli is ready for cutting when it forms a head, which is a cluster of tiny buds. The head should be cut before the buds open and flower. The first head will appear in the centre of the plant. After it has been cut out, smaller heads will start to form in other parts of the stem. If you keep cutting the heads as they form and don't let them flower, you will get several crops of broccoli from one plant.

Pests

The list of creatures that might attack your broccoli includes cutworms, cabbage worms, maggots, aphids, slugs, snails, and various other crawlers. You can guard against cutworms by wrapping a collar of tinfoil or tarpaper around the stem to prevent the worm crawling up it. This also deters slugs. A deterrent against many of the others is to sprinkle the broccoli lightly with salt early in the morning. If this fails, there are various organic sprays and dusts that will usually keep the pests at bay, and it should not be necessary to resort to anything stronger. A summer crop is more likely to be infested than one that matures late in the year. Because of the cooler weather, fall broccoli is often nice and clean.

Broccoli Recipes

Broccoli suffers from the reputation of being "good for you" and is therefore expected to taste horrible. Yet it can be a delicacy when treated right – which simply means not overcooking it. When broccoli is cooked for too long, it gets mushy and develops a slightly stale taste, which is accentuated when combined with incompatible flavours. Broccoli is not one of those vegetables that can be mixed with anything and still taste good. It is best when limited to the flavours that really suit it, such as cheese or nutmeg. With such accompaniments, it can be delicious.

How to Prepare and Cook

Dip the broccoli in a pail of salted water to free it of any insects or grubs that may be lurking among the tightly packed buds. Then cut off the tough lower stalk, remove the leaves, and divide the head into sprigs. Wash the sprigs thoroughly in the sink, together with the more tender stalks.

One of the nicest ways to eat broccoli is plain, cooked briefly in unsalted water. It is surprisingly tasty like this. Cut the stalks into bite-sized pieces, place them in a small saucepan, and add water just to cover. Stand up the "trees" between the pieces of stalk so that their greenery is above water level. Place a lid on the pan, and cook over a high heat for no more than 5 minutes – just enough to steam the tops to a deep green and to boil the stalks tender. Drain, dry on paper towels, and sprinkle with salt. Serve immediately.

BROCCOLI WITH NUTMEG

A pleasant accompaniment to roast beef, this version of steamed broccoli makes excellent dinner-party fare. It can be cooked in advance and reheated in butter at the last minute.

2.2 lbs	broccoli	1 kg
	salt	
1 Tbsp	butter	15 mL
	grated nutmeg	

Cook the broccoli in a covered pan for 5 minutes, steaming the tops and boiling the stalks as described above. Drain, sprinkle with salt, and leave to dry on paper towels. Just before serving, melt the butter in a saucepan, add the broccoli and a sprinkling of nutmeg, and toss gently while heating. One or two minutes should be enough to heat the broccoli through. Do not overcook. *Makes 4 servings.*

BROCCOLI AND EGG SALAD

Broccoli can be eaten raw as a crudité with a dip, and it is also good almost raw, served as a salad with a garlic vinaigrette. This broccoli and egg salad makes a nourishing and easy supper dish that goes well with cold ham and wholemeal bread.

3	eggs	3
1½ lbs	broccoli	680 g
1	small garlic clove	1
1 tsp	chopped raw onion (optional)	5 mL
2 Tbsp	canola or corn oil	30 mL
1 Tbsp	wine vinegar	15 mL
	salt and pepper	

Place the eggs in a pan of cold water, bring to the boil, and cook for 10 minutes. Then plunge the eggs into cold water, leaving them there for 5 minutes. This makes them easy to peel. Meanwhile, divide the broccoli into spears and cook in boiling salted water for no more than 2 minutes. Drain, dry on paper towels, and leave to cool.

Peel and mince the garlic, and place it in a bowl together with the chopped onion and the oil and vinegar. Add about 10 shakes of salt and some freshly ground black pepper. Whisk briskly with a fork.

Shell and slice the eggs and arrange them in a serving dish with the broccoli. Just before eating, give the vinaigrette a final whisk and add it to the salad, mixing it in thoroughly with a spoon and fork. *Makes 4 servings.*

BROCCOLI QUICHE

This quiche is particularly good when served with baked tomatoes, which can be cooked at the same time. To bake the tomatoes, cut them in half, place them cut-side up in an ovenproof dish, and sprinkle with salt and pepper. If desired, add butter. Place in the oven 20 minutes after the quiche has gone in.

PASTRY

½ lb	flour	225 g
¼ lb	fat	112 g
½ tsp	salt	2 mL
⅓ cup	water	83 mL

FILLING

½ lb	broccoli	225 g
2	eggs	2
1 cup	milk	250 mL
½ cup	grated parmesan cheese	125 mL
	salt	
1 tsp	butter	5 mL
2 Tbsp	chopped almonds	30 mL

Combine the first four ingredients to make the pastry (page 251) and roll it out to line a 23-centimetre (9-inch) pie dish (or take the labour-saving route and thaw a ready-made pie shell). Bake the pastry shell in a preheated 425°F/220°C oven for 10 to 12 minutes. While it is cooking, divide the broccoli into sprigs and cut the more tender pieces of stalk into bite-sized chunks. Cook both sprigs and stalks in boiling salted water for 3 minutes, drain, and dry on paper towels.

When the pie shell is cooked, lay the broccoli in it, arranging the "trees" around the outside and the chopped stalks in the centre. Break the eggs into a bowl, whisk with a fork, and continue to whisk as you add the milk and grated cheese. Season with salt to taste, pour the mixture over the broccoli, and bake in a preheated 350°F/180°C oven for about 40 minutes. When cooked, the quiche will be puffed up and lightly brown on top, and a knife slipped into the centre will come out clean.

Just before serving, melt the butter in a skillet, add the chopped almonds and a sprinkle of salt, sauté quickly, and scatter the almonds over the quiche. *Makes 4 servings.*

 Freezing

Frozen broccoli keeps its colour beautifully but inevitably becomes rather flabby. It will last up to a year at 0°F/–18°C. To freeze, divide the broccoli into sprigs and blanch in boiling water for 2 minutes. Drain, cool, and pack in plastic bags, sucking out the air with a straw. To serve after freezing, thaw the frozen broccoli in a saucepan with a little butter, turning gently until it is piping hot. This produces better results than cooking the frozen broccoli in boiling water.

Brussels Sprouts

L ike all green-leaf vegetables, Brussels sprouts are very nutritious, and they can be fun to grow. They like a cool climate and plenty of water, but hybrids have been developed that can withstand the heat of Canadian summers.

Your best course is to buy the sprouts as bedding plants. Brussels sprouts need a long growing season, so it is only worth raising them from seed if you have the facilities to start them indoors in March.

The sprouts should be planted in the garden in mid- to late May. They will do best in a bed that gets shade for half the day and one where no fellow *brassica* crops grew the previous year (this includes broccoli, cauliflower, and other members of the cabbage family). Dig over the bed, add plenty of manure, water well, and then press in the seedlings, setting them about 45 centimetres (18 inches) apart.

How to Grow
Planting

To keep the soil cool, water regularly. You can also add a mulch by surrounding the roots with some form of covering, such as wood chips or grass clippings – but don't use grass clippings if your lawn has been sprayed. Some gardeners like to cover the soil with

Ongoing Care

a black plastic sheet. This has the double advantage of keeping the weeds down, but it has the disadvantage of looking ugly.

The sprouts grow directly from the stem of the plant, each one forming just above a leaf. To encourage growth, pull off the leaves from the bottom of the stem. As the plant grows, you can continue to pull off the lower leaves. The sprouts will be ready for picking when they are about the length of a thumb and feel firmly packed. Remove those that are ready, leaving the others to carry on growing.

 Pests

Brussels sprouts attract the same range of insects as broccoli, but they seem less vulnerable and it is easier to see whether they are being attacked. If they are, some organic powder or insecticidal soap should do the trick. Or give the plants a fierce spray with the hose. If rabbits or groundhogs are nibbling the leaves, sprinkle blood meal around the base of the plants. As well as scaring off the animals, the blood meal will enrich the soil and increase the growth of the sprouts. (See also the homemade organic repellant on page 237.)

Brussels Sprouts Recipes

Sprouts are a traditional accompaniment to roast turkey and cranberry sauce – a perfect match in tastes – but they also go well with any roast or chop. I like them best served plain or sautéed with braised chestnuts. When cooked in a cream sauce, such as béchamel or hollandaise, their delicate flavour tends to get lost and they run the risk of getting soggy. Sprouts are best cooked briefly so that they are tender but still firm.

How to Prepare and Cook

Wash the sprouts in salted water, making sure you clean them of any grit and, possibly, aphids. Strip off the outer leaves, and score a cross into the stem to help all parts of the sprout cook evenly. Bring a pan of salted water to the boil, add the sprouts, and boil briskly for 15 minutes. Drain and serve immediately.

BRUSSELS SPROUTS AND PEA SOUP

If you have a large crop of Brussels sprouts, those that aren't eaten as vegetables can be made into soup. This recipe includes peas to give extra flavour.

1	onion	1
1 Tbsp	butter	15 mL
2 cups	chopped Brussels sprouts	500 mL
2 cups	peas (fresh or frozen)	500 mL
3 cups	chicken stock	750 mL
2 cups	milk	500 mL
	salt and pepper	
2	Brussels sprouts for garnish	2

Peel and chop the onion and cook it gently in butter. Add the sprouts, peas, stock, and milk. Bring to a boil and simmer for 30 minutes. Blend and return to the pan. Add pepper and salt to taste. Chop the remaining two sprouts, add them to the soup, and cook 3 or 4 minutes. *Makes 4 to 6 servings.*

SAUTÉED SPROUTS AND CHESTNUTS

Fresh chestnuts are usually on sale in the supermarkets in the fall, around the same time Brussels sprouts are at their peak. They contrast well with the taste of the sprouts.

½ lb	chestnuts	225 g
1 cup	chicken stock	250 mL
1½ lb	Brussels sprouts	680 g
2 Tbsp	butter	30 mL
	salt and pepper	

With a sharp knife, pierce the skins of the chestnuts on each side, penetrating deeply with the knife (this prevents them from exploding during cooking). Place the chestnuts on a baking sheet and grill them 2 minutes on each side. They should now be easy to peel. Break off the skins, chop the chestnuts in two, and boil them in the stock for 10 minutes. Meanwhile, prepare the sprouts as described on page 33 and boil them in salted water for 15 minutes. Drain the sprouts and the chestnuts. Heat the butter in a pan, add the chestnuts and sauté quickly. Add the sprouts. Add black pepper, and serve. *Makes 4 servings.*

 ## Storing and Freezing

Brussels sprouts can be stored for a limited time in a cool cellar. They also freeze well, though they lose some of their crispness in the process. (They will last up to a year in the freezer.) To freeze the sprouts, prepare them as usual and blanch them in boiling water for 3 minutes. Cool quickly by rinsing in cold water. Dry, and pack in airtight plastic bags from which you have sucked the air with a straw. To serve after freezing, tip the frozen sprouts into boiling salted water and cook for 10 minutes.

Cabbages and Kale

Cabbages are easy to grow, but they take up a lot of space, and I would not place them near the top of the list for backyard gardeners. Store-bought cabbage tastes much the same as freshly picked cabbage and it is usually conveniently cheap. However, enthusiasts for sauerkraut may want to grow large quantities. And, of course, anyone with a big enough garden will find cabbages well worth growing, just as every vegetable is if you have the space.

The various types of cabbage include Savoy, Chinese, and red cabbage, as well as kale, which is a near cousin in the cabbage family. All varieties can be sown directly into the ground or bought as seedlings and transplanted into the garden in May or June. Cabbages do well in almost any soil but preferably should not be planted where members of the *brassica* family grew the previous year (this includes broccoli, Brussels sprouts, and cauliflower as well as cabbage and kale).

If you are growing the plants from seed, wait until the temperature is around 24°C/75°F. Dig some manure into the bed, rake the surface smooth, and drop the seeds at intervals of about 10 centimetres (4 inches). This is nearer than you will want the

How to Grow
Planting

cabbages, but it allows for wastage, and you can always thin and reposition later on. Cover the seed with 1 centimetre (⅓ inch) of soil, press down firmly, and water lightly – enough to wet the soil but not disturb the seed.

If you have bought the seedlings as bedding plants, space them at least 30 centimetres (12 inches) apart. Dig a hole for each plant and add water and a handful of manure. After the water has soaked in, drop in the roots and press the earth down firmly around them. If you believe in "folk" methods, you can try burying a stick of rhubarb underneath each plant to ward off clubroot (a disease that prevents cabbage from maturing and producing a large, well-packed head).

Ongoing Care

Cabbages have shallow roots, so be careful not to damage them when weeding around the plants; and keep the bed well watered, for the roots dry out easily. When the cabbage heads approach full size, they may start to split if they are growing too strongly. You can stop this by breaking or loosening some of the roots (take hold of the head and give it a twist to the right; then press down the surrounding soil so that the cabbage is again firmly embedded).

Flea beetles and cutworms are likely to be the greatest threat to your cabbages. Flea beetles attack the seedlings, and you can get a plague of these tiny black jumping insects during hot dry spells. Fortunately, they can be kept at bay by hand-held organic dusts and sprays. Fossil Flower dust seems particularly effective. It also kills cabbage looper and cabbage worm, two other possible predators.

For cutworms and slugs, the strategy is prevention rather than murder. Either buy some "cabbage collars" or twist a spiral of newspaper or tinfoil around the base of each stalk so that nothing can crawl up it; and cut off any leaves that are touching the ground. Another effective strategy, if you are an early riser, is to go into the garden at dawn while there is heavy dew on the cabbages and sprinkle salt on them – the same trick that works on broccoli and Brussels sprouts. While doing this, you may well catch some slugs or caterpillars in the act, in which case you can simply remove them or squash them. You could also try growing mint, rosemary, or thyme in your cabbage patch. All are said to repel the white cabbage butterfly, which lays the eggs that produce cabbage worms.

Cabbage Recipes

Cabbage can be a delight or a disaster, depending on how it is cooked. When boiled to a pulp, it not only tastes revolting but gives off a penetrating stale odour. When cooked with imagination, cabbage seems a totally different vegetable and can be a veritable taste treat. Yet it is just as easy to cook cabbage well as badly. The main thing to remember is not to boil all the taste out of it, and that means not boiling it too long.

 ## How to Prepare and Cook

Cabbage is so tightly packed that you don't normally need to wash it. Just tear off the outer leaves and chop as much of the rest as you need. It can then be cooked in boiling salted water for about 10 minutes, but by far the nicest way is to use no water at all, sautéing the cabbage quickly in butter.

CABBAGE SAUTÉED IN BUTTER

I learned this method years ago from a friend who lived in Hong Kong and I have used it ever since. It is a delicious way of serving cabbage.

1 Tbsp	butter	15 mL
6 cups	finely sliced cabbage	1.5 L
1 Tbsp	sugar	15 mL
	salt and black pepper	

Melt the butter in a saucepan. Add the cabbage, sugar, a few shakes of salt, and some freshly ground black pepper. Cook quickly over a moderate heat, tossing constantly until all the cabbage is just wilted but still firm. Drain thoroughly and serve immediately. Cabbage cooked this way makes an excellent accompaniment for roast duck. *Makes 4 servings.*

CABBAGE ROLLS

There are countless recipes for stuffed cabbage leaves, with varying ingredients and flavours. This one is particularly meaty and uses no rice.

4 large or 8 small	cabbage leaves	4 large or 8 small
1 lb	lean ground beef	450 g
1	chopped onion	1
1	minced garlic clove	1
1 tsp	dried thyme (or fresh 1 Tbsp/15 mL)	5 mL
1 tsp	Bovril (or similar meat extract)	5 mL
½ cup	tomato paste	125 mL
2 cups	tomato sauce	500 mL
½ cup	red wine	125 mL

With a long sharp knife, cut out the core of a cabbage. Then ease off the outer leaves and boil them in salted water for 5 minutes. Dry on paper towels and cut out any ribs that are inflexible.

Sauté the ground beef in a frying pan, stirring briskly. Drain off the fat and add the onion, garlic, thyme, Bovril, and tomato paste. Cook, stirring, for 5 minutes, moistening with a little water if necessary. Season to taste and fill the cabbage leaves with the mixture, rolling up the leaves and tucking in the ends to make 4 or 8 rolls. Place the rolls in a shallow casserole. Combine the tomato sauce with the wine and pour over the rolls. Cook, covered, in a preheated 350°F/180°C oven for 1 hour. *Makes 4 servings.*

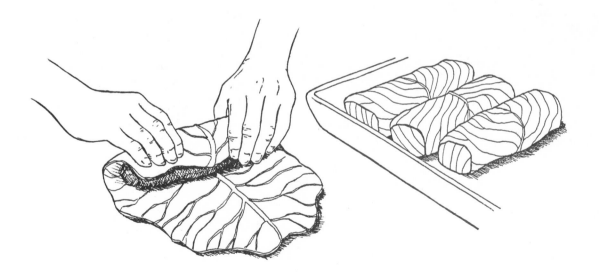

Place a portion of the filling on the rib end of a large cabbage leaf. Roll towards the tip and tuck in both ends.

COTTAGE CHEESE COLESLAW

Cabbage can be particularly tasty raw, especially as coleslaw. This recipe is less fattening than coleslaws made with sour cream, and I think it tastes even better. Try it plain, as given here, or with a few more ingredients such as grated carrots and finely chopped young leek leaves.

½ cup	cottage cheese	125 mL
½ cup	mayonnaise	125 mL
1 Tbsp	Dijon mustard	15 mL
2 Tbsp	lemon juice	30 mL
4 cups	finely shredded cabbage	1 L

Mash or sieve the cottage cheese to form a smooth paste and mix it with the mayonnaise, mustard, and lemon juice. Add the shredded cabbage and mix thoroughly. *Makes 4 to 6 servings.*

KALE

Tender young kale leaves are very good – as well as good for you – served raw in a lettuce salad. Kale is also pleasant cooked, though I wouldn't rank it as gourmet fare. It works best with a flavouring such as nutmeg sauce.

2 lbs	kale	900 g
1 Tbsp	butter	15 mL
2 Tbsp	flour	30 mL
1 cup	milk	250 mL
	nutmeg	
	salt and white pepper	

Wash the kale carefully, removing all grit. Cut off and discard any tough stalks, chop the leaves, and boil in salted water for 10 minutes. Drain thoroughly. Melt the butter in a saucepan and gradually add the flour and milk to make a white sauce (page 248). Season to taste with salt, white pepper, and nutmeg. Boil the sauce gently for a few minutes and then stir in the kale. *Makes 4 servings.*

 Storing

Heads of cabbage store well in a cool environment, the cooler the better, providing it is not below freezing. Store them either unwrapped or in perforated plastic bags. They will keep for several months.

Carrots

Freshly dug carrots straight from the garden have a crispness and sweetness that is unique. If you want to get your children to like carrot sticks, you stand a good chance if you grow your own – and carrots are very easy to grow. They don't seem to mind what the weather is like – hot or cold, wet or dry – and they require very little time or effort.

How to Grow
Planting

Carrots do best in loose soil, but they will also grow in heavy clay – they are simply more difficult to dig up. You should fertilize the bed the previous autumn, since too much fresh manure can make the carrots knobbly and hairy; if this was not possible, mix a rich topsoil such as black earth into the bed. Peat moss can be added to lighten the soil.

Like other root crops, carrots are grown from seed, which should be sown as early as possible in spring. As soon as the ground can be worked, dig over your carrot bed, rake it smooth, and then lightly water the row or rows where you will be sowing the seed. The fine carrot seed blows away easily, and wetting the earth helps keep it in place. Scatter the seed by hand and cover it with a light sprinkling of earth. You can sow the seed quite thickly, since birds and other hungry creatures are sure to eat some of it.

Ongoing Care

Carrots take two or three weeks to germinate, so don't give up hope if nothing seems to be happening. If possible, keep the bed damp; this will speed germination.

Once the carrots have pushed up their first green shoots and are well established, you should give them a thorough thinning. Water the bed so that the shoots can be pulled up easily and then pull those that are crowded. Unlike beets, the pulled seedlings cannot be replanted. (I've tried it, and all you get are gnarled and twisted roots which would be a nightmare to peel.) Weed the bed at the same time as you thin it. This entire process of thinning and weeding can be time-consuming, but it is the only major work you will have to do on your carrot bed.

As the carrots grow larger, they will again become crowded, but future thinnings will in fact be harvesting. In midsummer, for instance, if you want a meal of tender young carrots, you simply pull up those that are competing for space with their neighbours. Or you can thin only around those you want to grow really big, leaving the rest to manage as best they can. You will still get a good crop – some large and suitable for stews, others small and ideal for cooking whole.

Whenever you work on your carrot bed, build up earth over any roots that are protruding above ground. This will prevent their tops from turning green. It is also good protection against frost. In regions that do not have too harsh a winter, carrots can be left in the ground to be dug up during thaws or in spring. But where the climate is more severe – in the prairies, for instance, and Quebec – you should harvest all your carrots in October.

Pests

You will be unlikely to have trouble with insects. If you see holes in carrots that are protruding above ground, this will probably be due to slugs. Unless the damage is widespread, it's not worth worrying about. Simply cut off the affected portions when you harvest the crop.

If the carrots have clearly been chewed or their greenery has been bitten off, you can blame rabbits or other rodents. A handful of blood meal sprinkled lightly around the bed will frighten them away, and it will also help the carrots grow big and juicy.

Carrot Recipes

I like to grow a large crop of carrots because they have so many uses. They are one of the basic flavours of cooking, an essential ingredient in soup stocks and most stews. They make an excellent salad and, of course, can also be served boiled, though I find them least tasty this way. Carrots seem to work better as an ingredient rather than as a vegetable on their own, though baby carrots tossed in parsley are certainly very good, as are roast carrots.

How to Prepare and Cook

Cut off the feathery greenery, wash the carrots, and scrape or scrub them if they are young; peel them if they are large and old. Baby carrots can be cooked whole, added to boiling water and cooked for about 10 minutes. They keep more of their flavour if the water is not salted. Sprinkle them with salt after you have drained them; then reheat in a saucepan with a little butter and chopped parsley. Larger carrots will need to be sliced before boiling. They take 20 minutes or more.

Carrots are particularly tasty when cooked in the oven alongside a roast, in the same way as potatoes. You will need large carrots for this. Peel them, halve them lengthwise if they are more than 2 centimetres (¾ inch) thick, smear them with margarine or butter, and lay them on the bottom of the roasting pan, adding pepper and salt. After 20 minutes, move the carrots onto a wire rack in the roasting pan and cook for a further 20 to 30 minutes. When cooked, they should be malleable but still firm. If they begin to look wizened, remove them from the pan and return them to the oven to reheat shortly before serving.

CARROT, LENTIL, AND HAM POTAGE

Halfway between a soup and a stew, this potage is marvellously nourishing and sustaining, and very savoury too. It is great as a lunchtime filler and can be kept for two or three days if it doesn't all go the first day – as it so often does in our house. If you do make it last over several days, remember that all soups more than a day old should be brought to the boil and then simmered for 10 minutes before serving.

1 lb	carrots, peeled and chopped	450 g
½ lb	ham	225 g
1	potato, peeled and chopped	1
1	onion, peeled and chopped	1
1	celery stalk, chopped	1
3	chicken cubes	3
2	bay leaves	2
1 tsp	rosemary	5 mL
1 Tbsp	lemon juice	15 mL
1 cup	lentils	250 mL

Bring 10 cups of water to a boil and add all the ingredients except the lentils. Simmer for 1 hour. Meanwhile, pick over the lentils to remove any grit and wash thoroughly. At the end of the hour, add the lentils and simmer for a further 30 minutes.

Remove the ham and the bay leaves, and blend about half of the soup in a blender. Return it to the saucepan. Chop the ham into bite-sized pieces and add it too. Add salt to taste. You now have your basic potage, which you can serve as it is or with additions. I like to add some chopped celery leaves and perhaps a little more carrot and potato. When diced, the carrot and potato will be suitably tender after simmering in the soup for about ten minutes. *Makes 10 to 12 servings.*

CARROT AND LEEK SALAD

Grated carrots make a refreshing salad that can have any amount of variations, depending on what you choose to add: raisins, chopped cabbage, chopped nuts, grated cheese, sliced red pepper, and so on. My favourite combination includes young leek leaves and yogurt. The leeks add a spicy tang, and the yogurt prevents it from becoming too powerful. For perfection, this salad should be made with crisp and juicy carrots dug straight from the garden.

2 Tbsp	young leek leaves	30 mL
1 lb	carrots	450 g
2 Tbsp	chopped walnuts	30 mL
2 Tbsp	plain yogurt	30 mL
	salt and pepper	

Choose tender young leek leaves that are less than 2 centimetres (¾ inch) wide. Wash them thoroughly and cut them into 1-centimetre (½-inch) lengths. Peel and grate the carrots, and mix with the leeks and the chopped walnuts. Just before serving, stir in the yogurt and season with salt and freshly ground black pepper. *Makes 4 to 6 servings.*

CARROT AND CHERVIL SOUP

This is a delicious way to eat carrots, especially when based on a rich homemade chicken stock. To taste especially good, the soup should be quite peppery, so don't hold back on the pepper during the final seasoning.

1 large or 2 small	leeks	1 large or 2 small
1 Tbsp	butter	15 mL
1 lb	carrots	450 g
1	potato	1
3 cups	chicken stock	750 mL
2 cups	milk	500 mL
1 Tbsp	fresh chervil (or dried 1 tsp/5 mL)	15 mL
	salt and pepper	
	fresh chervil leaves, parsley, or chives for garnish	

Wash the leeks thoroughly, chop into short lengths, and cook gently in the butter over a low heat for about 5 minutes. Peel and chop the carrots and potato, and add them to the saucepan, together with the chicken stock, milk, and chervil. Bring to a boil and simmer gently for 45 minutes. Blend in a blender, return to the saucepan, reheat, and adjust the seasoning by adding salt if necessary and freshly ground black pepper. If the soup is too thick, dilute with a little milk or chicken stock. Serve with a garnish of chopped chervil leaves, parsley, or chives. *Makes 4 to 6 servings.*

🥗 Storing and Freezing 🥫

Carrots will keep for several months when stored in a cool environment. Wash them under a hose, rubbing gently to remove all earth; as soon as they are completely dry, pack them for storage. If they are to be stored in a cellar or garage, pack them in boxes of sawdust or peat moss. If they are to be kept in the bottom drawer of a refrigerator, package them in plastic bags. Remember to punch air holes in the bags, otherwise the carrots may get slimy and rot. The perfect temperature for carrots stored in boxes is 32°F/0°C, but they will also keep well at slightly higher temperatures.

Only perfect carrots, without cuts or blemishes, are suitable for storage, but you can always freeze the others. Peel and dice the carrots, blanch in boiling water for 3 minutes, drain, cool, and pack in plastic bags, sucking out the air with a straw. These frozen carrots will not be as crisp as the fresh ones, but they keep their taste well and are handy for soup stocks and stews. To serve after freezing, drop them frozen straight into the stew or stock.

Cauliflower

Cauliflower is not an ideal crop for Canadian home gardeners. It can be difficult to grow, since humid weather can cause stem rot, which destroys the plant, and dry weather can cause the plant to bolt (go to seed). There is also the problem that you can't see what is happening inside the cauliflower head. Are caterpillars and other critters making a home there, or is it nice and clean? The only way to be sure is to spray or dust regularly, and if you are going to do that, you might as well buy cauliflower that has been raised by farmers who know from experience how much – or how little – insecticide need be used.

Of course, there are some Canadian backyard gardeners who do grow cauliflower successfully. You stand the best chance if you live in British Columbia and have an average summer without sudden heat or cold. In other parts of the country, your best bet is to aim for a fall crop, sowing the seed in June in order to get the flower heads to form after the heat of summer is past.

If you want an early crop, the easiest method is to buy the plants as seedlings, setting them in the ground towards the end of May. For a late crop, you can start the plants from seed, sowing them in flowerpots or flats in early June and transplanting into the garden in late June or early July. If possible, grow your cauliflower in a

How to Grow
Planting

bed that has shade for at least half the day and one where no fellow *brassica* crop (such as cabbage, broccoli, and Brussels sprouts) was grown the previous year.

Cauliflower likes a rich soil, so prepare the bed well by digging in plenty of manure. The plants will eventually take up a lot of space and should therefore be set well apart, at intervals of about 45 centimetres (18 inches). Dig a small hole for each seedling, add a little manure, and fill the hole with water twice, letting it sink in and penetrate the surrounding soil. Then drop in the roots, firming the earth tightly around them.

🛠 Ongoing Care

Your most important task in growing cauliflower is to make sure that the roots do not dry out, and this means watering regularly. Try and keep the soil slightly moist at all times.

When the flowering heads start to form, you will need to blanch them to make them white and tender. Blanching simply involves keeping out the sunlight. The simplest way is to pull the outer leaves up over the head and tie them together at the top. After about eight days, unwrap the head and take a peek to see if the cauliflower looks nice and white and ready for cutting. If it doesn't, simply tie the leaves back and wait a little longer.

Pests

Cabbage worms, cutworms, and a whole range of crawlies will get into cauliflowers given half a chance. If you decide to keep them off with an insecticide, consult your local garden centre or department of agriculture so that you can pick one that best suits your priorities. If you do not spray, the "folk" method of getting a clean cauliflower at harvest time is to dip each head in a bucket of heavily salted water. This is said to cause the caterpillars to float to the surface. And it's true, some do. But others get stuck in the branches.

Cauliflower Recipes

Cauliflower may be difficult to grow, but it is certainly delicious to eat. I particularly like it raw, either as a crudité with a dip or in a salad with a vinaigrette dressing. For many people, it is a favourite in homemade pickles. It is also excellent boiled – but not for so long that it goes mushy. Like so many vegetables, cauliflower can be spoiled by overcooking.

How to Prepare and Cook

To cook cauliflower whole, tear off the leaves, cut off the lower end of the stalk, and wash the flower head. Place upright in a large saucepan and add about 5 centimetres (2 inches) of lightly salted water. The water should cover only the lower part of the cauliflower so that the thick base will be boiled while the more tender top will be steamed. Place a lid on the saucepan, bring to the boil, and cook over a moderate heat for 15 minutes. Drain thoroughly before serving.

If you have grown your cauliflower organically, you may want to break up the head before cooking so that you can wash it extra thoroughly, making sure there are no caterpillars. In this case, place the pieces in a pan of boiling water and cook over a high heat for 5 to 8 minutes, depending on the size of the pieces. Drain thoroughly before serving.

CAULIFLOWER IN PARSLEY SAUCE

My favourite way of eating cauliflower – and indeed one of my all-time vegetable favourites – is to serve it in a light white sauce flavoured with parsley and black pepper. I usually prepare about twice as much as we are likely to eat, because any leftovers can be made into an equally delicious soup.

1	cauliflower	1
1 Tbsp	butter	15 mL
1½ cups	milk	375 mL
2 Tbsp	flour	30 mL
	salt and black pepper	
2 Tbsp	chopped parsley	30 mL

Cook the cauliflower, steaming or boiling it as described above. Drain and keep warm. Melt the butter in a saucepan and slowly add the flour and the milk to make a white sauce (page 248). Add pepper and salt to taste. Let the sauce bubble gently for a few minutes and then add the chopped parsley. Pour over the cauliflower and serve immediately. If you need to wait before serving, hold the sauce in the pan rather than on the cauliflower. *Makes 4 servings.*

QUICK AND EASY CAULIFLOWER SOUP

Any leftover cauliflower can be transformed into a remarkably flavourful soup, with very little effort.

Cauliflower in Parsley Sauce
   (as above)
milk, in equal portion
salt and black pepper

Chop up your leftover Cauliflower in Parsley Sauce and place it in a blender with an equal portion of milk. Blend thoroughly. Heat to boiling in a saucepan, stirring to prevent sticking, and dilute with more milk if necessary. Add more salt as needed and plenty of black pepper. Cauliflower soup should be noticeably peppery. Serve piping hot. This soup freezes well and can be stored for later use if your family objects to having cauliflower two days running.

CAULIFLOWER CHEESE

Cauliflower cheese can be made in a variety of ways, both with and without a sauce. This recipe has the advantage that it can be prepared in advance, to be heated up just before the meal.

1	cauliflower	1
2 Tbsp	butter	30 mL
3 Tbsp	flour	45 mL
2 cups	milk	500 mL
1 cup	grated cheddar cheese	250 mL
	salt and pepper	

Break the cauliflower into pieces and cook in lightly salted boiling water for 5 minutes. Drain and keep warm. Melt the butter in a saucepan and slowly add the flour and milk to make a white sauce (page 248). Bring to a boil and add salt and pepper to taste. Simmer, stirring constantly, for 3 minutes. Lay the cauliflower pieces in a shallow baking dish, add the sauce, and top with grated cheddar. Heat in a 375°F/190°C oven for 30 minutes or until the top is crisp and bubbling. *Makes 4 to 6 servings.*

CRUNCHY CAULIFLOWER SALAD

Raw cauliflower is excellent in a salad. This salad, which includes raw mushrooms, is best made at least 10 minutes before the meal so that the vegetables have time to absorb the taste of the dressing.

SALAD

1 lb	cauliflower pieces	450 g
6	mushrooms	6
2 Tbsp	chopped green pepper	30 mL
1 Tbsp	chopped green onion	15 mL
1 Tbsp	sunflower seed	15 mL

DRESSING

2 Tbsp	white vinegar	30 mL
4 Tbsp	canola or corn oil	60 mL
1 tsp	Dijon mustard	5 mL
	salt and pepper	

Cut the cauliflower into bite-sized pieces, peel and slice the mushrooms, and place in a bowl together with the green pepper and onion. In a separate bowl, combine the vinegar, oil, and mustard to make the dressing. Season with salt and pepper, and pour over the salad. Mix thoroughly, then sprinkle the sunflower seeds on top. Place the salad in the refrigerator and leave to marinate for at least 10 minutes before serving. *Makes 4 to 6 servings.*

 **Freezing**

Cauliflower can be frozen, but like broccoli it tends to go limp and flabby. If you have grown too much, you would do better to make it into soup and freeze that (page 250). However, if you do want to freeze cauliflower, it's very easy. Break it into branches, blanch in boiling water for 2 minutes, and then drain, cool, and pack in freezer bags, sucking out the air with a straw. To serve after freezing, remove the frozen cauliflower from the bag, drop it into boiling salted water, and cook for up to 5 minutes.

Celery

Every cook-gardener should grow celery – just a few clumps conveniently near the kitchen door. The leaves are one of the building blocks of cookery, adding a subtle richness to the taste of soup stocks, stews, and various sauces. Fresh young celery leaves have the strongest flavour, and this is the great advantage of growing your own: you don't have to buy a whole bunch whenever you need a few leaves.

Many gardeners are put off growing celery because the business of blanching the stalks (to make them pale and tender) sounds complicated. But if you are growing celery for the leaves, you don't need to do any blanching. I like to grow celery both ways – some near the kitchen for flavouring, and others at the end of the garden for harvesting as blanched ribs when the plant is fully grown. Another alternative is to grow self-blanching celery, raising the plants as an all-purpose crop.

Celery takes a long time to grow and therefore needs to be started indoors two or three months before it is transplanted into the garden. Since this is impractical for most people, my advice is to buy young plants from a garden centre rather than trying to grow celery from seed.

To grow unblanched celery, dig the required number of holes in rich well-manured soil, fill the holes with water, let it soak in,

How to Grow
Planting

and then add the young plants, pressing the earth firmly around them. The holes can be quite small – just large enough to take the roots comfortably – and they can be spaced as near as 15 centimetres (6 inches).

To grow blanched celery, the easiest way is to dig a ditch about 20 centimetres (8 inches) deep. Add plenty of well-rotted manure, mix it with earth, and then water liberally. After the water has soaked in, gently press in the celery plants, firming the soil around them. Space the plants about 25 centimetres (10 inches) apart.

To blanch celery, plant the seedlings at the bottom of a trench. Fill up the trench as the plants grow.

Unblanched celery requires virtually no attention. Just keep the plants well watered and pick a handful of leaves or stalks whenever you need them.

Blanched celery has to be kept free of light, so you should gradually fill in your trench with earth as the stalks grow. Keep on building up the soil around the plants so that only the topmost leaves are showing. The celery will be ready for harvesting in late summer. Lift the entire plant, hose down thoroughly to remove all earth, and cut off the roots.

If you don't like this earthy way of blanching celery, there are several alternatives. You can grow a row of celery between planks to keep out the light; or you can wrap the plants in newspaper or black polythene. I find the latter unsatisfactory, for it creates a cosy environment for slugs, though it certainly blanches the stalks effectively.

Celeriac tastes much like celery but is grown for its turnip-like root rather than its stalks. It can be grown the same way as celery, except that celeriac does not need blanching. Space about 15 centimetres (6 inches) apart. If you are fond of celeriac, it is worth planting a row, since it is normally a trouble-free crop and needs little attention. Lift the plant when the root is about 8 centimetres (3 inches) thick.

Insects don't seem to like celery, so your only predators are likely to be a few slugs, which may feed on the insides of the ribs. The best way to deal with them is to pick them off by hand early in the morning . . . if, indeed, there are any. Chances are that you and your family will be the only celery eaters in your garden.

Celery Recipes

Celery stalks taste so good raw that it often seems a shame to cook them. On the other hand, the leaves taste best when cooked; all but the inner leaves tend to be too strong and pungent to be pleasant raw – but, of course, that is precisely why they work such wonders as a flavouring in soups and stews.

There are countless ways of eating raw celery. It can be a crudité with a dip, or an appetizer spread with cheese (almost any type of cheese, though camembert tastes particularly good). You can mix chopped celery with chicken pieces and mayonnaise to make a chicken salad. Or you can just eat the celery as it is, savouring every crunchy mouthful.

How to Prepare and Cook

To my mind, cooked celery served plain is very uninspiring. Celery tastes better as an ingredient in something else rather than as a cooked vegetable on its own. Nevertheless, it does have its fans and it can be a useful standby.

To prepare the celery, wash the stalks, peeling away any coarse strings and removing the leaves, and chop into bite-sized lengths. The celery can then be steamed, braised, or boiled. Try boiling it in chicken stock until it is just tender (about 5 minutes). Then spread it with a little butter or add a white sauce (page 248).

CELERY AND DRIED PEA SOUP

This recipe gives one of my favourite ways of using celery as an ingredient. It produces a wonderfully appetizing soup, one that lines your ribs as well as tickling your taste buds. Although the soup takes two days to prepare, you can save time overall by making a large batch and freezing most of it for later use. I always freeze vast quantities in early autumn so that it can be brought out as a hearty "instant soup" in the depths of winter. This is the perfect soup to have after an icy bout of snow shovelling. It is made in two steps: first the stock and then the soup.

STOCK

1	onion	1
3	garlic cloves	3
2 cups	chopped celery leaves (the leaves of about 8 young stalks)	500 mL
2	chopped celery stalks	2
2	bay leaves	2
2 Tbsp	lemon juice	30 mL
2	chicken cubes	2
2.2 lbs	smoked ham hock, ham bones, or leftover ham end	1 kg

Pour 10 cups (2.5 L) of water into your largest cooking pot and bring it to the boil. Peel and chop the onion and garlic, and add them to the pot together with all the other ingredients. Simmer for about 3 hours. Strain the stock, keeping only the liquid. Cool overnight and skim off the fat next morning.

SOUP

2½ cups	whole dried green peas	625 mL
	ham stock	
2	potatoes	2
2	celery stalks	2

Soak the peas overnight. Rinse thoroughly. Bring the ham stock to a boil, add the peas, and skim off any scum as the stock simmers. Add the peeled and chopped potatoes and boil for 1½ hours. Then remove 4 or 5 cups of the soup, blend to a smooth liquid, and return to the pot. If the soup is now too thick, dilute with 2 cups (500 mL) of water. Add the chopped celery sticks and cook for 10 minutes more. Adjust the seasoning and serve; or cool in preparation for freezing (page 250). *Makes about 12 servings.*

CELERY AND CRISPY CHICKEN WINGS

This dish is a winner for a dinner party – decorative, delicious, and drudgery-free. All but the deep frying can be done in advance, and you can have fun arranging the table, placing little bowls for the dips beside each place setting, and fingerbowls of water with a flower floating in each.

For each person, you will need two bowls of dip (one for a spicy sauce and one for a cool sauce) as well as a bowl of chicken wings set on a plate of crudités. The crudités can be celery sticks alone or a mixture of celery and carrot sticks, or whatever most appeals to you and is available in the garden. My favourite combination is the one given here: celery, carrots, snow peas, and zucchini. For the spicy dip, I particularly like Pickapeppa Sauce (available at West Indian stores and some supermarkets), but if you can't get it, substitute another hot sauce.

	CRUDITÉS	
12	large celery stalks	12
4	large carrots	4
4	small zucchini	4
20	snow peas	20

	HOT SAUCE	
¼ cup	Pickapeppa Sauce	62 mL

	COOL SAUCE	
½ cup	blue cheese	125 mL
1 cup	sour cream	250 mL
1	garlic clove (or garlic salt)	1
2 Tbsp	chopped chives	30 mL
1 Tbsp	chopped parsley	15 mL
	salt	

	CHICKEN	
16	chicken wings	16
4 cups	cooking oil	1 L

Chop the celery stalks into two or three lengths crosswise and then slice them lengthwise into thin sticks. Peel and slice the carrots into sticks. Slice the zucchini into sticks. Trim the top off the snow peas. Arrange all the crudités on four plates so that there is an equal number of celery sticks, carrot sticks, etcetera, on each plate. Cover with plastic wrap to keep moist.

Pour the Pickapeppa Sauce into four bowls, one for each plate. To make the cool sauce, soften the blue cheese with a spoon or fork and blend it thoroughly with the sour cream. Peel and mince the garlic and add it to the mixture, together with the chopped chives and parsley. Add salt to taste. Spoon into four

bowls, cover with plastic wrap, and keep cool in the refrigerator until dinner time.

Cut the tip off each chicken wing and discard it. Then cut the main wing bone in two at the joint, so that you have 32 pieces altogether (8 for each plate). Sprinkle lightly with salt.

The dinner is now prepared. All it needs is last-minute assembling and cooking. The chicken wings will take about 10 to 15 minutes to deep fry in oil. When done, they should be crisp and lightly brown. Fry the chicken in two batches, keeping the first warm while you cook the second. To fry, pat the wings dry with paper towels and lay them in a frying basket. Heat the oil in a saucepan until it is quite hot and then lower the basket into it. Stir the wings occasionally to prevent sticking. When cooked, remove and dry on paper towels.

To serve, portion the wings into four bowls, and take them to the table along with the plates of crudités and bowls of dip. The

meal is designed to be eaten entirely with your fingers, dipping the chicken and crudités first into the spicy sauce and then into the cooling one. *Makes 4 servings.*

CELERY, BEET, AND APPLE SALAD

These three tastes blend beautifully together to make a pleasantly refreshing salad. It tastes particularly good with a slightly sweet dressing, which is why Russian mustard is used in the vinaigrette.

2 Tbsp	wine or cider vinegar	30 mL
4 Tbsp	canola or corn oil	60 mL
1 tsp	Russian mustard	5 mL
	salt and pepper	
2 cups	chopped celery stalks	500 mL
2 cups	peeled and chopped beets	500 mL
2 cups	peeled and chopped apple	500 mL

You can use either pickled or boiled beets for this recipe. The celery and apple should both be raw, and the dressing should be added as soon as possible after peeling the apple to prevent it from turning brown. Make the dressing by combining the vinegar, oil, and mustard. Whisk vigorously and add salt and pepper to taste. Mix the chopped celery, beets, and apple in a salad bowl. Add the vinaigrette dressing and toss. *Makes 4 to 6 servings.*

Storing and Freezing

To freeze celery, wash the stalks and strip off the leaves and any coarse strings, then cut into pieces and blanch for 5 minutes in boiling water. Drain, cool, and pack in plastic bags, sucking out the air with a straw. Like other vegetables, frozen celery will keep for a year. To serve after freezing, remove the frozen celery from the bag, drop it into boiling water or stock, and cook for 5 to 10 minutes.

Celery does not store well raw, but the plants can withstand slight frosts, and if you live in one of the milder parts of Canada you may be able to pick celery leaves from your garden right through until late November (or all winter long in parts of British Columbia). In the colder parts of the country, you could try lifting some celery plants in the fall. Dig up the entire plant, disturbing the roots as little as possible, and replant it in a flower pot. Vigorously hose the stalks and leaves to discourage any aphids that may have taken refuge there, then stand the pots in a tray of water and place in a cool environment. You can blanch this indoor celery by cutting off both ends of a milk carton and easing it over the plant so that it covers the stalks. Harvest these plants whenever you need them. With luck, you will be eating your own fresh celery far into the winter.

Corn

One of the joys of backyard gardening is that you can eat really fresh corn – corn that was picked not yesterday or this morning but less than an hour ago. There is nothing quite like it. Even if you are short of space, it's worth squeezing in a few corn stalks. You could plant them as a corner clump at the back of the garden, or you could combine them with pole beans, using the stalks as support for the beans to climb. This does no harm to either crop.

How to Grow
Planting

Corn will grow in virtually any type of soil, but it likes lots of fertilizer. In late autumn or early spring, dig in plenty of well-rotted manure or compost; or, if you prefer, use artificial fertilizer. Some gardeners prefer artificial fertilizer because manure and compost are said to be risky; being organic fertilizers, they can encourage the development of micro-organisms, which may attack the seed or the young roots. However, I have never experienced these problems myself, and I always use organic fertilizers.

Corn is a warm-weather crop and will not germinate in cool soil. In most parts of Canada, the best time to plant it is mid- to late May, but wait for a warm spell before doing so. Choose a spot where the corn will not shade other plants; it will be tall when fully grown. Then build up the soil into low hills and push about six seeds into each. The seed should be 2 to 3 centimetres deep (about 1 inch) and about 10 centimetres (4 inches) apart. Corn is wind-pollinated, so you will have more success if you plant it as a clump, or in two or three small rows, rather than in one single row.

If the temperature is around 20°C/68°F or more, you may see the first shoots in five or six days. Once they are established, thin them and if necessary rearrange them so that they stand about 20 centimetres (8 inches) apart. When doing this replanting, be sure to prepare a welcoming muddy environment for the seedlings to be moved into; then gently press them in, firming down the surrounding soil.

Now there is nothing more to do, except weeding, until the corn ripens. How can you tell when the corn top is ripe? In late summer, when the heads look nice and plump, slit or strip part of the husk and then press your thumbnail into a kernel. If a white milky liquid spurts out, the corn is ready for eating and can be picked. If you don't get the desired result, leave it for another week.

If you live near a ravine, you may discover that your corn is ripe the hard way – by having it knocked down in the night by hungry raccoons. A tangle of netting laid around the bed can sometimes help; the raccoons panic when their feet catch in the mesh. If that doesn't work, you can try sprinkling pepper on the husks. But your best bet is to beat the raccoons to it by eating the corn before they do – cutting it the moment it seems ready. Birds, too, love to feed on ripe corn. A cat in the neighbourhood often prevents them doing so, simply by its presence. If the birds cause serious damage, try constructing a mesh of strings and tinfoil to keep them off during the ripening period. Birds can be a nuisance at the beginning of the season also, scratching up the seed or eating the seedlings. A little netting over the bed will help (it needs to be there only temporarily, while the shoots are young and tender).

As for insects, there is the European corn borer, which lays masses of fishscale-like eggs on the underside of the leaves. Cut off such leaves immediately if you get an infestation (which you

probably won't). You are more likely to have trouble with corn earworms, which work their way through the husks and feed on the kernels, generally near the tip. In this case, simply cut off the spoiled part before cooking the cob. You can lessen the likelihood of both these pests by removing the corn stalks as soon as the crop is harvested. If you have the time and energy, chop up the stalks rather than throwing them out, and then dig them back into the bed. This will help enrich the soil.

Corn Recipes

Corn on the cob, whether boiled, barbecued, or roast, is best picked immediately before cooking. The longer the delay between picking and cooking, the more there is a loss in flavour. According to folklore, you should put on the water to boil before you go out to pick the corn.

How to Prepare and Cook

To boil corn, remove the husks and trim the stem with a sharp knife. Plunge the cobs into a large cauldron of unsalted boiling water, cover, and cook for 3 to 5 minutes. Remove from the water immediately, drain, and serve with plenty of butter and with salt if desired. If you like the corn very sweet, add 2 or 3 tablespoons (30 or 45 mL) of sugar to the cooking water.

To barbecue corn, do not remove the husks. Simply place the cobs on a grill and cook for about 10 minutes, turning frequently. Serve with butter.

To roast corn in an oven, tear off the husks, spread the cobs with butter, and wrap in tinfoil. Cook in a preheated 350°F/180°C oven for 30 to 40 minutes.

To cut corn kernels from the cob, slice them off with a sharp knife.

CORN CHOWDER

This soup is one of those that I like to make in bulk and store in the freezer. It is a wonderful soup for midwinter – rich with subtle flavours, and very sustaining. And like so many soups, it is little trouble to make.

2	potatoes	2
4 cups	milk	1 L
1 cup	water	250 mL
1 Tbsp	fresh marjoram	15 mL
	(or dried 1 tsp/5 mL)	
4 cups	corn kernels	1 L
	salt and black pepper	
1 cup	chopped celery	250 mL
2 Tbsp	chopped parsley	30 mL
	for garnish	

Peel and slice the potatoes and place in a saucepan together with the milk, water, marjoram, 2 cups (500 mL) of the corn kernels, and 1 teaspoon (5 mL) of salt. Bring to the boil (watching carefully to prevent the water from boiling over) and simmer gently for 30 minutes. Blend, then return to the pan along with 2 more cups (500 mL) of corn kernels and the chopped celery. Season to taste with freshly ground black pepper and a little more salt if necessary. Simmer for 10 minutes, stirring to prevent sticking. Serve with a garnish of chopped parsley. *Makes 6 to 8 servings.*

CORN CASSEROLE

Here is an easy supper or lunch dish that takes little time to prepare.

3	eggs	3
1½ cups	milk	375 mL
1 cup	grated cheddar cheese	250 mL
2 cups	corn kernels	500 mL
1 tsp	salt	5 mL
½ tsp	black pepper	2.5 mL

Beat the eggs well and then beat in the milk and cheese. Add the corn and the salt and pepper, and pour into a buttered casserole. Bake in a preheated 350°F/180°C oven for between 50 minutes and one hour, by which time the mixture should be firm and slightly risen. If it is still runny in the centre, cook a little longer. *Makes 4 servings.*

 **Freezing**

If you have any corn left over, it will freeze superbly. I find the easiest method is to boil the cobs for 4 minutes, cool quickly under running cold water, and then cut off the kernels. (This is easier than cutting kernels off uncooked cobs.) Place all the well-formed kernels on a metal baking dish and freeze quickly. Then crumble them apart and pack into plastic bags, sucking out the air with a straw. To serve after freezing, pour as much as you need from the bag and boil for 3 or 4 minutes, or toss in butter until heated through. The remainder of the kernels can be frozen as cream-style corn, together with all the milk you can scrape from the cobs. Pack in plastic bags, sucking out all air with a straw. To serve after freezing, remove from the bag, tip into a saucepan and heat gently with a little milk or water. Season with salt or sugar. Like other frozen vegetables, corn will last a year in the freezer – long enough to see you through to the next season.

Cucumber

Ever since growing my own cucumbers, I have found it hard to enjoy any that are not homegrown. They just don't have the same crispness. Nor is there the same choice in the stores, for the seed catalogues offer a wonderful range: tiny pickling cucumbers, bush cucumbers, English long cucumbers, Chinese varieties, and various novelties such as the pale green serpent cucumber. My current favourite is a variety called Gourmet II; slender, meaty, and with few seeds, it is a "burpless" variety that does not cause flatulence, and it never gets bitter as some cucumbers do.

Fortunately, you do not need a big garden in order to grow cucumbers. Although the vines will cover a large area once they are growing vigorously, they can be trained to climb a chain-link fence or to wind up the steps of a deck. Cucumbers can even be grown in flowerpots on a balcony; for although the vines spread, the roots take up very little space. However, if you decide to grow cucumbers on your balcony, be sure to have more than one plant, since this will make pollination easier.

Cucumbers are very easy to grow. The only important thing to know is that they do not like having "wet feet." You can kill a young cucumber plant in less than an hour if you let it stand with soggy roots under a blazing sun.

How to Grow
Planting

To avoid soaking the roots, gardening books generally recommend growing the cucumber on mounds, but I prefer to provide the required drainage by placing a layer of peat moss under the roots. By this method, surplus water does not drain off uselessly into the surrounding soil; it soaks through to the peat moss, forming a type of underground reservoir for the plant to use when needed. This procedure can be adapted for flowerpot-grown cucumbers. Fill the bottom of the pot with peat moss, add a rich mixture of manure and potting soil, then a thin layer of potting soil on which you place the seed, covering it with a sprinkling of earth. Stand the flowerpot in a tray of water and keep it indoors in a sunny window until the temperature is well over 20°C/68°F outside. It can then be moved onto the balcony.

Cucumbers need heat for the seed to germinate and plenty of heat for the plant to grow strongly. The best temperature for germination is about 20°C/68°F, and I like to start an early crop indoors to plant out in mid-June, after summer has arrived. I then sow a second crop directly into the garden. This method of planting prolongs the cucumber season at both ends and generally means that we are eating our first cucumbers in late June.

Seed started indoors should be sown about one month before planting out, and the seedlings should be grown in Jiffy-7s so that their roots will not be disturbed (see pages 229–34 for indoor sowing). When transplanting into the garden, choose a spot that gets plenty of sun and is sheltered from the wind. Dig a hole for each plant 15 centimetres (6 inches) or more deep, give it a bottom layer of peat moss, then add some well-rotted manure and a small amount of topsoil. Fill the hole with water, letting it soak right in. Then press in the seedling, firming the soil around it. The plants can be quite near one another – about 20 centimetres (8 inches) apart. When sowing seed directly in the garden, follow the same principles. First, dig plenty of manure into the bed and then lay a porous layer of peat moss underneath the places where you put the seed. Cover this with earth and lay the seed on top, pressing it down firmly so that it can't blow away. Top with a light sprinkling of crumbled earth.

Since cucumber uses lots of fertilizer, you should add more as soon as the vines start to grow if you want a really good crop. Dig in the fertilizer around the plants, taking care not to disturb the roots. Bone meal is excellent for this purpose because it acts as a slow-release fertilizer and will continue to nourish the plants over a long period.

Ongoing Care

Cucumbers need plenty of water to produce a good crop. Watering from above can encourage mildew on the leaves, so it is better to ease a hose or watering can under the leaves and water only the patch of earth where the roots are located. In very hot dry weather, water every evening. If you have prepared a good porous base for your plants, there will be no danger of overwatering.

You can start picking the first cucumbers when they are still quite small; this will encourage more blossoms to appear and more cucumbers to be formed. Do not let the cucumbers grow too large before picking them. Overripe fruit slows production. Also, large cucumbers do not taste as good.

If the vines begin to grow rampantly – as if they are trying to take over the entire neighbourhood – you can slow them down by pinching off the fuzzy ends with your fingers. This will direct the plant's strength into producing cucumbers rather than producing record-length vines.

If any leaves turn dry and brittle or get a grey mildew on them, pick them immediately and discard them so that the mildew will not spread. Bad attacks of powdery mildew can be controlled with organic fungicide, which is available in hand-spray dispensers.

Pests

Watch out for cucumber beetles – rather pretty little things, yellow with black stripes or yellow with black spots. If there are enough of them, they can kill young cucumber plants, and they are so agile that they are not easy to catch with your fingers. To kill them, give them a squirt of organic dust or hand spray, but be careful to do this when there are no bees around. You will find that bees are regular visitors to the cucumber blossoms.

If the vines or infant cucumbers look as if they have been

chewed, they are probably being eaten by rodents during the night. This problem is more likely to occur when the plants are young and tender than when they are mature. A tangle of netting around the plants will generally keep the animals off, as will a sprinkling of blood meal. Slugs are not usually a problem with cucumbers, since the prickly stalks keep them off, but if some cucumbers look as if they are being nibbled by slugs, simply lift the cucumbers off the ground and tuck a leaf underneath them.

Cucumber Recipes

Cucumber was surely made to be eaten raw. It is totally uninteresting cooked, except as a soup, since cooking turns it into a dreary marrow-type vegetable, and a rather slushy one at that. But why even bother to cook cucumber when it is so good raw? One of the great treats of each summer is the first sandwich made with homegrown cucumber. Then there is cucumber salad – or, rather, all sorts of different cucumber salads. And there is that very simple delicacy, cucumber as a side dish: thinly sliced and sprinkled with salt, pepper, and parsley. At the height of summer, this makes the perfect accompaniment to almost any main dish.

The most nutritious part of a cucumber is said to be the skin, but in this age of chemical sprays, the skin of most cucumbers is likely to be the most poisonous part. If you grow your own, however, you can confidently eat the skin – and that means wonderfully crunchy slices. Cucumbers are at their most crunchy when served straight after picking, but homegrown cucumbers will keep their crispness for several days if stored in the refrigerator, covered tightly in plastic wrap. The wrap is essential, otherwise the cucumbers will go flabby.

Perhaps cooked cucumber was invented to cope with the glut that always happens at some point in the summer – usually when your neighbours are having a glut of cucumber too. Even home picklers find it hard to cope when the plants are producing so abundantly. It can seem as if there's a cucumber hiding under every leaf. But none need be wasted or concocted into an uninspiring cooked-up novelty if you are prepared to spend less than an hour making soup. The soup can then be frozen and stored for later use.

CREAM OF CUCUMBER SOUP

My favourite cucumber soup is simple to make and very tasty. It can be served either hot or cold, but is best when very cold indeed.

1 Tbsp	butter	15 mL
6 cups	peeled and chopped cucumber	1.5 L
3 Tbsp	flour	45 mL
2 cups	chicken stock	500 mL
2 cups	milk	500 mL
1	peeled and chopped onion	1
	nutmeg or dill	
	salt and pepper	
1 cup	table cream	250 mL
	sliced unpeeled cucumber and chopped chives for garnish	

Melt the butter in a saucepan, add the peeled and chopped cucumber, and cook over a low heat for 5 minutes. Sprinkle with flour and gradually add the chicken stock and milk, stirring constantly. Add the onion and boil gently for 15 minutes. Blend, cool, and season to taste with salt, pepper, and a little nutmeg or dill. Place the soup in your refrigerator's freezer compartment until it is icy cold but not forming crystals. Just before serving, stir in the cream and sliced cucumber. Sprinkle with chopped chives. *Makes 6 to 8 servings.*

Note: If you are intending to freeze the soup, package it without adding the cream, sliced cucumber, and chives. To serve after freezing, thaw in a saucepan with a little water. Bring to a boil and cook for 5 minutes. Cool and then proceed as above.

THE PERFECT CUCUMBER SANDWICH

The two essentials are white pepper and thin slices – thinly sliced bread and thinly sliced cucumber. Butter the bread before cutting it, then gently saw off a very thin slice. The choice of bread is up to you, but small brown loaves work best; being tightly packed, they don't fall apart when cut very thin.

After buttering and cutting sufficient slices, layer half of them with a generous amount of cucumber slices cut from an unpeeled cucumber. Sprinkle with salt and white pepper, top with another slice of bread, and cut off the crusts. Traditionally, such sandwiches are served with an English tea, but they also make excellent lunchtime fare on a hot summer's day.

CUCUMBER AND COTTAGE CHEESE OPEN SANDWICH

Here is another taste treat. In this case, you need crisp rolls rather than bread. Cut the rolls in half and top each half with cottage cheese, unpeeled cucumber slices, salt, and a sprinkle of cayenne pepper. The hotness of the cayenne is balanced by the cooling effect of the cucumber and cottage cheese, and the total is both delicious and filling.

CUCUMBER SALAD

There are all sorts of ways of making cucumber salad. You can toss sliced cucumber in sour cream or mix it with mayonnaise or serve it with a vinaigrette. Or you can make a more complex salad dressing based on one of

the above or on cottage cheese, adding chives or parsley and various other ingredients. All are good, but in the heat of summer I prefer a simple yogurt dressing. As well as being virtuously low-fat, it is wonderfully cooling – the perfect accompaniment to a backyard barbecue.

1	cucumber (preferably a long, seedless variety)	1
½ cup	yogurt	125 mL
¼ cup	chopped fresh mint	62 mL
	salt	

Wash but do not peel the cucumber. Slice it thinly and lay the slices on a plate. Sprinkle with salt, cover with another plate, place a weight on top, and leave for about an hour. By the end of the hour, the cucumber will have given off a liquid. Drain it off, squeezing the plates together to obtain the maximum amount, and then dry the cucumber slices on paper towels. Mix the slices with the yogurt and finely chopped mint leaves, and season with additional salt and pepper if desired. *Makes 4 servings.*

Currant and Berry Bushes

If you can find space in your garden for some currant and berry bushes, you will never regret it. Red currants, black currants, gooseberries, and blueberries are all perennials and will bear fruit year after year, in great profusion, and with virtually no effort on your part. They can be grown in all provinces, though high-bush blueberries are not suitable for places where winter temperatures drop below –29°C/–20°F. If you live in the prairies or southern Yukon, you may want to try some native species, such as Saskatoon berries or chokecherries. Although the latter are bitter raw, they make excellent jelly.

 **How to Grow**
Planting

Garden centres usually have a good selection of young berry bushes, and the varieties they stock are those most suitable for the local area. The best time to plant the bushes is early spring. They will do best in full sun, but a partially shaded spot is possible as a second choice. For blueberries, you should choose a well-drained location, since they very quickly die if the soil becomes at all waterlogged.

Dig a large hole to receive each plant, spacing the holes at least 60 centimetres (24 inches) apart. Although the plants may consist

of only a few twigs right now, they will eventually grow into wide bushes. Ideally, they should be set at least a metre (3 feet) apart. Black currants will take up the most space. If you have difficulty fitting them in, try planting them as a hedge dividing one part of the lawn from another.

When digging the holes, make them deeper and broader than the containers the bushes are standing in so that there will be plenty of room to add some fertilizer. For currants and gooseberries, a mix of well-rotted manure and peat moss makes a good fertilizer mixture. For blueberries, which need a sandy, acidic soil, use just a little manure and plenty of peat moss mixed with sandy topsoil. If your garden has a heavy clay soil, make the holes for the blueberry plants extra deep and line them with a layer of pebbles before adding the sand and fertilizer mixture. The pebbles will help give the plants adequate drainage.

After mixing the fertilizer into the holes, pour in water. Let the water soak in and then fill up the holes again. You have now provided food and drink to help the roots get started. When the water has again soaked through, ease the plants carefully out of their containers, disturbing the roots as little as possible, and place them in the holes you have prepared for them. Add earth as necessary to fill in the edges and press them down firmly.

To help the bushes start growing, you can do a little pruning at this time. Simply cut off the end of each branch. (For more about pruning, see Fruit Trees, page 85.)

✑ Ongoing Care

The first year, remove any blossoms that form. (By doing so, you will help the plants put all their strength into growing.) Water regularly. The following spring you may get a pleasing number of blossoms. But beware of spring frosts, especially on currants and gooseberries, which bloom early. If there is a frost warning after your bushes have come into blossom, be sure to cover them at night, otherwise the blossoms will be killed and will drop off rather than developing into berries. I use an old nylon tent fly as a covering, weighting it down at the edges with bricks. It is light enough not to crush the bushes and it provides the necessary protection.

The fruit will be ready for picking in early summer. Black currants and blueberries bear fruit on the previous season's shoots. Red currants and gooseberries bear fruit on spurs that grow from two- and three-year-old wood. Unless you are sure of what you are doing, it is best not to prune the bushes, since you run the risk of cutting off branches that are due to give you your next crop. However, there is a way you can safely do a bit of yearly pruning on black currants (but not red currants). When picking the crop, cut off the stem bearing the fruit rather than picking off the currants individually. By doing this, you will be removing the appropriate branches from the black currant bush and allowing space for the growth of new branches.

Since all currant and berry bushes will bear well without any pruning, especially during the first few years, all you need do is cut off any dead or injured branches and any that are trailing on the ground. After four or five years, if you feel like pruning more vigorously, cut off the oldest shoots at the base. This "thinning out" will encourage the production of new berries and will open up the bushes, allowing space for new growth. The best time for pruning is early spring, before bud break, though it can also be done in the fall.

The only other thing you need do is to keep a watch for powdery mildew and leaf spot, especially in warm, humid weather and especially on currant bushes. These are the diseases that are most likely to occur. If you notice a white powdery fungus on the leaves, or brown spots, treat immediately with a fungicide. There are organic fungicides in hand-spray dispensers that are easy to apply.

Pests

You are unlikely to have trouble with insects, though there are several species that do attack currants and berries. These range from the currant borer and cranberry fruitworm to the ubiquitous aphid. What you will have trouble from, for sure, are birds – How can they be expected to resist such luscious berries so early in the year? If you don't take measures against them, they will strip your bushes even before the fruit is ripe. Stretch netting will help – indeed, it has been made specifically for this purpose. Usually, it does not need to be kept over the bushes until all the fruit is picked. After a few weeks, the birds have so many other things to eat that they tend to lose interest in currants.

Currant and Berry Recipes

I t was the love of homemade black currant jam and red currant jelly that first inspired me to plant fruit bushes, but nowadays very few of my currants go to make jam or jelly. Ever since discovering currant and blueberry pie, I have been very stingy about using the fruit in any other way, though in fact blueberries and black currants are both excellent raw, served with fresh cream.

CURRANT AND BLUEBERRY PIE

Made in a deep pie dish or soufflé dish, this pie must be served cold to enjoy the exquisite flavour to the full. Hot, it is quite nice. Cold, it is heavenly. If you have no black currant bushes, use equal amounts of red currants and blueberries. If you have no red currants either, don't bother to make it.

PASTRY

½ lb	flour	225 g
¼ lb	fat	112 g
⅓ cup	water	83 mL
½ tsp	salt	2 mL

FILLING

1 cup	red currants	250 mL
1 cup	black currants	250 mL
2 cups	blueberries	500 mL
1 cup	sugar	250 mL

Wash the fruit, remove any stalks, and nip the tops off the black currants. Mix all but ½ cup (125 mL) of the fruit with the sugar and pour it into a deep pie dish about 18 centimetres (7 inches) in diameter. Heap the fruit so that it is slightly domed and then top with the unsugared ½ cup (125 mL) of fruit (to prevent any sugar touching the pastry and causing the crust to get soggy).

Make the pastry (page 251) and roll it flat, shaping it to form a circle that is larger than the pie dish. Cut a narrow strip off the edge of the pastry, wet the lip of the pie dish, and press this strip on it. Lightly moisten the strip with cold water. Roll the remaining pastry round the rolling pin in order to lift it easily, and gently lay it over the pie. Use your fingers and thumbs to seal the edges of the pastry by pressing it down firmly on the dampened strip. Neaten the edges by cutting off any surplus pastry.

Roll the surplus pastry into a rectangle and cut it into squares or fingers. These can be cooked on a baking sheet to serve as extra pastry pieces.

Leave the pie to settle for 10 minutes and then place it in the centre of a preheated 425°F/220°C oven. After 10 minutes, reduce the heat to 350°F/180°C and continue to cook for a further 30 minutes. Cool and sprinkle with a dusting of icing sugar (optional). Serve cold with a generous helping of table cream. *Makes 4 to 6 servings.*

GOOSEBERRY FOOL

Delicious, and so simple to make, gooseberry fool has been enjoyed for centuries and is still a delicacy today. For this recipe, there is no need to go through the fiddly business of topping and tailing the gooseberries, because the fruit will be sieved through a strainer, which will keep the coarser bits back. Just pick the berries and then wash them.

2 cups	gooseberries	500 mL
½ cup	sugar	125 mL
½ cup	whipping cream	125 mL

Place the gooseberries in a saucepan with the sugar and ¼ cup (62 mL) of water, and stew gently until soft. Press through a strainer or moulin (food mill). Cool. Whip the cream and fold it into the gooseberries. Spoon into individual bowls. *Makes 4 servings.*

 Freezing

Currants and berries can be frozen raw. Simply wash and stem them, dry thoroughly, and then pack in plastic bags, sucking out the air with a straw. Alternatively, the fruit can be frozen in dry sugar: gooseberries and currants, 1 cup (250 mL) of sugar mixed with 4 cups (1 L) of fruit; blueberries, ⅔ cup (166 mL) of sugar to 4 cups (1 L) of fruit. These, too, are packed in airtight freezer bags. Frozen fruit will keep for a year. To serve after freezing, thaw slowly in the bag and eat or cook as soon as possible.

Eggplant

Eggplant (*aubergine*) belongs to the same family as tomatoes, and like tomatoes it is a hot-weather plant – the hotter the better. Summer conditions in many parts of Canada suit it just fine, provided you choose a variety that has a short growing season. Some varieties take as much as 120 days to mature, and this is too long for most regions.

How to Grow
Planting

In late May, after the danger of frost is past, buy the plants from a garden centre or nursery. This is better than growing eggplant from seed, since it cannot be sown outdoors until the soil temperature is around 29°C/85°F and it is only worth starting indoors if you have plenty of room for indoor gardening.

Choose a part of the garden that gets full sun and dig a hole for each eggplant at intervals of about 40 centimetres (16 inches). Half-fill the holes with a rich mixture of well-rotted manure and peat moss. If available, add some bone meal too; eggplant does best with plenty of fertilizer, and the bone meal will act as a slow-release nutrient. After mixing in the fertilizer, fill the holes with water, let it soak in, and then gently press in the plants, firming down the soil around them.

Ongoing Care

Water regularly throughout the summer and weed with care, since the roots lie close to the surface. You can begin to pick the eggplant before it has reached its full size – it is excellent young

and tender. On the other hand, eggplant does not need to be picked even when it is fully grown. Ripe eggplant can be left on the vine for a week or more.

Keep a watch out for the Colorado potato beetle. In its larval form, it is a red grub with rows of black dots. Pick it off by hand and squash it or drop it in soapy water. The grub does more harm than the adult beetle, which has yellow and black stripes and also can be picked off by hand.

Pests

Eggplant Recipes

The Greeks, Turks, French, and many other nationalities have invented a great variety of ways of cooking eggplant. There is a Turkish recipe called *Imam Baaldi* ("the priest has fainted") because an important Imam apparently fainted with joy on tasting the dish. It seems to me that the Imam overreacted – eggplant isn't all *that* delectable, though it can make a pleasant meal when its distinctive flavour is combined with compatible ingredients.

 **How to Prepare and Cook**

Simply wash the eggplant and cut off the end. Most recipes do not require that it be skinned, but tradition states that it should be cut into thick slices and then soaked in salt to draw off excess liquid. This is not necessary, but some cooks like to do it before broiling or frying, and it does leach out the moisture. Simply sprinkle the slices liberally with salt, let them stand for 30 minutes, and then drain off the liquid. Blot on paper towels before cooking.

To broil eggplant, brush with oil, season with freshly ground black pepper and, if desired, with garlic salt, and broil under a hot grill (or on the broiling rack of a barbecue) for 5 minutes on each side.

To fry eggplant, dust the slices in flour, otherwise the eggplant will soak up too much cooking fat and will be unpleasantly greasy; alternatively, roll the slices in flour, then in beaten egg, and then in breadcrumbs. Season with pepper and salt, and cook quickly in hot oil. Blot dry on paper towels and serve immediately.

STUFFED EGGPLANT WITH TOMATOES

A pleasant mix of flavours that combine well with the taste of the eggplant, this dish is a good standby for informal supper parties, since it looks nice as well as tasting good, and it can be prepared in advance.

2	eggs	2
2	small eggplants	2
1 Tbsp	butter	15 mL
1	onion	1
1	small garlic clove	1
1 Tbsp	parsley	15 mL
2 Tbsp	breadcrumbs	30 mL
	pepper and salt	
2	tomatoes	2
4 Tbsp	grated mozzarella cheese	60 mL

Hard boil the eggs, peel and mash them. Split the eggplants in half lengthwise, scoop out the flesh, and sauté it in butter until soft. Add the peeled and finely chopped onion and garlic and the chopped parsley. Cook a further 3 to 5 minutes. Combine with the mashed egg and with fresh breadcrumbs (page 253). Season with pepper and salt. Spoon this mixture into the eggplant halves. Cover with the tomatoes, thickly sliced, and top with grated mozzarella. Set in a baking dish with a little water and bake in a preheated 375°F/190°C oven for 45 minutes. Serve with baked tomatoes (page 212). *Makes 4 servings.*

EGGPLANT DIP

This Middle Eastern dip includes tahini *(which is made from crushed sesame seeds and is rather like peanut butter). It is readily available at specialty and health food stores, as well as at some delicatessens. If you have any* tahini *over after making the dip, it can be used on lunchtime sandwiches instead of peanut butter.*

2 small or 1 large	eggplants	2 small or 1 large
1 Tbsp	cooking oil	15 mL
1	garlic clove	1
½ cup	tahini	125 mL
¼ cup	fresh lemon juice	62 mL
2 Tbsp	chopped parsley	30 mL
	salt	

Lightly oil the eggplant and bake it in a 350°F/180°C oven until soft (between 45 minutes and one hour). Strip off the skin, and mash the flesh with a fork. Peel and mince the garlic and mix it into the eggplant, then combine with the remaining ingredients, seasoning to taste with salt. Serve cold with black olives and pita bread. *Makes about 8 servings.*

Fruit Trees

Now that dwarf trees are readily available, it is no longer necessary to have a large garden in order to experience the pleasure of growing fruit trees. And it is indeed a pleasure – a gorgeous display of blossoms in the spring and then the gradual ripening of the fruit, with an increasingly large yield each year.

People are sometimes put off planting fruit trees because it seems such a costly outlay, but in fact trees are wonderfully inexpensive compared to most things nowadays. You can get yourself an orchard of six trees for less than a quarter of the price of an average television set, and the trees will still be growing strongly and bearing fruit for years after you have traded in the TV for an updated model.

Nor are fruit trees difficult to care for. You can just plant them and let them grow, giving them little if any pruning. On the other hand, a backyard orchard can become a full-time hobby for those who want to get into the whole business of training and shaping and pruning the trees, spraying regularly, inspecting for insects and diseases, and generally investing hours of loving care with the aim of producing utterly perfect fruit.

 How to Grow
Selecting the Trees

Buy the trees from a reputable garden centre or nursery. They are going to live a long time, so it is worth getting good stock, preferably with a guarantee. Your choice of fruit trees will be dictated by the part of Canada you live in. One cannot grow peaches on the prairies, for instance, but it is possible to grow some varieties of pear, as well as apples and plums.

Some trees need a cross pollinator nearby in order to produce fruit; you will need to get two apple trees, for instance, or one apple and one crabapple. Other trees, such as peaches and apricots, are self-fertilizing, setting their fruit with their own pollen; in this case, you need only one tree of that particular group. The salespeople where you buy the trees will be able to tell you precisely which ones need a cross-fertilizer and which do not.

Planting

The trees can be planted either in the fall or in the spring, but it is safer to plant them in the spring. Very early spring is best, before the weather begins to warm up.

First, consider carefully where you are going to put the trees. Remember that they will provide shade as they grow and should not be in a place where they will overshadow anything that needs full sun. Also, do not plant them too close together. They may be small now, but even dwarf trees spread considerably as they grow.

The hole you dig for each tree should be large enough to fit its roots comfortably and allow them to grow outward. For balled and burlapped trees, make the hole at least twice as wide as the root ball; allow a similar amount of space for trees that come in containers. In both cases, make the opening deep enough for a layer of topsoil to be laid at the bottom of the hole.

Fill the hole with water, but do not add any type of fertilizer or manure. After the water has soaked in, refill the hole with water and let it soak in again. Now add a layer of good topsoil, such as black earth.

To plant a balled and burlapped tree, stand it in the hole and surround it with topsoil. You can either leave the root ball fully wrapped or you can untie the burlap and pull it open to allow the roots to spread more easily – but try not to disturb the roots when doing so. Similarly, try not to disturb the roots when planting a

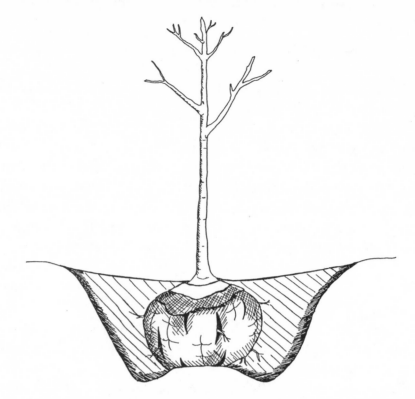

When planting a balled and burlapped tree, dig a hole that is wider than the ball and deep enough to allow the tree to grow at the same level it grew in the garden centre. Line the hole with good topsoil, such as black earth.

tree that comes in a container. Cut away the container carefully and lower the tree into the hole.

An alternative method of planting intentionally disturbs the roots by removing them from the soil and clipping off their ends to stimulate growth. If you choose this course, water the hole thoroughly as described above, build a small mound of soil at the bottom of the hole, and plant the tree on top of this, spreading the roots around it.

Whichever system is used, be careful not to plant the trees too deeply; with dwarf fruit trees, the union between the root and trunk should be above ground. Fill in the holes with topsoil to a height that is just below ground level, so that the surface of the earth around the trunk is a little lower than the surrounding soil, forming a basin to catch rainwater. Press the trees in firmly, and drive in stakes to which the trees can be tied to hold them steady in their first years.

A third possibility is to get someone to do the planting for you. Digging the holes can be slow and heavy work in some soils, and in spring local newspapers always have advertisements from people offering to do garden work. Shop around for the best bargain, preferably for someone who is knowledgeable and yet won't charge too much. Many of the freelance gardeners offer very reasonable hourly rates.

Pruning

The experts say that one should prune fruit trees severely immediately after planting in order to stimulate new growth. If you have hired a professional to do your planting, he or she will do this first pruning for you. If you are doing the planting yourself, you may hesitate to cut back the tree. Severe pruning means cutting off most of the branches, leaving only the centre leader and a few side branches, which should be shortened drastically. A compromise is simply to snip the end off each branch. When in doubt, it is always safer to do too little than too much.

Pruning fruit trees is both an art and a science, and if you want to get into it in a big way, the best course is to buy a book on the subject or visit your local department of agriculture and pick up the available leaflets. Ontario, for instance, has a large number of factsheets on fruit trees, as well as a 39-page booklet called *Training and Pruning Fruit Trees* which, like the factsheets, is given out free.

If you don't want to be bothered to learn about pruning, here are a few simple rules to follow. First, always do the pruning in early spring before budbreak. Second, until the trees begin to bear fruit, do as little pruning as possible. Cut away only dead branches or those that are growing towards the centre of the tree or are rubbing against other branches. Do not shorten branches by cutting their ends off, for although this encourages new growth, it delays the formation of blossoms and hence fruit. Third, always cut off any suckers growing from the base of the tree. Fourth, always seal large cuts with a dollop of pruning paint (available from hardware and gardening supply stores).

Cuts should be made diagonally just above an outward-facing bud.

After the trees bear fruit, you can prune more energetically. There are two types of pruning: *heading back* (which simply means shortening the branches) and *thinning out* (cutting off entire branches or shoots). When heading back, always make the cut diagonally and just above a bud facing outward, and remember that heading back will stimulate growth but will not encourage fruit formation. Thinning-out cuts have less effect on the tree's production and are therefore safer for the novice pruner. Pruning can be particularly tricky on apples and pears, because they have two types of bud – thin, pointed wood buds and fat, stumpy fruit buds – so you need to know precisely what you are cutting off. If you are not sure what you are doing, it is better to limit yourself to very little pruning. The trees will still bear fruit (which they may not do if you prune incorrectly).

Ongoing Care

Different fruit trees take different lengths of time to produce fruit. You might get some peaches the year after planting a tree, whereas you will have to wait longer for apples and probably longer still for pears. But have patience. All will bear fruit eventually.

In the meantime, there is little to do except water the trees during hot dry weather and, in late fall, to wrap the lower part of the trunks to prevent rabbits and mice from nibbling the bark over winter. The wrapping can be bought at hardware and garden stores, and it should be removed from the trees in spring.

It is always exciting when the trees bear their first fruit, but don't be dismayed if a lot of it falls off early in the summer. This is known as the "June drop" and it is nature's way of ensuring that the trees do not grow more fruit than they can sustain. Once your trees are bearing abundantly, you can aid this process by picking off the smaller fruit or any that are very close together. This will allow the tree to put its strength into the remaining fruit, increasing their size and quality.

Most fruit can be picked as it ripens, but pears are best picked before they are ripe, when they are firm and still slightly green. If left to ripen on the tree, they may turn brown and soft inside.

Pests

Fruit trees can be attacked by a formidable range of insects and diseases whose names alone are enough to put anyone off even thinking of planting an orchard: brown rot, peach canker, apple scab, black knot on plums and cherries, peach leaf-curl, pear leaf blister mite, peach tree borer, cherry maggot, apple maggot, and so on.

The alarmist sprays regularly to avoid such horrors, but there is no need to do so. If you bought healthy trees, they are likely to escape most forms of infestation, and there may be some forms that you find you can live with. For instance, it is not the end of the world if a maggot gets into an apple. Apple maggots usually head straight for the core, leaving the flesh juicy and unblemished; you simply cut out the maggoty part. As a child, eating from our own trees, I always bit into apples carefully, aware of my brother's joke: "Which would you rather find in your apple – a maggot or half a maggot?" Apple maggots were a fact of life, and they were far less harmful (even when accidentally swallowed) than a modern apple that has been sprayed with chemicals. However, there may be occasions when you have to resort to spraying. If a tree is obviously suffering from something serious, with blistered and curled leaves or rotting fruit, you should act promptly. But don't use an all-purpose spray. Consult your local garden store for one that will deal with that particular condition.

In any case, there is no spray that will protect the trees from the creatures that are most likely to cause trouble: birds and squirrels. Some years they can be a thorough nuisance, eating a vast amount of fruit just as it is ripening. Cherry trees are definitely for the birds; it's hard to get any cherries for yourself unless you cover the trees with netting. Apples are usually safe from predators, but plums, pears, apricots, and peaches are popular with wasps as well as birds and squirrels. Sprinkling blood meal around the base of a tree sometimes frightens squirrels away; and you can protect fruit from wasps and birds by wrapping it in clear plastic bags while it is ripening. But, of course, this is impractical if a tree is bearing abundantly – though in that case there is generally enough for everybody: humans, birds, squirrels, the lot. If you want to be sure of getting your share, you can always pick the fruit early and let it ripen on a sunny windowsill. This is easier than covering the entire tree in netting. (See also the homemade organic recipes, pages 237–38.)

Fruit Tree Recipes

Orchard fruit is at its most delicious uncooked, eaten just as nature made it. The crisp juiciness of freshly picked apples, the luscious succulence of sunripened plums and pears . . . merely thinking of them can make your mouth water. But you won't want to eat all the fruit plain, since there are so many scrumptious ways of preparing it: jams and jellies, compotes and fruit salads, pies and tarts, and wonderful concoctions with flaming brandy or rum. Fresh fruit inspires inventiveness, though it is equally good when served very simply, without any fanfare.

How to Prepare and Cook

Stewed peaches and pears are an old-fashioned delicacy that is all too often overlooked. Served icy cold, this is a delicious way of eating the fruit.

PEACHES Dip the peaches in boiling water for about 30 seconds, then plunge them into cold water. This will enable you to slip off their skins. Cut the peaches into quarters, remove the stones, and place the peaches in a bowl of water and lemon juice. (The juice of one lemon will be sufficient; the purpose is to prevent the fruit from discolouring during preparation.) When all the peaches are prepared, cook them in a syrup of water, sugar, and lemon juice. The proportions will depend on how sweet you like the fruit, but begin by trying 2 cups (500 mL) of water, 1 cup (250 mL) of sugar, and the juice of 3 lemons for every 4 lbs (or 2 kg) of peaches. If the fruit is perfectly ripe, about 5 minutes of stewing will be sufficient. If unripe, simmer until soft.

PEARS An identical syrup can be used. To prepare pears, peel them, cut in quarters, remove the core, and soak in a bath of salted water to prevent discoloration. Then rinse and simmer gently in the syrup until soft. Pears will take up to 20 minutes to cook, depending on their ripeness.

During the fruit season, it is well worth freezing some stewed pears and peaches, since they retain their flavour marvellously and make an excellent base for all sorts of desserts. You can make a fruit salad simply by adding whatever fruit is available, for you already have the basic syrup. Or you can do the hot-and-cold trick, heating the peaches to boiling and then pouring them over vanilla ice cream – so easy and so delicious. PLUMS also can be cooked in syrup, with the stones removed and the skins left on, but they are not nearly as appetizing as stewed pears and peaches. Plums are better eaten raw or made into jam.

APPLES disintegrate when stewed, becoming apple sauce. Dip them, too, in a solution of water and lemon juice during preparation. This is particularly important, because fresh tart apples quickly turn brown. To make apple sauce, peel, core, and slice the apples and simmer gently in very little water with sugar and lemon juice to taste. When most of the water has evaporated, mash the apples with a potato masher or fork.

PEARS AND BLUE CHEESE

Ripe pears, blue cheese, and red wine work magic together, creating a beautiful symphony of tastes. They are the perfect end to a formal dinner that has had a complicated first course, since they need no preparation whatsoever, and yet are definitely gourmet fare.

Any blue cheese will do, though a creamy one is best. The red wine should be French, but it can be the cheapest and roughest *vin ordinaire*. The pears should of course be from your own trees.

Let the guests serve themselves – a slice of pear, spread with a wedge of cheese, washed down with a sip of red wine. Bliss!

APPLE FRITTERS

Here is a recipe that is popular with children – and often with adults too. Apple rings dipped in batter and fried in oil may not make the gourmet's "top ten," but there's no denying that these crisp and juicy fritters taste very good.

2	eggs	2
1 cup	flour	250 mL
1 cup	milk	250 mL
2 Tbsp	canola or corn oil	30 mL
¼ tsp	salt	1 mL
3	large apples	3
2 Tbsp	sugar	30 mL

To make the batter, beat the eggs in a bowl and add the flour, milk, oil, and salt. Whisk thoroughly and leave to settle for 2 hours. Peel and core the apples, cut them into slices, and dip them in the batter to coat. Lightly grease the surface of a frying pan, place over a moderate heat and, when the pan is hot, add the batter-coated apple slices. Cook on each side until brown, sprinkle with sugar, and keep warm while cooking the next batch of fritters. *Makes 4 servings.*

TUTTI FRUTTI

If you grow your own fruit, it is hard to resist making Tutti Frutti, that rich miscellany of fermented peaches, pears, plums, nectarines, strawberries, raspberries, cherries, grapes . . . any or all of the above. You will need a large stone crock to hold the fruit, and it is best to include some brandy as a starter to help the fermentation.

1½ cups	brandy	375 mL
	(1 small bottle)	
8 lbs	assorted fruit	3.60 kg
8 lbs	sugar	3.60 kg

Pour the brandy into the stone crock and add 1 lb (450 g) of fruit covered with 1 lb (450 g) of sugar. Cover the crock tightly. A larger quantity of fruit can be used to start with if you like, but it must be accompanied by an equal quantity of sugar. Then, as each fruit comes into season, add it to the crock, always with an equal weight of sugar.

The fruit should be added whole and prepared as follows: raspberries, wash; strawberries, hull and wash; peaches, wash, rub off the fuzz, and prick all over with a fork; plums, pears, and nectarines, wash and prick all over with a fork; grapes, remove the stems but not the seeds and do not prick with a fork; cherries, cut in half and remove the stones.

Stir every few days to help dissolve the sugar and prevent it from lying on the bottom of the crock. When the fruit begins to float to the surface, weight it down with a plate or other non-metal weight.

The fruit will need about two months to ferment. After the last addition of fruit and sugar – and when the juice has ceased to bubble up – the Tutti Frutti can be bottled. Remove any loose stones and pour the mixture into sterile jars. The easiest way to sterilize jars is to place them in a large cauldron of cold water, bring to the boil, and simmer for 10 minutes. Sterilize the caps in the same manner. Seal the jars tightly and store in a cool dry place. Store for 2 to 3 months before eating. Serve the Tutti Frutti with ice cream or cake, or use it as a flavouring for puddings.

PEACH TARTS

At the height of the peach season, I always make several batches of these tarts and stash them away in the freezer. Each small pie makes a greedy portion for one person, and they can transform a cold-meat supper in midwinter, offering an evocative taste of summer in the dessert. The peaches retain their flavour even after months in the freezer. The only drawback is that the pies do take time to make, but the effort is more than compensated for later on, because they can go straight from the freezer to the oven.

	PASTRY	
½ lb	flour	225 g
¼ lb	fat	112 g
½ tsp	salt	2 mL
⅓ cup	water	83 mL

JAM SAUCE

1	peach	1
¼ cup	water	62 mL
¼ lb	sugar	112 g
	quarter of a lemon	

FILLING

6	peaches	6

Combine the first four ingredients to make the pastry (page 251) and line six 114-millimetre (4½-inch) tart pans. Bake the pie shells in a preheated 425°F/220°C oven for about 10 minutes.

While the pastry is cooking, you can start making the jam sauce. Dip a peach into boiling water for about 30 seconds, then into cold water. Slip off the skin, remove the stone, and chop into small pieces. Place in a small saucepan with ¼ cup (62 mL) of water and simmer for 10 minutes. Blend, and then return to the saucepan, along with the sugar and lemon juice. Cook, stirring, until the sauce begins to thicken (about 5 minutes).

Skin the remaining 6 peaches by dipping them in boiling and then cold water. Cut 3 of the peaches in half, discard the stones, and place the halves dome-side up in the centre of the 6 pie shells. Cut each of the remaining 3 peaches into eighths and arrange 4 pieces around each dome. Cover with jam sauce and bake in a preheated 350°F/180°C oven for 30 minutes.

To freeze, cool the tarts, then place in the freezer compartment of the refrigerator. When they are frozen solid, slip each into its own freezer bag, sucking out all air with a straw.

To serve after freezing, remove from the bag and place the frozen tart in a preheated 425°F/220°C oven. Cook for 30 minutes. *Makes 6 servings.*

FLAMBÉED APPLES IN MAPLE SYRUP

This recipe has everything going for it. It's quick and easy to prepare, exquisitely tasty, and the flaming finale turns what would otherwise be an ordinary dessert into a spectacular happening.

4	apples	4
1 Tbsp	butter	15 mL
½ cup	maple syrup	125 mL
½ cup	water	125 mL
1 or 2 Tbsp	rum	15 or 30 mL

Core the apples and place them in a baking dish greased with butter. Add the water and cook in a preheated 350°F/180°C oven for 40 minutes to one hour, depending on the size of the apples. Baste frequently with maple syrup and the juices in the pan.

Take two precautions before flambéing. First, have a saucepan lid on hand with which to smother the flame if necessary. Second, measure the rum and pour it into a frying pan well away from the stove (bottles of spirits can explode when near a source of heat). To flambé, place the frying pan on a burner to warm the rum, set the rum alight with a long match, and pour over the apples. *Makes 4 servings.*

 **Storing and Freezing**

Apples store well in a cool temperature – the McIntosh at just above freezing, other varieties at 32°F/0°C. Lay the apples on planks or shelves, leaving space between them for the air to circulate. Do not store them piled in a barrel.

Peaches, pears, apricots, and nectarines retain their flavour best if they are cooked before freezing. Stew them as described above in How to Prepare and Cook fruit (page 88). (The apricots and nectarines do not need to be skinned; simply remove their stones before cooking.) Cool the fruit in its syrup and then ladle it into plastic sandwich boxes. When it has frozen into a solid block, pop it out (like ice cubes) and place in plastic freezer bags, sucking out the air with a straw. To serve after freezing, thaw slowly in the bag. Eat as soon as possible after thawing. Do not refreeze any leftovers; throw them away.

Apples, too, keep their taste best when cooked before freezing. The simplest way to freeze them is to make them into apple sauce, as described in How to Prepare and Cook fruit (page 89), and then freeze in sandwich boxes before transferring to freezer bags. To thaw after freezing, remove from the bag, tip into a saucepan with a little water and slowly heat to boiling. Simmer for a few minutes and either serve or leave to cool.

The best way to freeze plums is to stone and then stew them, but it is hardly worth the effort since they lose much of their quality when frozen. Cherries, on the other hand, taste excellent after freezing. Stone them and then stew gently, allowing 1 cup (250 mL) of water and ½ cup (125 mL) of sugar to every 2 cups (500 mL) of pitted cherries. Package the same way as peaches and pears. To serve after freezing, thaw slowly in the bag or remove from the bag, heat in a pan, and serve as a hot sauce over ice cream. All frozen fruit will last a year.

Garlic

Many people love to eat garlic, declaring it the most savoury of flavours. Others can't stand it. Even if you are among the latter, garlic is well worth growing because it works as a systemic insecticide. Plant it in a rose bed, and it will help keep aphids away from the roses. Garlic plants are not unattractive – they have a rather exotic appearance – and they can fit anywhere in the garden near any plant that seems in need of help.

Garlic is a long-season crop that must be planted in September or October if it is to have time to mature by the following August. Since it cannot withstand harsh winters, garlic can be difficult to grow in the colder parts of Canada. In much of British Columbia, Ontario, and the Maritimes, you should have no problems, but in colder zones you will need to mulch the plants over winter by building up a protective covering of earth and leaves. Of course, if you are growing garlic simply as an insecticide, anywhere in Canada is suitable. Plant it at any time of year and just let it grow.

Garlic is easier to grow from bulbs than from seed, and you can use the bulbs that are sold at vegetable counters. Break them into cloves and plant the cloves base down about 5 centimetres (2 inches) below the surface of the soil and at least 6 centimetres (2½ inches) apart. In colder zones, plant the cloves at least 8 centimetres (3 inches) deep. The garlic will do best in well-fertilized soil and in a bed that gets full sun.

How to Grow
Planting

✐ Ongoing Care

Garlic plants need little care, apart from occasional weeding, and even that is not essential. Soon after planting, a small green shoot will emerge from the tip of the clove, and this will develop into a stalk and leaves similar to those of an onion. As with onions, if a seedpod forms at the top of the stem, you should break it off. This will encourage the plant to concentrate its strength on developing the bulb.

Towards the end of summer, when the tops fall over and begin to wither, pull up the plant. You will find that each clove has divided to become a bulb of a dozen or more cloves. Brush off the earth and leave the bulbs to dry in the sun for a few days before taking them indoors.

Garlic Recipes

Many recipes that include garlic do not noticeably taste of it. Instead of dominating, the garlic acts as a catalyst, imbuing the whole with a subtle richness of flavour, an indefinable mellowness that makes the dish taste particularly good. In other cases, nobody could miss the fact that garlic is an ingredient. I have chosen a selection of the latter to include here, since people who like garlic will enjoy savouring it undisguised.

GARLIC BOURSIN

This homemade Boursin is perfect for a party, when it can be served attractively in small earthenware pots surrounded by crackers or melba toast. Although the taste of garlic is quite strong, there are unlikely to be any leftovers; this is the type of cheese one wants to have "just a little bit more of" . . . and then just a little bit more again. Because of the high proportion of cottage cheese, it is relatively low-fat and can be made in large quantities at little cost.

9 oz	2% cottage cheese	250 g
9 oz	cream cheese	250 g
1	medium-sized garlic clove	1
2 Tbsp	chopped fresh chives	30 mL
	salt and black pepper	

Sieve the cottage cheese by pressing it through a strainer. Combine it with the cream cheese, beating it in thoroughly with a spoon. Skin and mince the garlic. Stir it into the cheese, together with the chopped chives. Add salt and freshly ground black pepper to taste.

Shape the cheese into a round, or spoon it into small earthenware pots or bowls. Dust with black pepper and a sprinkling of chives, and keep in the refrigerator until needed. Serve with crackers or melba toast, or spread on celery sticks. *Makes about 20 servings.*

GARLIC BREAD

Here is another great standby for a party – though not the same party at which you serve the Garlic Boursin. You don't want to lose the effect of either by overdoing the flavour.

1	garlic clove	1
½ cup	melted butter	125 mL
2	loaves French bread	2

Skin and mince the garlic and combine it with the butter. Cut the loaves into thick slices and brush both sides of each slice with the garlic butter. Wrap each loaf in tinfoil and bake in a preheated 350°F/180°C oven for 10 to 15 minutes. *Makes about 20 servings.*

BROILED GARLIC SHRIMPS

I first tasted shrimps cooked this way in a small family restaurant in Montreal, and it has been one of my favourites ever since. The actual cooking takes very little time, and the preparation doesn't take long either. Allow between 4 and 6 shrimps per person, depending on the size of the shrimps.

2 lbs	large shrimps	900 g
2 Tbsp	parsley	30 mL
1	garlic clove	1
2 cups	canola or corn oil	500 mL
	salt and black pepper	
2 Tbsp	breadcrumbs	30 mL
	half a lemon	

Cut the shell of each shrimp down the back, using kitchen scissors, and remove the black vein. Cut off the legs but leave the shell on. Then take a sharp knife and make a deep cut down the back so that the shrimp can be opened flat in a butterfly position. Chop the parsley, peel and mince the garlic, and place in a bowl together with the oil and a little salt and pepper. Stir, then add the shrimp and let it marinate for an hour or more, turning occasionally.

Shortly before the meal, lay a piece of tinfoil on a large flat baking dish. (This is not essential, but it makes the washing-up easy, since you simply roll up the tinfoil and don't have to scrub the dish.) Lay the shrimp flat on the tinfoil, shell side down, and sprinkle lightly with freshly made breadcrumbs (page 253). Tilt the baking dish slightly to drain off any oil from the shrimp and spoon off all the oil that flows down. Then squeeze the lemon over the shrimp.

To cook, place under a hot grill for 5 to 8 minutes until the shrimp is cooked through and bubbly. Serve with lemon wedges and melted butter. *Makes 4 to 6 servings.*

 **Storing**

After bringing the garlic indoors, hang it in a mesh bag in an airy place for a week or two to complete the drying process. It can then be transferred to the basement or anywhere that is cool and dry. Some people like to weave the tops together so that it can be hung as a string.

Grapes

Grapes grow well in southwestern Ontario, the interior valleys of British Columbia, and other parts of Canada where the winter is not too severe. There is something wonderfully romantic about growing your own grapes, and the vines can form an attractive feature even in the smallest backyard. They can be grown as a trellis dividing off the vegetable patch or as a canopy covering a patio – a great show-off gimmick in the fall, when you can casually lean up and pluck a few grapes to offer admiring visitors. In a larger garden, they can be trained to form a leafy bower, where you can bask away hot summer afternoons, enjoying the dappled shade and the gentle rustling of the leaves. Then there is a grapevine's use as camouflage, tumbling over railings or crumbling walls. I know of one ancient vine that has spread itself almost the entire length of a backyard, its huge leaves giving a luxuriant display of greenery while hiding a broken-down old fence.

How to Grow
Planting

The best time to plant grapes is early spring. Besides the well-known Canadian blue grapes such as Concord and Fredonia, you have the choice of a range of green and red grapes, including seedless varieties.

Buy the young grapevines from a reputable garden centre or nursery that will give you a guarantee. The vines will probably be growing in containers, and this makes planting easy. Dig a hole wider and deeper than the container and shovel in a rich mix of manure and peat moss. If available, some bone meal should be added too, since it will act as a slow-release fertilizer, feeding the vine throughout the first summer. Fill the hole with water and let it soak in. Then carefully cut away the container and ease the vine into the hole, trying to disturb its roots as little as possible. The vine should be planted a little deeper than it stood in its container. Press it in firmly, adding more earth if necessary to hold it steady.

If you are planting more than one vine, space them about 2 metres (6 feet) apart. Ideally, they should be in full sun, but they will still give a good crop of grapes if planted on a patio, for instance, that is shaded by the house for part of the day. More important is that they be planted in well-drained soil; grapes will not do well in swampy ground.

Grapevines can be trained to grow in any shape or direction simply by tying the canes the way you want them to grow and by cutting off any shoots that are growing where you don't want them to. But it is best not to cut off anything the first year. Let the vine establish itself and gather strength before you begin to prune.

The pruning should be done while the grapevine is dormant. The best time is early spring before budbreak. If you plan to prune aggressively, consult a book that details the various methods and styles; all sorts of fancy training systems have been devised to shape grapevines. Such expertise is not necessary for the average backyard gardener, who simply wants a leafy vine and a crop of grapes. In this case, all that needs to be done is to cut off any canes that are crowding out others or heading where you don't want them to. If you feel like being more adventurous, you can also cut off the canes that bore fruit last summer, since this will encourage the growth of new fruit. But be careful what you cut. Grapes bear fruit on the previous year's shoots, so be sure not to cut off any newly grown canes – unless you are intentionally doing so in order to shape the vine.

When the grapes begin to form, you can thin them by picking the smaller fruit from a bunch or by removing whole bunches. You will get fewer grapes this way, but those you do get will be bigger.

Grapes require lots of food and drink, so water them well during hot spells and give them more fertilizer every year. I once had a grapevine that seemed very unwilling to grow, so one spring I spread a whole bag of sheep manure on the earth around its roots and then added some bone meal for good measure. The results were amazing. That grapevine more than doubled its size during the summer. In fact, it grew more in that one year than it had in all previous years, producing a marvellous effulgence of large green leaves as well as countless new canes. And I had a bumper crop of grapes into the bargain. However, it is not a good idea to load on fertilizer to such an extent very often, since too much fertilizer can cause the grapevine to put its energies into vegetative growth rather than fruit production.

In humid weather, watch for mildew on the leaves. Some varieties of grape are particularly susceptible to powdery mildew.

This can usually be halted by spraying with organic fungicides, which are available in convenient hand-held dispensers (but check to make sure that the fungicide will not damage your particular variety of grape).

 Pests

Although two hundred or so pests can cause damage to grapes, the only ones you are likely to encounter are a few beetles and leafhoppers, and possibly the grape berry moth. The most likely is the grape flea beetle, an attractive looking insect about 5 millimetres long with a greenish-blue metallic sheen. Its larvae are black-spotted grubs that feed on the leaves. If you don't want to spray, it is fairly easy to pick off the grubs by hand and to flick the adults into a pail of soapy water. Search for them and deal with them soon after the leaves appear in May. You won't get them all, but it doesn't do much harm to have a few around feeding on the fully grown leaves.

The grape berry moth is more of a problem because it attacks the fruit. If you see what look like tiny spider webs among the grapes, pick off and destroy those bunches. If there is a massive infestation, you will probably have to spray, in which case you should consult your local garden store to decide which of the available sprays best suits your priorities.

As soon as the grapes are ripe, birds and squirrels will come visiting, but there are usually more than enough grapes to feed everybody. To be sure of getting your share, pick the bunches as soon as they ripen. In fact, the birds may prove to be allies in the spring, so don't scare them away if you see them pecking at the vines; they will be feeding off insect eggs and small grubs.

Grape Recipes

Like all fruit, grapes are best eaten raw, either on their own or combined with other fruit. But a mature grapevine will likely produce far more than you will want to eat raw. The obvious solution is wine making, and it can be fun to stock up with the equipment and get busy in the basement, though the enjoyment is usually in making the wine rather than drinking it. In my experience, homemade wine all too often tastes curious rather than delicious.

For those who enjoy preserving, grape jelly is a sure winner, especially when made with the pungent Canadian blue grapes. But this, too, entails a good deal of time and trouble. The easiest way of dealing with an overabundance of grapes is to make them into juice. Simply boil the grapes in a little water, then strain the liquid and add sugar to taste. Served with ice, this drink is very refreshing.

GRAPES AND MELON BALLS

Seedless grapes are preferable for this dessert, which is a form of fresh fruit salad. Simple to make, it meets the "three d's" that I like to aim for: decorative, delicious, and drudgery-free.

2	oranges	2
1	lime	1
2 Tbsp	instant dissolving sugar	30 mL
2	cantaloupes	2
4 cups	grapes	1 L

Squeeze the juice from the oranges and lime, and add the sugar to make a fairly tart syrup. Stir well to dissolve the sugar. With a melon-ball cutter, scoop out the flesh of the cantaloupes. Toss together with the grapes and syrup, and serve chilled. *Makes 4 to 6 servings.*

GRAPES AND DUCKLING

This is a low-fat way of enjoying duck, because the skin is removed before cooking. For perfection, green grapes should be used in the recipe because of the contrast in colours, though red grapes work equally well.

1	duckling	1
2 cups	red wine	500 mL
½ cup	freshly squeezed orange juice	125 mL
2 cups	water	500 mL
3	chicken cubes	3
4	cloves	4
1 Tbsp	butter	15 mL
1 Tbsp	flour	15 mL
1 cup	seedless grapes	250 mL

Strip the skin from the duck by pulling it from the flesh while running a knife underneath it. Cut the duck into serving portions (setting aside the wings and giblets, which can later be boiled up to make soup stock, page 249) and place the pieces of duck in a saucepan with the wine, orange juice, water, chicken cubes, and cloves. Bring to a boil and simmer, covered, for 40 minutes.

Remove the pieces of duck onto a platter and keep warm. Boil the liquid briskly for about 15 minutes until it is reduced to 2 cups (500 mL). In a small saucepan, melt the butter and add the flour. Gradually add ½ cup (125 mL) of the liquid. Stir until the sauce is smooth. Add the remaining liquid and heat to boiling, stirring constantly. Cut the grapes in half and add them to the sauce. Simmer for 3 or 4 minutes and pour over the duck. *Makes 4 servings.*

GRAPE JELLY DESSERT

Canadian blue grapes are ideal for this recipe. The raspberries are optional, but if you grow everbearing raspberries, they will be producing their fall crop at the same time as the grapes are ripe, and the two flavours work superbly together.

2 lbs	Canadian blue grapes	900 g
4 cups	water	1 L
⅔ oz	gelatin powder (2 pkts)	20 g
⅓ cup	sugar	83 mL
¼ cup	raspberries	62 mL

Simmer the grapes in the water for 30 minutes. Strain to separate the pips and skin from the juice and then strain again through a fine sieve, such as a coffee strainer, to catch any further residue. Keep only the juice. When cool, return it to the saucepan. Sprinkle on the powdered gelatin and stir until dissolved. Add the sugar and heat to boiling, stirring constantly. Pour the juice into individual serving dishes and allow to cool. When the jelly has set, decorate the top with raspberries. A couple of grape leaves surrounding each dish adds a final decorative touch. *Makes 4 to 6 servings.*

CANADIAN GRAPE PIE

Concord and other Canadian blue grapes make a marvellously tasty pie, which I think is even better than blueberry pie, and it's quite easy to prepare. If you don't have time to make the pastry, you can always use two ready-made pie shells (one for the top and one for the bottom).

PASTRY

¾ lb	flour	340 g
6 oz	fat	170 g
½ tsp	salt	2 mL
6 Tbsp	water	90 mL

FILLING

2 cups	skinned grapes	500 mL
⅔ cup	sugar	166 mL
2½ Tbsp	flour	37 mL

First, pinch the grapes out of their skins until you have enough to fill 2 cups (500 mL). Keep the skins. Cook the pulp gently for about 10 minutes, until you can separate the seeds. Strain and discard the seeds. Then mix the pulp with the skins, the sugar, and the flour. (At this stage, the mixture will look thoroughly unappetizing, but don't be put off. During the baking, the grape skins will soften and blend in with the rest of the pulp to make a rich purple filling.)

Make the pastry (page 251) and roll out half to line a 23-centimetre (9-inch) pie plate. Pour the grape mixture into the pie shell. Lightly dampen the edges all round, then roll out the rest of the pastry and lay it on top, sealing the edges firmly. Cut a few vents in the top crust. Place on a metal baking tray and bake in a preheated 400°F/200°C oven for 15 minutes. Then turn down the heat to 350°F/180°C and cook a further 30 minutes. Cool and serve very cold, accompanied with table cream. *Makes 6 to 8 servings.*

Herbs

Surely it is every gardener's dream to have a herb garden. Thumbing through the glossy "house and garden" magazines with their entrancing photos, it is so easy to fantasize about creating your own garden of aromatic herbs set among flagstone paths, with an ancient stone sundial as the centrepiece and perhaps low box hedges surrounding each bed.

For the average gardener, such dreams must remain dreams, but the experience can be enjoyed to some extent by devoting a whole bed to herbs. Just outside the kitchen door is the best place, for the obvious reason that it is so convenient. Which herbs you grow will depend on which you commonly use in your cooking. Parsley, chives, and thyme are those I class as the basics, but my personal choice also includes basil, because it tastes so exquisite fresh. Other people will have different preferences. In making the selection of which herbs to describe here, I have focused on those that I think most people would want to grow.

 **How to Grow**

All herbs can be grown from seed, but it is easier to buy them as bedding plants. Although most herbs are said to require full sun, they will do well in a bed near the house that may be in shade for part of the day. Before planting the herbs, dig some peat moss and well-rotted manure into the bed to make the soil light and rich, then water the soil to create a muddy environment and gently press in the plants.

There are two types of basil: small leaf and large leaf. Both will become bushy, pushing out side branches, if you pinch off the central shoot; but wait until the plant has several leaves before doing this. As soon as the flower buds form, pinch them off too. Basil is said to repel mosquitoes, so it is a good plant to grow beside a patio.

To harvest basil, simply pick the leaves as you need them. If you want fresh basil during the winter, dig up some of the plants before the first frost, replant in flowerpots, and run under the hose to wash off any insects. Although basil is treated as an annual in Canada, it is in fact a perennial and will continue to grow if placed in a sunny window.

Chives are perennials and are usually the first shoots to push up in spring. Early in the summer they produce pretty mauve flowers that look like pompoms. By the time the flowers have bloomed, the chives may be so tall that they are falling over, making a convenient hiding place for slugs. When this happens, give them a crew cut. Take a pair of scissors and cut off the whole bunch about 2 centimetres (¾ inch) from the base. Within a few days, new shoots will begin to appear, giving you a second crop.

Chives can be picked for the table as soon as they begin to grow, regardless of their length. If you want fresh chives over winter, take a sharp spade or cutter and bring it down fiercely, cutting the plant in two. Dig up one half, give it a very close crew cut, and wash the roots under a hose to get rid of most of the soil and any insects. Place a mix of peat moss and manure in the bottom of a flowerpot, add the chives root-side down, and cover over with potting soil. Within a week, the plant will begin to push up new shoots.

To thin chives, cut away parts of them in the same manner. Once chives get established, they spread considerably and you will probably need to thin them every year.

Dill

Dill is one of the few herbs that are best grown from seed, especially if you need a large amount for pickling cucumbers. Sow it early in spring. Rake over the earth, lightly water where you are going to sow, and sprinkle the seed by hand, adding a light covering of crumbled earth. The dill may take as much as two weeks to germinate, and you will then probably need to do some thinning by pulling out seedlings that are growing too close together.

Dill leaves can be cut at any time but are most tasty in late summer, just before the plant flowers. This usually coincides most conveniently with the height of the cucumber season. Dill can also be harvested after flowering by collecting the ripe seeds.

Fennel is a perennial and it is best not planted near dill. The two are so closely related that they can be cross pollinated; this mingles the flavours, making both taste much the same.

    Like dill, fennel is best cut just before flowering or after the seeds have ripened. In the fall, cut the plants down to about 10 centimetres (4 inches) above the ground.

Marjoram comes in two forms: pot marjoram and sweet marjoram. The latter is the most commonly grown, since it has a sweeter taste. Sweet marjoram is treated as an annual in Canada because it cannot survive a frost. Grow it in the same way as basil, picking the leaves whenever you need them.

Mint is a perennial and is the easiest to grow of all herbs. Indeed, the problem with mint is how to stop it from growing. It usually acts as if it is trying to take over the entire garden, pushing out a vigorous network of roots that spread through and under neighbouring plants, under walls, and even through cracks in concrete. Each spring I pull up large quantities of mint – a wonderfully fragrant task, since the smell of mint intensifies when it is crushed.

    Mint will grow even if all you plant is a length of root, but garden centres usually sell it as a small bedding plant. To prevent the mint from spreading, some people advise removing the base from a bucket, burying it in the soil, and planting the mint inside it. But this does not really solve the problem, since the roots soon become overcrowded in the bucket and inevitably find a way out. It makes more sense to plant the mint among annuals which die off each year, leaving you a clear field so that you can pull up all unwanted roots the following spring.

    To harvest mint, pick it whenever you need it. The flowers are deliciously fragrant, but they attract flies and should be picked off as soon as they form. Around midsummer, when the mint is getting leggy, cut half of it down to ground level. This will cause it to send up a new crop of shoots. As soon as these leaves begin to appear, cut the remaining mint down to ground level so that it will produce a second crop as well. By doing this cutback in two stages, there are always some mint leaves available for you to pick.

If you want to grow mint on a windowsill during the winter, simply fill a flowerpot with potting soil and bury some lengths of root in it.

Oregano

Also called wild marjoram, oregano is a hardy perennial. Like mint, it needs cutting back each year, though its roots do not spread as aggressively as mint roots. Oregano has small and very fragrant flowers. They can be left on a mature plant that has plenty of leaves but should be picked off if you want maximum leaf production. To harvest oregano, pick the leaves as you need them.

Parsley

Parsley does best in a very rich soil, so as well as digging in peat moss and manure, it helps to sprinkle some blood meal on and around the plants. The blood meal can have a magical effect, causing frail little clumps of parsley to transform themselves into large healthy plants with thick stems and masses of curly leaves.

To harvest parsley, cut off the stems as you need them. This encourages new growth; but do not take more than two or three stems at a time from any one plant, otherwise you may weaken it. Water well in hot weather to discourage the plants from flowering and going to seed. If any flower pods do form, pick them off immediately. Parsley becomes straggly and bitter after it has flowered.

Parsley will survive a mild winter, but in most regions of Canada it is best to take it indoors in the fall. When you dig up the plant, you will find it has developed a long root, rather like a parsnip. Wash the root and the stalks thoroughly under a strong hose, then plant the parsley in a flowerpot with a mix of well-rotted manure and light potting soil. Be careful not to plant the parsley too deeply. It may rot and die if the crown is below the soil. Allow the top of each root to poke up just above the surface. In spring the parsley can be replanted in the garden, again with the crown just above soil level.

Rosemary is an evergreen that can be grown as a perennial where the ground does not freeze solid. It will grow into a wide bush and should be planted at least 30 centimetres (12 inches) from neighbouring herbs. Rosemary is suitable for a flower bed as well as a herb garden, for it produces heavily scented flowers, rather like lavendar. To harvest, cut the sprigs as you need them.

Rosemary

Thyme is a perennial shrub that will spread as it grows, so it too should be given plenty of room. Plant it at least 30 centimetres (12 inches) from other perennials. The stalks can be picked at any time, though it is easiest to harvest them when they are not in flower. The more you cut thyme, the more bushy it will grow.

Thyme

In parts of Canada where the winters are severe, it is advisable to give the plants winter protection by building up the earth around them. After a few years, thyme tends to get straggly and may lose its pungency. This can be avoided by dividing the plant whenever it gets too large. Simply cut part of it off. Provided there are roots in both parts, the thyme will continue to grow. If you do this in the autumn, you can replant the smaller part of the thyme in a flowerpot and take it indoors to provide you with fresh thyme all winter. When doing this, wash the thyme thoroughly before potting so that you clean its branches of any insects.

Herb Recipes

My favourite recipes all rely on fresh herbs for their savoury taste. Commercially dried herbs just don't give the same flavour, and even home-dried herbs are far inferior to fresh.

The marvellous thing about fresh herbs is that they can create a gourmet meal from the most simple ingredients. Take eggs, tomatoes, and bread, for example. The bread is made into toast to accompany a herb omelette, made by beating chopped parsley and a little thyme in with the eggs (plus a little salt, of course). The tomatoes are served as a side salad, cut into thin slices and sprinkled with chopped basil, salt, and black pepper. The result is a quick and easy supper that tastes like a feast. And all because of the fresh herbs.

For a tasty low-fat lunch, try a parsley sandwich: light rye bread, spread with a little margarine, together with a light sprinkling of salt and plenty of chopped parsley.

MINT SAUCE

Everyone who grows mint is likely to want to make mint sauce at some time. It is simple to make, and it smells wonderful while you are doing so.

½ cup	mint leaves	125 mL
¼ cup	brown sugar	62 mL
½ cup	cider vinegar	125 mL

Wash the mint, discard the stems, and chop the leaves very finely. Place in a small bowl and pour on just enough boiling water to cover. It is important to use as little water as possible, otherwise the sauce will be too diluted. Add brown sugar and stir to help it dissolve. When cool, add the vinegar. *Makes 4 to 6 servings.*

MINT TABBOULEH

This salad has everything going for it. It's nutritious, delicious, decorative, filling, and easy to prepare. If you can't find the cracked wheat at your supermarket, try a health-food store. Specialty stores usually carry it too. Both the mint and the parsley must be fresh, of course, and don't hold back on the mint. The predominant flavours should be mint and lemon.

SALAD

1 cup	cracked wheat (bulgur)	250 mL
1 cup	chopped mint	250 mL
4	chopped tomatoes	4
6	sliced green onions	6
1 cup	chopped cucumber	250 mL
4 Tbsp	chopped parsley	60 mL
	salt and black pepper	

DRESSING

3 Tbsp	lemon juice	45 mL
1 Tbsp	vinegar	15 mL
2 Tbsp	canola or corn oil	30 mL

Soak the cracked wheat in 2 cups (500 mL) of water for 30 minutes. Drain thoroughly and empty into a salad bowl. Add all the other salad ingredients with plenty of salt and a little freshly ground black pepper. In a separate bowl, mix the lemon juice, vinegar, and oil. Whisk briskly with a fork, pour over the salad, and toss gently. *Makes 4 to 6 servings.*

ROSEMARY WITH EYE OF THE ROUND

Rosemary adds a pleasant flavour to meat – sprinkled on a roast of lamb or on duck or spare ribs – and it gives a superb flavour to an eye of the round roast of beef. I once served this dish to an old family friend who was well into his eighties, and he told me he had never in his life tasted such good meat. Whether that was a reflection on his usual eating habits or my cooking, I don't know, but this is certainly a delicious way of cooking beef.

1	eye of the round roast	1
1	garlic clove	1
	rosemary	
	salt and black pepper	
1	small onion	1
2	bay leaves	2

If there is any fat on the roast, cut it off and discard it. Peel the garlic and cut it into thin slices. With a sharp knife, pierce the roast and slip a sliver of garlic into each deep gash. Sprinkle liberally with rosemary and season with salt and black pepper. Peel the onion, slice it thinly, then lay the bay leaves on the meat, topped by a layer of onion slices. Roast in a preheated 400°F/200°C oven for about an hour. Do not overcook. The roast should be slightly pink in the middle when served. Slice thinly.

Serve with roast carrots (page 44) or a green salad.

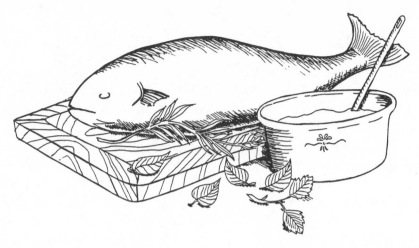

HERB STUFFING FOR TROUT

When made with fresh herbs and fresh bread-crumbs, this makes a superb stuffing for trout. Fill the cavity with the stuffing and then roll the trout in flour and fry for 6 minutes on each side: or roll in flour, brush with butter, and grill for 5 or 6 minutes a side, depending on the size of the trout. This stuffing is also good for bass.

3	green onions	3
2 Tbsp	butter	30 mL
2	peeled and chopped tomatoes	2
2 Tbsp	chopped basil leaves	30 mL
2 Tbsp	chopped parsley	30 mL
	salt and pepper	
1 cup	breadcrumbs	250 mL

Chop the green onions and sauté them in the butter. Add the finely chopped tomatoes, chopped basil, and parsley, and simmer for about 5 minutes until the tomatoes are soft.

Season with salt and black pepper, and stir in the breadcrumbs. If the mixture is too dry and crumbly to hold together, add a little white wine or lemon juice. *Makes stuffing for 4 trout or one bass.*

HERB STUFFING FOR POULTRY

I first sampled this recipe as a stuffing for roast squab but have since tried it with turkey, chicken, and goose, and it is equally good with all of them.

1	peeled onion	1
1	celery stalk	1
2 Tbsp	butter	30 mL
1 Tbsp	fresh thyme leaves	15 mL
2 Tbsp	chopped parsley	30 mL
2 Tbsp	lemon juice	30 mL
1 cup	breadcrumbs	250 mL
	salt and pepper	

Finely chop the onion and celery, and sauté them in butter for 2 minutes. Add the thyme and parsley, and cook a further 2 minutes. Stir in the lemon juice and breadcrumbs, and season to taste with salt and freshly ground black pepper. If the mixture is too dry, moisten with wine, chicken stock, or more lemon juice. The stuffing should be moist enough to hold together but should not be soggy. *Makes enough for 4 squab or one medium-sized bird.*

HERB STUFFING FOR LAMB

This stuffing is particularly tasty as a filling for rolled breast of lamb, which is tied around the stuffing and then roasted. It works well also as a stuffing for other roasts of lamb and for roast veal.

1	peeled onion	1
2 Tbsp	fresh marjoram	30 mL
2 Tbsp	chopped parsley	30 mL
1 tsp	grated lemon peel	5 mL
1 cup	breadcrumbs	250 mL
	salt and pepper	
1	egg	1

Chop the onion very finely and mash it together with the chopped marjoram and chopped parsley. Add the lemon peel and breadcrumbs, and season with salt and pepper. Whisk the egg and stir it into the mixture. If the stuffing then seems too runny, add more breadcrumbs and adjust the seasoning accordingly.

HERBED CHICKEN

When I am tired at the end of a busy day, longing for a delicious meal yet not wanting to make the effort, I often choose this recipe. It is so easy that even non-cooks can pose as gourmet chefs, but you do have to use fresh herbs to give it the succulent aroma and flavour that make it so special. If you grow beans as well as herbs, you really have a winner, because the perfect accompaniment is lightly cooked green beans. Failing that, any fresh vegetable will do, or serve it with pasta sprinkled with parsley.

4	chicken breasts	4
1 Tbsp	fresh thyme	15 mL
1 Tbsp	fresh chives	15 mL
1 Tbsp	chopped parsley	15 mL
	salt and pepper	

Tear off a length of tinfoil that is large enough to double over, holding all four chicken breasts. Lay it on a flat baking dish. Cut the chicken breasts from the bone, skin them, and place them on half the tinfoil. Sprinkle with thyme, chopped chives, parsley, and a little salt and pepper. Fold over the other half of the tinfoil to make an envelope enclosing the chicken. Seal tightly at the edges. Turn on the grill and, when it is red hot, place the baking dish directly under it. Close the oven door and cook for 18 minutes. When you open the envelope, a delicious waft of herbs will greet you. The chicken will be just cooked and still moist, surrounded by its own juices. Spoon the juices over the chicken as you serve. *Makes 4 servings.*

🍅 Storing 🥫

The best way to store herbs is to dry them. This can be done at any time of year but is easiest early in summer before the herbs flower. You will get the best results if you process the herbs in small batches so that none are lying around wilting while waiting to be dried. The old-fashioned way was to let the herbs wilt, hanging them in bunches from rafters, but they retain far more flavour if you dry them quickly, preferably in a microwave.

All herbs should be washed first, and large-leaved herbs such as mint and oregano should be picked from their stalks so that only the leaves get dried. With small-leaved herbs such as thyme, it is simpler to dry the whole twigs, since they are easier to crumble and strip of their leaves after drying.

The procedure is as follows: cut a small amount of the chosen herb, wash it, blot on paper towels or a cloth, and remove the stalks if appropriate. Place in a microwave between paper towels for 1 or 2 minutes until crisp and crumbly. Cool and store in airtight jars. If neither you nor your friends have a microwave, the herbs can be dried slowly on a baking tray in a low oven (about 150°F/70°C), but they will not retain quite as much flavour as those dried in a microwave.

Kohlrabi

Kohlrabi is a member of the cabbage family, though it looks and tastes more like a turnip than a cabbage. It can be grown throughout Canada but does best where it is not subject to extreme heat.

Kohlrabi is a quick-growing plant and can therefore be sown directly into the garden. It is only worth starting indoors if you want an early crop. When all danger of frost is past, dig over the bed, adding well-rotted manure and peat moss if the soil is heavy or has not been fertilized. Rake the surface flat and sow the seeds about 1 centimetre (1/3 inch) deep and about 2.5 centimetres (1 inch) apart. Cover with earth and then water lightly with a watering can.

How to Grow
Planting

The kohlrabi will need thinning as it grows. After the seedlings have appeared, pull up those that are close together so that the remaining seedlings are about 15 centimetres (6 inches) apart. Water regularly, especially if the temperature suddenly soars. In very hot weather, kohlrabi may bolt rather than forming a round bulb on the lower part of the stem, and a long heatwave can cause kohlrabi bulbs to become tough and woody. By keeping the crop well watered and as cool as possible, you will encourage fast growth and tender bulbs.

Ongoing Care

Kohlrabi can be picked when the bulbs are barely 5 centimetres (2 inches) in diameter. They are at their most tender when small, and it is best to pull them up at this stage rather than waiting for them to grow large and risk them getting tough. They will remain crisp for several weeks if stored in plastic bags in the refrigerator.

Pests

All the insects that attack cabbage also attack kohlrabi, but you are most likely to have trouble from flea beetles, which may descend on the seedlings in great numbers. Take action as soon as you notice them, giving them a burst of organic dust or liquid soap from a hand-held spray. (See also organic repellants, pages 237–38.)

Kohlrabi Recipes

I f you have never tasted kohlrabi, be adventurous and try it. You will be pleasantly surprised if you eat it raw. The bulbous stem has a sweet, spicy flavour, rather like a radish, only better . . . perhaps halfway between a radish and a water chestnut. When cooked, kohlrabi loses this distinctive flavour and does not taste much of anything, though there is a faint hint of turnip. Cooked kohlrabi works best combined with something that has a pronounced taste.

How to Prepare and Cook

To prepare kohlrabi, cut off the leaves and peel and slice the round bulblike stem. If you want to try it as a cooked vegetable, either boil or steam it until it loses its crispness (10 to 15 minutes). Sprinkle with salt and add a pat of butter; or sauté the boiled slices in butter together with fresh thyme, adding the chopped kohlrabi leaves after 3 minutes and then cooking for a few minutes longer.

KOHLRABI AND TOMATO SALAD

Kohlrabi adds a spicy crispness to almost any salad, and it goes particularly well with tomatoes. This colourful salad has the advantage of being quick to prepare.

2	kohlrabi	2
4	tomatoes	4
3 Tbsp	parsley	45 mL
1 Tbsp	vinegar	15 mL
2 Tbsp	canola or corn oil	30 mL
	salt and black pepper	

Remove and discard the leaves. Peel the kohlrabi, slice finely, then chop the slices into quarters. Add the chopped tomatoes and chopped parsley. Make the dressing in a separate bowl, combining the vinegar, oil, salt, and pepper. Whisk briskly with a fork, pour over the salad, and toss lightly. *Makes 4 servings.*

KOHLRABI CRUNCH IN BACON ROLLS

When deep fried in bacon, kohlrabi is an epicure's delight. These crunchy morsels can be served as appetizers or as part of a buffet lunch. You can cook them in a fondue dish at the table or in a deep pan in the kitchen, depending on the type of entertaining you are doing. And for extra flavour you can add further ingredients to the rolls – smoked oysters or prunes or chicken livers.

	ROLLS	
6	kohlrabi	6
1 lb	bacon	450 g
	cooking oil	
	DIP	
½ cup	tomato ketchup	125 mL
¼ cup	Dijon mustard	62 mL

First, make the dip by combining the ketchup and mustard. Mix thoroughly and spoon into small bowls.

Peel the kohlrabi and cut into rectangular cubes about 1 centimetre thick and 3 centimetres long (⅓ inch by 1¼ inch). Cut the bacon slices in half crosswise and wrap each around a cube of kohlrabi. Secure with toothpicks or skewers and deep fry in oil until the bacon is crisp. Drain on paper towels and serve immediately, accompanied by the dip. *Makes about 20 servings.*

Storing and Freezing

Kohlrabi will keep for several weeks when stored in plastic bags in the refrigerator. Although it can also be frozen, I do not advise this form of storage; frozen kohlrabi tends to be mushy and tasteless.

Leeks

When living on the prairies I made the surprising discovery that leeks can survive a Canadian winter, even with temperatures of forty below. This was a real breakthrough, not because they are anything special in themselves, but because of the inimitable flavour they give to soups and ragouts. With the short prairie summers, it had been hard to get good-sized leeks, but then came the year when the ground froze before I had harvested them. I thought I had lost them, but the following spring most pushed up green shoots, and by the end of the summer they had developed satisfyingly thick stalks as large as I have ever seen.

Since then, I have always grown leeks on a rotational basis so that there are some large enough to be harvested throughout the summer and fall, others that get overwintered, and still others that are very young, sown that year, with leaves that are tender and slender – perfect for chopping into salads or adding as a garnish to soups.

It is worth growing leeks for these young leaves alone. Fully grown leeks can be bought in the stores, but I know of nowhere that you can get the delicately pungent young leaves – except in the vegetable patch at the side of the house.

How to Grow
Planting

Leeks are a long-season crop that can take as long as 130 days to mature, so it is best to buy them as seedlings if you want to harvest them the same year. At this stage, they will look like young green onions. If you have not fertilized the bed recently, dig in some well-rotted manure, and add peat moss too if the soil is heavy clay; otherwise, the leeks will be hard to pull up when the time comes for harvesting.

On the day of planting, put on rubber gloves, because this is going to be a muddy job. Water the row or rows where you are going to grow the leeks, poke a hole into the mud with your finger, drop in a leek, and gently squeeze the hole shut. The leeks should be spaced about 10 centimetres (4 inches) apart, with the roots and half the greenery below soil level.

If you prefer to raise the leeks from seed with the intention of overwintering those that are not fully grown, sow the seed as soon as the ground can be worked in spring. Dig over the bed, adding manure and peat moss if necessary, rake the earth flat, and then lightly water each row before scattering the seed. Leek seed is so fine that it blows away easily, but it will stick to soil that has been dampened. Cover the seeds with a light dusting of earth and pat down firmly. When the shoots are about 12 centimetres (5 inches) tall, put on rubber gloves and move those that are crowded, replanting them at 10 centimetre (4 inch) intervals as described above.

Ongoing Care

When the seedlings are young, you will need to keep the bed well weeded and watered, but it is not essential to do so as the leeks grow larger. If there are more urgent jobs to be done in the garden, you can ignore the leeks for weeks on end. You need not even blanch them, for the thick centres of the stalks will be pale even without this treatment.

However, if you want really tender white leeks, they will need to be blanched. This takes only an hour or so. One method is to build up earth around the leeks, but I prefer to dig them up and replant them deeper. Leeks don't mind being moved, provided they have a suitably muddy mess to be moved into, and here is a

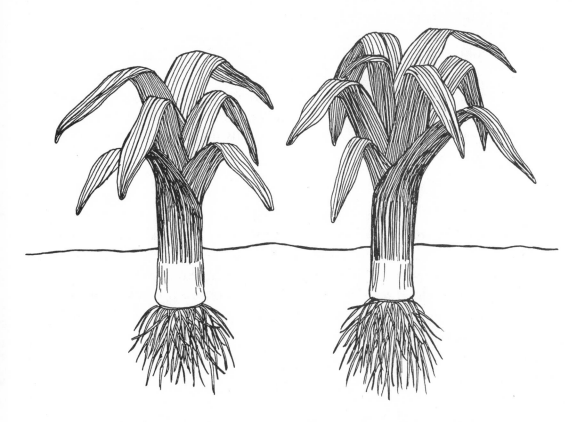

chance to give the plants more fertilizer. Move only the larger leeks, the ones that look as if they will be thick enough to eat that year. Dig a hole for each plant about 15 centimetres (6 inches) deep, mix some manure with the earth, water well to make a mud pie, then stand the leek in the mud and fill in the earth so that the leek is held straight and firm.

If you are growing leeks on a rotational system, there will be some large enough to harvest during most of the summer. Spring plantings, on the other hand, will probably not mature until late fall, though there is no need to wait until the leeks are full-sized before eating them. When digging up leeks, keep in mind how deep they are and dig carefully to avoid puncturing them with the fork. Then wash them thoroughly under a hose to remove all earth from the roots and as much as possible from the leaves.

Leeks that have overwintered often produce seedpods early in summer. If this happens, cut off the pods immediately – but don't throw them away; they make a superb flavouring for soups. After the seedpod has been removed, the stalk that held it will harden and wither, and the leek may look as if it is dying. In fact, it is propagating under the soil: the root divides to form two onion-like bulbs, each of which will grow to become a new leek. If you later separate these rejuvenated leeks so that they have space to develop, they can become fully mature before the end of the season.

Pests

Leeks seldom suffer from insect pests, but hungry rabbits are likely to chew any leaves that are exposed during winter. Their grazing does no harm to the leeks and it helps the rabbits survive. If new shoots are chewed in early spring, the best protection is to scatter blood meal on the bed. The blood meal will keep nearly all rodents away. (See also the recipe for an organic rodent repellant, page 237.)

Leek Recipes

Like onions, leeks are more important as a flavouring than as a vegetable in their own right. The chopped leaves of very young leeks add a whole new dimension to a tossed green salad. If you have never tasted leeks raw, be adventurous and sample some. Try them instead of spring onions in a lettuce salad with a vinaigrette dressing, or in a creamy coleslaw or carrot salad, or as a salad of their own with a dressing of yogurt and lemon juice.

Often, when I am chopping leeks for a soup, their pungent smell is so delicious that it seems a waste to cook them when they taste so good raw. But I always revise this opinion during the first stages of soup making, when the kitchen is redolent with the wonderful aroma of leeks cooking slowly in butter. Only boiled leeks smell and taste unappetizing. The boiling ruins them and makes them thoroughly unpalatable. It is a desecration of one of the most savoury of greens.

How to Prepare and Cook

A common complaint about leeks is that they are gritty, but they have no need to be if you wash them with care. Cut off the roots at the base and then make another crosswise cut just below where the green parts of the leaves begin. The green leaves, being separate, are now easy to wash thoroughly. To clean the tightly folded white part, slit it lengthwise on both sides for about 6 centimetres (2½ inches) so that you can get at the underside of each layer where the grit usually hides. If you immerse the leeks in water before cleaning them under a running tap, you should be able to get rid of all the grit. When a recipe calls for chopped leeks, you can slice the whites in half lengthwise to make them easier to clean. Young leeks that are to be added to a salad also can be sliced right through lengthwise and the leaves washed individually before being chopped.

The whites of leeks, kept whole, are an essential ingredient in flavouring oxtail ragouts and some stews. They will cook in 20 to 30 minutes, depending on their size, and should be added towards the end of the cooking time. Chopped young leeks can be added to a stew during the last 5 or 10 minutes of cooking. They are so tender that they don't need lengthy stewing, and they give a pleasant tang when cooked so briefly.

If you wish to serve leeks as a vegetable, which I do not advise, the most palatable way is to braise them in a little butter and water. Cook slowly in a saucepan with the lid on. They will take 30 to 40 minutes and can be served in their juices or with a white sauce (page 248).

Most recipes use only the white parts of the leeks, but the full length can be used, except for the very coarsest leaves, when making soups.

Each year I make vast amounts of leek soup – one of the best standbys anyone can have in a freezer. Heated up in midwinter, it makes a hearty soup just as it is, but it can also be transformed into other types of soup. Add potatoes, for instance, plus a little chopped parsley and pepper, and you have potato soup. Served cold with whipped cream, it becomes vichyssoise. Throw in some chopped celery and it's celery soup. Leek soup also makes an excellent base for clam chowder. And not only does each of these soups taste notably different, but each

is delicious in its own right. Nor is the stock base a problem. With leek soup, whatever its form, an instant stock of chicken powder and water works better than a rich, home-made chicken stock.

LEEK SOUP

This basic leek soup uses the green as well as the white of the leaves. Only the very coarsest green leaves need be discarded.

2 large or 6 small	leeks	2 large or 6 small
2 Tbsp	butter	30 mL
2	potatoes	2
4 cups	water	1 L
1 cup	milk	250 mL
2 Tbsp	chicken powder	30 mL
	nutmeg	
	salt and pepper	
1	small leek for garnish	1

Slit the leeks in two lengthwise and wash thoroughly. Slice the green parts again lengthwise before chopping them finely so that the pieces are about 1 centimetre (⅓ inch) square. Place in a large saucepan with the butter and sauté gently. Meanwhile, roughly chop the whites and add them to the pan. While they are sautéing, peel and chop the potatoes. Then add them to the pan, along with the water, milk, and chicken powder. Bring to a boil and simmer for 30 minutes.

Blend the soup in a blender until smooth. Return it to the saucepan and reheat, seasoning to taste with nutmeg, salt, and pepper. Wash and chop the small leek that is serving as garnish, place it in the pan, and simmer gently for 5 minutes. (Alternatively, the tender inside white of a large leek can be used for garnish.) *Makes 4 to 6 servings.*

VICHYSSOISE

This delicious cold soup is just an ordinary leek soup with additional cream, yet its exquisite taste makes it a luxuriously gourmet dish.

	Leek Soup (minus the garnish)	
½ cup	whipping cream	125 mL
2 Tbsp	chopped chives	30 mL

Cool the leek soup, whip the cream until thick and fold it into the cold soup. Taste for seasoning; a little more nutmeg or salt may be needed to accentuate the flavour. You may also wish to adjust the consistency; vichyssoise should be fairly thick, but it can be thinned if required by adding more cream or a little milk. Serve it very cold with a garnish of chopped chives. *Makes 4 to 6 servings.*

LEEK PIE

Only the tender white parts of the leeks are used in this dish, but the green tops can be kept for the next batch of leek soup. Although this recipe is always referred to as leek pie, it is really a leek quiche – more of a flan than a pie.

	PASTRY	
½ lb	flour	225 g
¼ lb	fat	112 g
½ tsp	salt	2 mL
⅓ cup	water	83 mL

	FILLING	
3	large leeks (whites only)	3
1 Tbsp	butter	15 mL
2 Tbsp	water	30 mL
2	eggs	2
1 cup	milk	250 mL
½ tsp	salt	2 mL
¼ tsp	white pepper	1mL
	nutmeg	

Make the pastry (page 251) and roll it out to line a 23-centimetre (9-inch) pie dish. (Alternatively, use a ready-made pie shell.) Bake the pastry shell in a preheated 425°F/220°C oven for 10 to 12 minutes. Cool and set aside.

Slice the leek whites lengthwise and wash them thoroughly, removing all grit. Then chop finely and braise in the butter and water until soft.

Break the eggs into a bowl and whisk briskly with a fork. Stir in the milk, salt, and pepper. Spread the leeks and their juices on the pie shell. On top of this pour the egg and milk mixture. Sprinkle with nutmeg and cook in a preheated 350°F/180°C oven for 40 minutes. *Makes 4 servings.*

Storing and Freezing

If you cut the roots off the leeks and package them in plastic bags, they will keep in the refrigerator for a month or more. For long-term storage, they should be frozen. Wash them thoroughly, chop, and blanch in boiling water for 2 minutes. Drain, cool, and pack in plastic bags, sucking out the air with a straw. To serve after freezing, place the frozen leeks in boiling water to break them up. Then sauté in butter or boil, according to the recipe they are being used in. Like all frozen vegetables, leeks can be kept for a year in the freezer.

Lettuce
and Other Salad Greens

Most gardeners like to grow lettuce, despite its tendency to bolt when the weather suddenly turns hot and dry. There is something very satisfying about picking your own lettuce leaves – indeed, of having all the salad vegetables within picking distance of the kitchen. The seed catalogues offer a wide choice: Boston, iceberg, romaine, buttercrunch, and many others, including escarole and curled-leaf endive (or chicory).

How to Grow
Planting

Lettuce can be sown as soon as the ground can be worked in spring. It grows best in cool weather and in loose soil that is rich in humus, so if the bed has not been fertilized, dig in some well-rotted manure or rich topsoil. If your soil is heavy clay, lighten it by adding peat moss. And if you live in a region that has very hot summers, choose a bed that gets shade for part of the day. Rake the bed smooth and then drag the handle of the rake lengthwise along the bed so that it makes a slight indentation along the line where the seed is to be sown. Water lightly so that the seed will stick to the earth (lettuce seed is so fine that it blows away easily), then scatter the seed by hand and cover it with a light dusting of crumbled earth.

Some gardeners like to start the seed indoors about four weeks before planting out. If you do this, water the row well before planting and then press in the seedlings, spacing them about 5 centimetres (2 inches) apart.

Ongoing Care

It is important to keep the bed well watered, especially for the first few weeks. If the bed is nice and damp, the seed will germinate more quickly and the young seedlings will not be in danger of drying out. Soon after the seed has germinated and pushed up the first green leaves, the seedlings will be ready for their first thinning. Pull out the most crowded seedlings so that those remaining stand about 5 centimetres (2 inches) apart – the same distance apart as any that you started indoors and then transplanted into the garden.

If you have space to spare, you can replant the pulled seedlings rather than throwing them away. They will be slower to mature than those that have not been moved and will be ready for picking around the time the other lettuces are finishing. Replanting is a good way of prolonging the season. Gardening manuals normally tell you to prolong the season by sowing every two weeks throughout the summer. I tried this once, and I had enough lettuce to start a vegetable stall. It makes far more sense to replant each time you thin the lettuce beds. By doing so, you don't waste seed, you don't get inundated with far more lettuce than you need, and you still spread the picking season over most of the summer.

The lettuce can be thinned whenever it has grown so much that it looks crowded. Obviously, some of those that are thinned out will go straight to the kitchen, but there are sure to be others that need replanting. When replanting, tear off the outer leaves (since this will help the plant to form a head) and always prepare a moist and muddy environment for the lettuce to be moved into.

Although this system avoids sowing a new crop every two weeks, you will need to sow again in late June or early July if you want to be able to pick right until frost. Often this late crop does particularly well because of the cooler weather in the fall, though it will need plenty of water in midsummer when it is getting started. So will all your lettuce plants. Remember that hot dry

weather can cause lettuce to get coarse or go to seed; make a point of watering the bed thoroughly during heatwaves.

You will probably have most trouble from slugs, which are not always easy to find, for they get down into the inner ribs. A slug hunt early in the morning while the plants are still wet with dew is an excellent way of catching them. Simply pick off the slugs and stamp on them. Sprinkling the leaves with salt can also be quite effective. This is preferable to using slug baits or powders, which can kill other creatures as well as slugs. Lettuce sometimes suffers from aphids. If the insects are seriously damaging the leaves, you can control them by squirting them with organic insecticide or a homemade repellant (page 238), but in most cases all that is necessary is to wash the leaves thoroughly in the sink before eating the lettuce.

Lettuce Recipes

Some imaginative recipes have been devised for cooked lettuce – combining it with melted cheese, for instance, or frying with bacon and pine nuts – but none of these concoctions tastes all that exciting and most require a lot of effort. In any case, I can't see the point of going to so much trouble when lettuce tastes superb just as it is, crisp and fresh.

Lettuce makes an excellent sandwich, either on its own or with peanut butter, and it combines well with other sandwich fillings. Above all, lettuce is a salad vegetable, and this is the best way to serve it. The salads can include tomato, cucumber, and so on, but it is hard to beat a simple salad made of lettuce only, using a mix of various types of leaf lettuce.

 **How to Prepare**

Homegrown lettuce should always be washed thoroughly. I like to give it a first wash in the garden, running the whole head under the hose, before washing the lettuce, leaf by leaf, in the kitchen sink. This avoids the unpleasantness of finding insects or slugs floating in the sink – they will have been rinsed off during the outdoor hosing.

After washing the lettuce, dry the leaves thoroughly, shaking off the water and then laying them on paper towels if they still have water clinging to them. The best lettuce for most salads is leaf lettuce, and its leaves should be torn apart, not cut. This treatment helps to keep the leaves crisp. If you are preparing the salad more than 30 minutes in advance, place it in a covered bowl in the refrigerator so that it will not go limp. The dressing should be added just before serving. If this happens to be halfway through a meal, place the dressing in a bowl beside the salad and toss it at the table. When dressing is added in advance, it makes the salad soggy.

The dressing should, of course, be home-made. It takes only a couple of minutes to mix a vinaigrette dressing, and a freshly made dressing can make a world of difference to a salad. Here are two of my favourites.

RUSSIAN MUSTARD VINAIGRETTE

Russian mustard adds a pleasant sweetness to a vinaigrette, but it also increases the oil content. This can be an advantage in salads that don't include lettuce, but if there is lettuce in the salad, the oil should be reduced to only one tablespoon (15 mL), as given here, otherwise the leaves will get limp. Which oil you use is a matter of preference. Canola is probably the most healthful, and it is my current favourite, followed closely by Mazola corn oil, since neither adds a taste to the dressing. Olive oil I find too heavy, both in consistency and flavour.

1 Tbsp	canola or corn oil	15 mL
1 Tbsp	wine vinegar	15 mL
1 tsp	Russian mustard	5 mL
	salt	

To make the vinaigrette, whisk the ingredients together with a fork. This dressing can be made in advance but should be kept at room temperature, not in the refrigerator,

and should be given a final whisk before being mixed into the salad.

GARLIC VINAIGRETTE

Two portions of oil to one of vinegar are the usual proportions for a vinaigrette, as in this garlic dressing. This is the perfect dressing for a tossed salad of leaf lettuce, served as a lightener after a sumptuous main course such as steak or grilled prawns.

1	garlic clove	1
2 Tbsp	canola or corn oil	30 mL
1 Tbsp	wine vinegar	15 mL
½ tsp	Dijon mustard	2 mL
1 tsp	chopped onion (optional)	5 mL
	salt	

Peel and mince the garlic and place it in a bowl with the other ingredients, adding the salt last according to taste. Whisk with a fork. Like all vinaigrettes, this can be made in advance but should be given a final whisk before being tossed over the salad.

MAYONNAISE

Iceberg lettuce tastes better with mayonnaise than with a vinegar dressing, and occasionally a mayonnaise is needed for other types of lettuce too. I find that the best oil for mayonnaise is Mazola because it does not add an oily taste. The mayonnaise given here not only goes well with lettuce and other salad vegetables but is superb with cold lobster.

2	egg yolks	2
1/4 tsp	dried mustard	1 mL
1 tsp	lime or lemon juice	5 mL
1/2–1 cup	Mazola oil	125–250 mL
	salt	

Mayonnaise is easy to make provided you are not in a hurry; it will curdle if the oil is added too quickly. It works best when made with a wire whisk and with the ingredients at room temperature, so leave your electric mixer in the cupboard but take the egg out of the refrigerator about an hour beforehand.

Break the egg yolks into a bowl and beat with the citrus juice and dried mustard powder. Then add a drop of oil with one hand while whisking with the other. Beat in the oil for a few seconds before adding a few more drops. The oil should be added drop by drop at first and should be well beaten in before adding more, but it can be added in larger quantities once the mayonnaise begins to coagulate.

If you have added too much oil too quickly, causing the mixture to curdle, break an egg yolk into a separate bowl, beat in a few drops of oil, and then slowly beat in the curdled mayonnaise. Continue to add oil until the mayonnaise is the required thickness. The salt should be added towards the end, after the mayonnaise has begun to thicken. Add it according to taste. If the mayonnaise then becomes too thick, beat in a little vinegar or cream. If it is too thin, beat in more oil.

Mayonnaise is best made the day you intend to eat it, and it should be kept in the refrigerator in a covered bowl. Since it is made with raw egg, it will not keep for long and should be discarded if there is still some left over after the second day.

LETTUCE AND SEAFOOD COCKTAIL

A mild and creamy pink mayonnaise is the key to this recipe, along with leaf lettuce. Don't try it with iceberg; it will not be the same thing at all. This is one of the few occasions when leaf lettuce is cut rather than torn. Chop it into thin strips with kitchen scissors, making each strip about 1/2 centimetre wide by 5 centimetres long (1/4 inch × 2 inches).

2 cups	chopped leaf lettuce	500 mL
1 cup	cooked shrimp or lobster	250 mL
1 Tbsp	tomato ketchup	15 mL
4 Tbsp	mayonnaise	60 mL

Divide the chopped lettuce into 4 small bowls or champagne glasses and top with the pieces of seafood. This can be done an hour or more before the meal. Just before serving, mix the tomato ketchup into the mayonnaise and spoon it over the seafood. Serve with lemon wedges and thinly sliced brown bread and butter. *Makes 4 servings.*

BOLTED LETTUCE SOUP

However systematically you grow your lettuce, there is bound to come a time when there are far too many ready for picking, all threatening to go to seed – or actually doing so. That is when it is handy to make bolted lettuce soup. In fact, the soup tastes the same whether or not the lettuce has gone to seed, since cooking removes the bitterness from bolted lettuce. All you need is plenty of lettuce leaves and a stock of some type, or it can be made with a flour and milk base. Of all the possible variations, I prefer the one given here which includes split peas to give the soup extra body.

½ cup	dried split peas	125 mL
2	large leaf lettuces	2
1	large potato	1
1	large onion	1
4 cups	chicken stock	1 L
1 cup	milk	250 mL

Rinse the split peas and wash the lettuce thoroughly. Roughly chop the lettuce, peel and chop the potato and onion, and place in a large saucepan together with the split peas and chicken stock. Simmer for 30 minutes or until the split peas are soft and cooked through. Blend in a blender, then return to the saucepan along with the milk, and season to taste with a little salt and pepper. Heat to boiling but do not boil the soup. *Makes 6 to 8 servings.*

Melons

The seed catalogues offer a mouth-watering selection of muskmelons and cantaloupes, and it is well worth experimenting with a few just for the novelty of being able to eat the luscious fruit straight from the vine. One of my late-summer pleasures is to go into the garden early in the morning and choose a melon for breakfast. Melon may not be as vauntedly healthful as oat bran, but it sure tastes good – sweet and juicy – and it's a great way to start a summer's day.

Melons don't need much space, since their roots remain compact even when the vines wander several metres. This makes them a good balcony plant, grown in flowerpots or a window box; or they can be tucked into the corner of a flower bed, so long as there is room nearby for the vines to roam – across the concrete of a patio, for instance, or up the steps of a deck. Concrete is particularly suitable, because it reflects heat, which helps the melons to ripen.

How to Grow
Planting

Melons need plenty of heat to provide a good crop. Even though some varieties can bear fruit within as little as 65 days, it is advisable to start the seed indoors and wait until June before transplanting into the garden. Sow the seed in late April or early May, and keep it in a very warm place until it germinates. Then, soon

Melons ripen more quickly when placed on inverted pie pans. The pans reflect the heat onto the underside of the fruit.

after the first pair of leaves appears, transfer the seedlings to Jiffy-7s (as described on page 233) and place them in a sunny window. Like cucumbers, melons do not like having their roots disturbed and they need to be grown in Jiffy-7s or similar peat pellets so that they can be transplanted without suffering shock.

If you are intending to grow the melons on a balcony, they can be transplanted into flowerpots soon after their second leaves appear. Melons need lots of fertilizer and lots of water – but dry feet. To fulfill these conditions, place some peat moss or sand at the bottom of the flowerpot to keep the roots well drained; then add well-rotted manure and stand the Jiffy-7 on this base, surrounding it with a rich mix of manure and earth.

Melons destined for the garden also can be placed in flowerpots as a temporary measure, or their Jiffy-7s can be stood in a tray and watered moderately so that they are dampened without getting soggy. As soon as the seedlings are sturdy and branching out with more leaves, I like to spoon a layer of well-rotted manure into the trays and stand the Jiffy-7s on it. If this manure base is watered regularly, the young melon plants have a store of food and moisture which they can draw on as needed, and there is no risk of overwatering the roots.

Providing the plants are getting plenty of sun on their windowsill, there is nothing to be gained by moving them into the garden until the weather is really hot. Choose a sunny and protected spot, such as a sun-warmed corner that is sheltered from the wind. Dig a hole for each plant, about 15 centimetres (6 inches) deep, and place a layer of peat moss on the bottom, followed by a generous amount of manure. Then stand the Jiffy-7 on the manure so that its top will be slightly below soil level. Surround it with more manure or with a rich mixture of compost and earth, and press in firmly. If you have some bone meal available, you can add it to the hole as a slow-release fertilizer. The plants can be as near as 15 centimetres (6 inches) from one another, and it is best to grow several in a clump, since this will aid pollination.

Ongoing Care

The plants will need regular watering, especially when the fruit begins to form, but there will be no danger of overwatering if you have given the plants a well-drained foundation of peat moss or even of sandy gravel.

The melons will look like tiny green balls to begin with, and the first to appear may fall off. But once the vine is growing vigorously and pushing out large leaves, more melons will form and will rapidly increase in size. When this happens, you should pick off the fuzzy ends of the vines. This temporarily halts growth and directs the plant's energies into developing the fruit. You can also pick off the tiniest melons, because this too will help to make the remaining melons large and juicy.

Plenty of water and heat at this stage will increase the quality of the fruit. A simple way of boosting the heat is to place each melon on an inverted aluminum pie case. This keeps the fruit from contact with cool soil at night, and in the daytime it reflects the sun's heat. Especially in the cooler parts of Canada, it is a good way of getting the fruit to ripen quickly.

Sometimes it is difficult to know when a melon is ripe, though one can often tell by the change of colour; for instance, a greyish-green skin will turn yellowy-orange. Another test is by smell; a ripe melon is notably aromatic. A third way is to lift the melon in your hand, putting a little strain on the stem. If the stem breaks easily, the melon is ready for eating.

Pests

Young melon seedlings are sometimes eaten by cutworms. If this happens, place a collar of newspaper or aluminum foil around the stem. Yellow and black cucumber beetles also may attack the plants. If you can't catch them with your fingers, use a hand spray of organic insecticide.

Melon Recipes

The delicate taste of a melon can easily be overpowered, and therefore one of the best ways to eat the fruit is plain, and not necessarily chilled. A sun-warmed melon can be as tasty as a cooled one. Simply cut it in half, remove the seeds, and then slice and eat. If using only half the melon, remove the seeds from the other half too, cover it with plastic wrap to keep it moist, and store in the refrigerator.

MELON AND PROSCIUTTO

The Italians gave us this dish, a delicate contrast of tastes. If you have no prosciutto, thin slices of ham are almost as good. Cut the rind off the melon and slice it fairly thinly, arranging the slices elegantly around the edge of the plate, with rolls of prosciutto or ham in the centre. Freshly ground black pepper, rather than mustard, is the perfect condiment. Grind it on the melon as well as on the prosciutto.

MELON FRUIT SALAD WITH KIRSCH

Melon halves piled high with a fruit salad mixture make a spectacular finale to a dinner. Almost any fruit will do, but I like to use those that are ripe at the same time as the melons –
everbearing raspberries and strawberries, for instance, and a few Canadian blue grapes.

2	oranges	2
1 Tbsp	instant dissolving sugar	15 mL
2 Tbsp	kirsch	30 mL
2	cantaloupe melons	2
½ cup	grapes	125 mL
1 cup	raspberries	250 mL
1 cup	strawberries	250 mL

First, prepare the juice. Squeeze the oranges into a bowl and stir in the sugar until it dissolves. Then add the kirsch. (If you have no kirsch, brandy can be used instead.)

Cut the melons in half and remove the seeds. Using a melon-ball cutter, scoop out the flesh of the melons and place it in the bowl with the juice. Wash the grapes and raspberries, wash and hull the strawberries, and add them to the bowl. Place in the refrigerator for at least an hour, stirring from time to time.

To serve, place the melon halves dome-side down and pile in the fruit salad and its juice. *Makes 4 servings*.

 ## Storing

Melons will keep for about a week in the refrigerator but are not suitable for long-term storing or freezing.

Onions

Most backyard gardeners don't bother to grow globe onions unless they have an exceptionally large vegetable patch, but green onions are very popular. When freshly picked, they are stronger than those sold in the stores, and for this reason they make a pleasantly pungent accompaniment to blue cheese – or, in fact, any cheese. But, of course, they are raised mostly for salads. All types of onion are grown much the same way and require very little attention.

How to Grow
Planting

Onions do best in a fairly loose, fertile soil, so dig in some rich topsoil or manure if the bed has not been fertilized recently. Onions can be planted as soon as the ground can be worked in spring, and they can be sown from seeds, bought as seedlings, or bought as sets (immature bulbs). The latter is the most common among home gardeners, who can obtain packets of these small bulbs at supermarkets as well as at garden centres.

To plant onion sets

Rake over the bed and then press in the bulbs base down, with their tops just below the surface of the soil. You can space green onions so closely together that they are almost touching, but globe onions should be about 10 centimetres (4 inches) apart. With green onions, rather than planting them all at once, try putting in a dozen or so every two weeks. This will give you a continuing crop throughout most of the summer.

Water the row well to make it suitably muddy and then press in the seedlings, spacing them as above.

To plant onions as seedlings

Water the row lightly, just enough to make the seeds stick to the soil, and then scatter the seed by hand, covering it with a light dusting of earth. Onions can be sown in fall as well as spring in the milder regions of Canada.

To sow onions

Onion that has been sown as seed will need thinning soon after the green shoots appear. Water beforehand so that the shoots can be pulled out easily, otherwise they may break off, leaving the roots in the ground. If you have space, the pulled seedlings can be replanted by being pressed into well-watered muddy soil. Space them 10 centimetres (4 inches) apart for globe onions but close together for green onions.

Ongoing Care

Like leeks, onions will grow well even when ignored, but if you want tender green onions, you should water regularly, and if you want large globe onions, you should keep the bed free of weeds. Globe onions also benefit from having most of the soil removed from around their bulbs. Only about one-third of the bulb should be below ground so that the plant looks as if it is standing on the soil rather then growing in it.

Globe onions grown from sets sometimes produce seedpods soon after being planted. If this happens, break off the pods as soon as they form. Towards the end of the summer, the green tops of the globe onions will begin to wither and some may fall over. In late August or early September, knock over the tops of all that are still standing, since this will increase the size of the bulbs. About three weeks later, loosen the bulbs gently with a fork; two weeks after that, lift them out of the ground. They should then be dried thoroughly. In hot and sunny weather, the drying can be done outside by laying the onions on concrete or on a deck. In wet weather, place the onions on shelves in the garage or in a warm and airy place indoors.

The drying process can take a week or more, but it is essential if you want to store the onions. On the other hand, if you are going to eat them immediately or within a week or two, none of this is necessary. Simply dig up the onions whenever you want them.

 Pests

Onion maggots are the main threat, though they are by no means a certainty. It is possible to grow onions year after year without ever encountering the creatures. If you do have an infestation, you will find the maggots in the bulbs. There is not much you can do about this, but you may be able to prevent an infestation the following year if you dig up and destroy all the onions in August, before the fall generation of maggots has hatched. This will prevent most of the maggots from overwintering in your garden and breeding a new generation in the spring. If this strategy doesn't work, your only solution is to apply diazinon when you next plant onions. This pesticide comes in granular form. Scatter the granules when planting, following the instructions on the container.

Onion Recipes

Many of the meals we eat would have far less flavour if there were no such things as onions, yet there are few really tasty recipes based on onions as the main ingredient. Although onion pie can be quite pleasant, it is little more than a second-rate copy of leek pie and far less savoury. And I have never been able to raise much enthusiasm for gussied-up dishes such as onions in cheese sauce. On the other hand, onions on their own – both cooked and raw – can be very tasty.

How to Prepare and Cook

Peeling and chopping onions really can make your eyes water, especially if the onions are fresh from the garden, so peel them under a running tap of cold water if you have trouble with your eyes. Always wash your hands in cold water immediately after handling raw onions, otherwise the onion smell will remain on your skin.

TO COOK ONIONS WHOLE Onions can be boiled in salted water, but their flavour is far richer when they are baked in the oven in their skins. Place them on a rack and bake at 350°F/180°C for 30 minutes or more, according to size, and slip off the skins before serving. The onions should be soft but still firm.

FRIED ONIONS Fried onions can come in at least three different forms: chopped finely and cooked gently in butter over a low heat until soft and golden; sliced and fried quickly over a high heat, using hardly any fat so that the slices are crisp and brown; or dipped in batter and deep-fried as onion rings.

GREEN ONIONS These onions are usually eaten raw. To prepare them, wash thoroughly, cut off the roots and trim the tops. Serve whole with cheese or chopped in salads, or as a garnish for sauces, rice dishes, etcetera.

FRENCH ONION SOUP

This tasty soup is a perennial favourite – wonderfully comforting on a cold day.

5 cups	beef stock	1.25 L
2	medium onions	2
1 Tbsp	cooking oil or butter	15 mL
4	slices bread	4
1 cup	grated mozzarella cheese	250 mL

If you have no beef stock, make an instant one by boiling some Bovril and 5 cups (1.25 L) water with 3 tablespoons (45 mL) of sherry and ½ teaspoon (2 mL) of dried thyme.

Peel and slice the onions, fry them fast in the fat so that they brown, and divide them among four ovenproof soup bowls. While heating the beef stock, make four pieces of toast and cut them into rounds the size of the soup bowls. Pour the stock into the bowls, cover with the toast, and top with grated cheese. Place the bowls under the grill for a few minutes until the cheese is brown and bubbling. *Makes 4 servings.*

ONION AND TOMATO RELISH

Whenever I make curry, I like to serve several side dishes: at least one genuine Indian chutney, a bowl of shredded coconut, a bowl of yogurt, a bowl of sliced bananas . . . and always a bowl of onion and tomato. Both are raw – they are simply chopped and mixed together – and they add a touch of freshness that blends well with the heavier taste of the curry.

3	white globe onions	3
2	tomatoes	2

Peel the onions, chop finely, and place in a covered bowl until mealtime. Core and chop the tomatoes and place in a separate covered bowl. Combine the two when serving the meal; they should not be mixed in advance or they will lose their crispness. *Makes 6 servings.*

ONION AND TUNA NIÇOISE

Here's a great recipe for those who enjoy raw onions – and it's well worth trying by those who think they don't. The dressing modifies the sharpness of the onions so that they are not too strong, and the result is a surprisingly good combination of tastes, as well as a filling supper dish.

	SALAD	
5 or 6	medium-sized new potatoes	5 or 6
2	medium-sized red onions	2
1	large red bell pepper	1
1 cup	olives	250 mL
1 cup	chopped celery	250 mL
14 oz	tuna (2 cans)	400 g
1	Boston lettuce	1
	chopped parsley for garnish	

DRESSING

2 Tbsp	red wine vinegar	30 mL
4 Tbsp	canola or corn oil	60 mL
½ tsp	Dijon mustard	2 mL
	salt and pepper	

Scrape the potatoes and boil in salted water until they are just cooked but still firm (about 15 minutes). Leave to cool in their water. Peel and slice the onions, core and slice the pepper, slice the potatoes, and combine in a large bowl, together with the olives and chopped celery. Make the dressing and add it to the mixture, tossing well. Do this about half an hour before the meal so that the vegetables marinate in the dressing.

When ready to serve, place the drained tuna in the centre of a large dish and arrange the lettuce leaves around it. Heap the salad mixture onto the lettuce and sprinkle liberally with chopped parsley. *Makes 4 servings*.

 Storing

Onions can be blanched and frozen, but it is hardly worth doing so since they store so well raw. They will keep for months when stored in cool conditions, provided they have first been dried in a warm environment, as described earlier. The best temperature for long-term storage is just above freezing. To store, braid the tops so that the onions can be hung in a string, or place the onions in shallow containers or in any place where the air can circulate around them.

Parsnips and Turnips
Including Rutabaga

Parsnips and turnips are not the most common garden crops because they are not something that most people eat in large quantity. But if you have a spare corner in your vegetable plot, you might want to try growing some, because they are among the most labour-free vegetables.

How to Grow
Planting

Parsnips take a long time to mature and should be planted early in spring, as soon as the ground can be worked. Rutabagas (swedes) also need a long growing season, but summer turnips will mature in about two months and can be planted in mid-summer for a fall crop as well as in early spring for a summer crop. All do best in a light soil that was fertilized the previous year. If the bed was not fertilized in advance, dig in some rich topsoil such as black earth.

Like other root crops, parsnips and turnips are grown from seed. After digging over the earth, rake it flat, water lightly so that the seed will stick to the soil, and then scatter the seed by hand. The turnips will germinate quickly, between three and ten days on average, but you may have to wait three or four weeks before the first tiny parsnip shoots appear.

All root crops do best if the bed is kept weeded while the seedlings are growing, but it is not so important to keep the bed free of weeds once the roots have grown fairly large. Obviously, weeds compete for the nutrients in the soil; but equally obviously, when the root crops have become established and are bigger than the weeds, they take in most of the nutrients. So apart from pulling up any oversized dandelions or other deep-rooted weeds, you can get by with very little weeding.

You will, however, need to thin the rows a few weeks after the seedlings have appeared. Water the bed first so that the seedlings will come out easily, then pull up all the crowded ones, leaving the remaining shoots at intervals of about 4 centimetres (1½ inches) for parsnips, 8 centimetres (3 inches) for summer turnips, and 13 centimetres (5 inches) for rutabagas.

All these root vegetables can withstand frost. In many parts of Canada, parsnips can survive over winter, which means that you don't have to harvest all of them in the fall. Dig up some after the first frost and build up the earth around the others to make sure that the roots are well covered. Harvest these overwintered parsnips early in the spring before the roots start growing new greenery. They will be wonderfully sweet and tender.

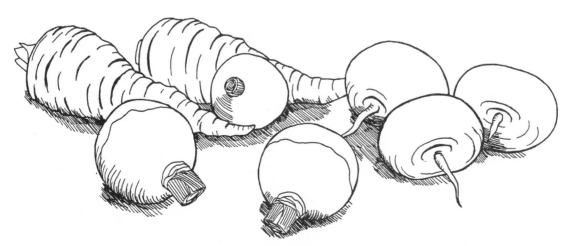

Rutabagas also can be left in the ground over winter provided they are totally covered, but don't let them grow too large. They become coarse when more than about 15 centimetres (6 inches) in diameter. Other types of turnip are best dug up when they are little more than 5 centimetres (2 inches) in diameter. They are said to be sweeter after a slight touch of frost, but they should be harvested before there is a deep frost.

 Pests

You are not likely to have insect problems with parsnips, but all turnips, including rutabagas, attract the same insects as cabbages (page 37). Fortunately, most of these creatures eat the leaves and do not seriously affect the roots, so you will probably need to do no more than remove a few caterpillars if you see them.

Parsnip and Turnip Recipes

"**F**ine words butter no parsnips" not only means that words are no good without action; it also means that parsnips are no good without butter, or at any rate that they do need butter. So do rutabagas and turnips. All these root vegetables are greatly enhanced by being mashed with butter.

 **How to Prepare and Cook**

Peel, slice, and cook in boiling salted water until soft. This will take from 20 to 30 minutes. Then mash thoroughly, adding butter and plenty of black pepper. Mashed rutabagas (swedes) are commonly served in Scotland as an accompaniment to haggis. Mashed parsnips go well with zucchini and some other squashes. Mashed turnips are the least tasty but can be palatable when combined with mashed carrots.

Some cooks like to stir-fry these vegetables, but I find fried turnips unappetizing, though fried parsnips can be pleasant. Parsnips are particularly good when parboiled and then fried in batter. The leaves of turnips can be eaten like cabbage.

CREAMED PARSNIP ON ZUCCHINI

With its subtle blend of tastes and its attractive appearance, this makes a pleasant change from the usual vegetables served with a roast. The zucchini slices should be barely cooked – still firm and crisp – so that they contrast with the puréed parsnips heaped on them.

1 lb	parsnips	450 g
3 Tbsp	cream	45 mL
1 Tbsp	butter	15 mL
	pepper and salt	
2 Tbsp	parsley	30 mL
2	medium-sized zucchini	2

Peel and slice the parsnips and boil in salted water for 30 minutes. Drain them, mash or purée them, and beat in the cream and butter. Season with pepper and with a little salt if desired. Place the mixture in a covered dish in a 300°F/150°C oven so that it continues to cook a little while you prepare the zucchini.

Cut the zucchini into slices about 1 centimetre (⅓ inch) thick, discarding the ends. Drop the slices into boiling salted water and cook for 3 minutes. Arrange the slices on a serving dish, place a dab of parsnip on each slice, and sprinkle with parsley. *Makes 4 servings.*

ROOT VEGETABLE GOULASH

Since root vegetables are harvested in fall and winter, they coincide with the type of weather that makes hearty stews very welcome. This stew uses most of the root vegetables, and you can add potatoes too if there is room in the pot.

1½ lbs	stewing steak	680 g
	flour	
2 Tbsp	butter or margarine	30 mL
4 cups	water	1 L
1 cup	red wine	250 mL
2 cups	tomato sauce	500 mL
2 Tbsp	Bovril	30 mL
6	cloves	6
4	bay leaves	4
2	garlic cloves	2
1	onion	1
2	turnips	2
4	parsnips	4
6	carrots	6
½	rutabaga	½

Cut the beef into cubes about 4 centimetres (1½ inches) square, roll in flour, and brown in butter in a frying pan over a high heat. Place the beef in a large cooking pot, together with the water, wine, tomato sauce, Bovril, cloves, bay leaves, the peeled and minced garlic, and the peeled and finely chopped onion. Simmer gently for 1½ hours. Peel the root vegetables, cut them into convenient sizes, and add them to the pot. Simmer for a further hour, adding a little water if the gravy gets too thick. *Makes 4 to 6 servings.*

 **Storing**

Parsnips and turnips keep well and will last all winter when stored at a temperature just above freezing. Clean them of all earth, cut off their stalks, and pack them loosely in boxes of sawdust or sand. They also last well when kept in the refrigerator. Although freezing is possible, I do not advise it. The vegetables lose out in both quality and crispness, and there is no need to freeze them when they store so well raw.

Peas

Peas taste best when picked within an hour or two of the meal. Since it is impossible to get them this fresh in the stores, they rank high on the list for backyard gardeners.

Fresh garden peas are surely one of the world's great delicacies. When I was a child, our first picking was always served as a course in itself, a heaped dish of succulent young peas lightly flavoured with mint leaves. They tasted all the better because we children had helped shell them.

I have always enjoyed podding peas, a pleasantly relaxing occupation – sitting in the sun or shade, according to the heat of the day, with a basket of full pods on one hand and a bowl of shelled peas in my lap. But of course there are now varieties that don't need shelling – snow peas and sugar snap – and these, too, are most satisfying to grow.

How to Grow
Planting

If you start early enough, you will be able to get in two crops of peas, the first being planted where you will later grow melons or cucumbers or anything that will not be moved into the garden until June.

The first crop can be planted as soon as the ground can be worked in spring; the second crop, two or three weeks later. Dig in plenty of well-rotted manure or compost and plant the peas about 5 centimetres (2 inches) deep and 5–8 centimetres

(2–3 inches) apart. The easiest way to do this is to push the peas in with your finger and then squeeze the hole shut.

Space the rows about 25 centimetres (10 inches) apart. Even if you have very little space, it is better to plant several rows, however short, rather than one long row, since this helps keep the roots shady. Peas grow best under cool conditions and will not do well if the earth around their roots gets hot and dry.

Some people have difficulty growing peas, finding that very few come up. This is usually a sign either that the seed has been eaten by insects or that the soil is too wet and the peas have rotted rather than germinating. One solution is to plant the peas in flats in the garage. The flats should be the type that have holes in the bottom so that water can run out. Fill them with light potting soil, water the soil to dampen it well, and push in the peas with your finger. You can crowd them in, setting them about 2.5 centimetres (1 inch) apart. Then leave them alone for a week or two. At this stage, they don't need light and don't normally need watering either.

After the shoots appear, move the flats outdoors onto a patio or driveway, but let the plants grow about 8 centimetres (3 inches) tall before planting them in the garden. Choose a cool day, because peas tend to wilt when transplanted. Dig a shallow trench along each row and mix in plenty of well-rotted manure and some peat moss. Fill the trench with water, let the water soak in, and then plant the peas, spacing them about 5 centimetres (2 inches) apart and giving them short sticks to lean against if they show signs of falling over. If the weather turns hot, they may look a bit sad for a few days, but they will soon perk up if you keep them well watered.

This procedure may seem to involve a lot of work, but it is a sure way of getting a good crop of peas. I usually plant my first crop in flats but sow my second crop directly into the garden.

Ongoing Care

Most peas need some form of support as they grow taller, and it is best put in place when the shoots are still quite short. I favour pea sticks (as many as are needed to keep the plants upright), but chicken wire and netting also work well. A chain-link fence

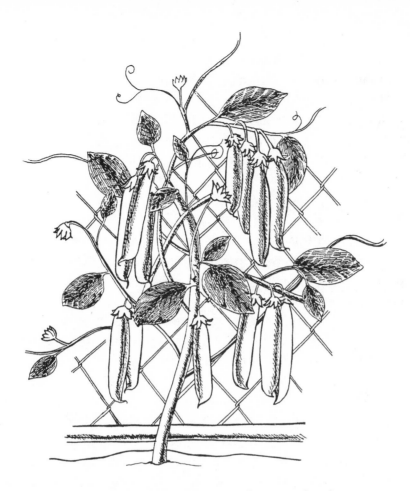

makes an excellent support, provided it does not back onto concrete or anything that absorbs heat. Peas do best when surrounded by moist, cool earth. This means watering the bed regularly – the roots rather than the leaves. If the weather turns very hot, take the nozzle off the hose and let the water flow gently over the soil for about 5 minutes each morning. This will give a more thorough soaking than watering with a sprinkler.

Soon after the flowers form, the pods will grow very quickly. When they begin to fill out, open and taste one or two to see if they are ready for picking. The great advantage of growing your own peas is that you can pick them while they are still young and tender. Don't wait until they are too large or they will become dry and mealy. On the other hand, snow peas and sugar snaps are equally good at any stage of growth, though you may have to string them if you let them grow very large.

It is always the lower pods of a plant that ripen first, so start picking from the bottom. By keeping mature pods picked, you will encourage the plants to form more farther up, and can therefore increase the length of the picking season. After all the pods have been picked, don't pull up the vines. They make excellent fertilizer. Dig them back into the bed so that they can help nourish the next crop.

☙ Pests

Insects are not usually a problem with peas, but you may need to protect the plants from birds and rabbits. The shoots that come up very early in spring are bound to attract birds, but this need not be a problem if you cover them with a tangle of netting. Usually, the netting can be removed after a week or two; by then the birds will have plenty of other food available (and in the meantime you can always salve your conscience by putting out bird seed).

Rabbits and other rodents are more of a long-term nuisance. They chew the young shoots down to the ground and also feed on mature plants. A homemade fence of netting sometimes keeps them off, but I find that blood meal is more effective. Sprinkled on the earth around the plants, it works like a magical barrier. The rabbits won't cross it; they are frightened by the smell. The only problem here is that you will need to sprinkle a new application after each heavy rainstorm, but this can work in your favour because blood meal is a superb fertilizer and peas need plenty of nutrients. (See also the recipe for Peppery Rodent Repellant, page 237.)

Pea Recipes

However many peas you grow, there never seem to be enough. Not only are they delicious on their own, but they go well with almost everything and can make a gourmet meal from the simplest ingredients. Softly scrambled eggs, for instance, with a helping of fresh garden peas make a delicious light supper. Whether served hot or cold, cooked or raw, peas can give that extra touch that transforms mere food into a feast.

How to Prepare and Cook

To savour peas at their best, you should pick and shell them as near to mealtime as possible, or at any rate as near as is convenient. If you have to pick them well in advance, don't shell them until shortly before cooking. Meanwhile, keep them somewhere cool, such as in the refrigerator; they lose their quality quickly when left lying on a counter.

FRESHLY PICKED PEAS Peas that have just been picked require hardly any cooking, but I like to take the time to prepare a broth of minted water to boil them in, since this makes them taste so very good. To make the broth, pick and wash a large bunch of mint; place it, stalks and all, in a saucepan of boiling water and simmer for half an hour or more. The most wonderful smell of mint will waft through the house while this brew is simmering. Just before the meal, remove the mint and add a spoonful of salt. Sugar can also be added, but this is not usually necessary with fresh young peas, since they are sweet enough in themselves. Bring the broth to a rolling boil before adding the peas, and then cook them very briefly: 1 or 2 minutes for small young peas, 3 or 4 minutes for large older peas. Drain and serve immediately.

SUGAR SNAP PEAS AND SNOW PEAS The full-podded sugar snap peas also can be boiled in mint broth, but snow peas taste better when cooked in chicken stock. If you have no stock, use chicken powder and water. Wash and trim the snow peas and bring the stock to a boil before adding them to the pan. Allow about 30 seconds, just enough for them to turn dark green, then remove the pan from the heat.

Drain and serve. This treatment not only heightens the flavour of the snow peas, but it retains their crispness. I find that it gives far better results than the more popular method of stir-frying snow peas in butter or oil.

POTAGE ST. GERMAIN

Fresh peas can be made into superb soups, usually cream soups with a flavouring of mint or curry. My favourite is this traditional French one made from peas and lettuce – a very suitable combination for home gardeners, since both crops are commonly at their peak at the same time.

2 Tbsp	butter	30 mL
1 cup	chopped leeks	250 mL
1	large leaf lettuce	1
4 cups	water	1 L
2 cups	milk	500 mL
6 cups	shelled peas	1.5 L
2	potatoes	2
	salt and pepper	
1 cup	table cream	250 mL

Melt the butter in a large saucepan and gently cook the chopped leeks. Wash and chop the lettuce and add it to the saucepan, together with the water, milk, 4½ cups (1.12 L) of the peas, and the peeled and sliced potatoes. Simmer for 30 minutes, then blend until smooth. Return the soup to the pan, add the remaining 1½ cups (375 mL) of peas, and season to taste with salt and pepper. Simmer for 3 or 4 minutes.

The cream should be added just before serving, and the soup must be poured into it rather than vice versa in order to avoid curdling. Pour the cream into a bowl and stir in about 1 cup (250 mL) of soup. Then stir this into the soup that is in the saucepan. Heat to boiling but do not allow to boil. *Makes about 10 servings.*

SNOW PEA DIP

Snow peas are pleasantly crisp and tasty eaten raw, and they go well with any dip. This dip includes shelled peas as one of the ingredients and is pale green. To add to the attractive appearance, you can surround it with bright red radishes as well as snow peas.

	CRUDITÉS	
½ lb	snow peas	225 g
½ lb	radishes	225 g
	DIP	
½ cup	shelled peas	125 mL
4 oz	cottage cheese	112 g
½ cup	mayonnaise	125 mL
1 tsp	Dijon mustard	5 mL
2 Tbsp	lemon juice	30 mL

First, make the dip. Cook the peas in boiling salted water until soft, then cool them and press through a sieve to make a thick paste. Press the cottage cheese through a sieve and combine it with the paste. Stir in the mayonnaise, mustard, and lemon juice.

Spoon the dip into a bowl and place it on a platter surrounded by the radishes and snow peas. *Makes 10 to 20 servings.*

PETITS POIS À LA FRANÇAISE

For a change, try cooking peas the French way, braised slowly with lettuce leaves. This gives them a subtly different flavour, and it can even make old and tough peas taste good.

1	small onion	1
2 Tbsp	butter	30 mL
4 cups	shelled peas	1 L
2 cups	shredded lettuce leaves	500 mL
3 Tbsp	water	45 mL
1 tsp	sugar	5 mL
1 tsp	salt	5 mL

Peel the onion, chop it finely, and sauté in butter for a few minutes before adding the remaining ingredients to the saucepan. Cover the pan, lower the heat, and simmer for about 20 minutes, until the peas are soft. *Makes 4 servings.*

PEAS WITH GREEN PASTA

A creamy sauce lightly flavoured with cheese is the catalyst in this dish, which combines fresh peas with fettuccine. For a more hearty meal, small cubes of cooked chicken can be added.

1 Tbsp	butter	15 mL
½ cup	table cream	125 mL
1 Tbsp	flour	15 mL
½ cup	chicken stock	125 mL
1 Tbsp	grated parmesan cheese	15 mL
	salt and pepper	
½ lb	green fettuccine (or linguine)	225 g
2 cups	shelled peas	500 mL

In a small saucepan, heat the butter and gradually add the flour, cream, and chicken stock to make a white sauce (page 248). Stir in the cheese and let the sauce bubble gently for 3 or 4 minutes. Season to taste with salt and pepper. Boil the fettuccine according to the directions on the package, adding the peas during the last 3 minutes of cooking. Drain, combine with the sauce, and serve immediately. *Makes 4 servings.*

 Freezing

Peas freeze superbly, including snow peas, though the latter inevitably lose their crispness. Blanch in boiling water for 2 minutes, then drain, cool, and pack in plastic bags, sucking out the air with a straw. To serve after freezing, remove from the bag, tip into boiling salted water, and cook for 1 or 2 minutes.

Peppers

Peppers are so decorative that they can be grown in a flower bed if there is no room in the vegetable patch. There are two types of peppers – sweet (or bell) peppers and hot peppers – and each type has a number of varieties. If you want to grow sweet red peppers, choose a variety that ripens quickly. All peppers turn either red or yellow when fully ripe, but some take longer than others and most tend to be picked and eaten while still green.

How to Grow
Planting

If grown from seed, peppers need to be started indoors 6 to 8 weeks in advance, so most home gardeners buy them as bedding plants. They should not be planted until all danger of frost is past, and it is best to wait until the onset of hot weather before setting them out. Dig a hole for each plant about 10 centimetres (4 inches) deep, add a handful of well-rotted manure, and fill the hole with water. After the water has soaked in, gently press in the pepper plants, firming down the soil around them. Space the plants about 30 centimetres (12 inches) apart.

Ongoing Care

After the peppers have grown two or more pairs of leaves, pinch off the top pair with your fingers. Although this treatment temporarily halts their growth, it will cause the plants to branch and grow bushy, and will result in more flowers and more fruit. The fruit grows quickly once it starts, but it remains green for a long time, and you may be tempted to pick all the peppers at this stage without waiting for them to turn red.

In fall, when the first frosts threaten, there are bound to be a number of peppers still at the green stage, but there is no need to pick them all, because you can take some of the plants indoors. In the tropics, peppers grow as perennial bushes, and they can be treated as perennials in Canada too if you give them a warm and sunny environment over winter. Dig them up carefully, disturbing the roots as little as possible, and wash them thoroughly with a hose before planting them in flowerpots. Add a little manure among the earth at the bottom of the flowerpot and place them in a sunny window. The green peppers will gradually turn red, and you may even get a second crop from flowers that start blooming in January. In early June, replant them in the garden. I once kept a pepper plant going like this for three years. Although the indoor fruit tends to be rather small, there is no loss in flavour, and it seems wonderfully exotic to be able to pick red peppers from your own plant in the midst of a Canadian winter.

Pends

Aphids are sometimes a nuisance, but in general peppers have little trouble from insects. Like tomatoes, they benefit from having marigolds grown nearby, since these flowers help to ward off insect pests.

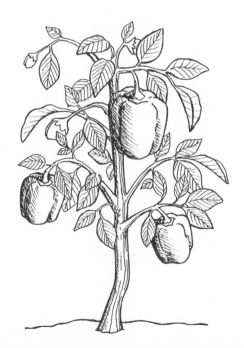

Pepper Recipes

Hot peppers tend to be very hot when freshly picked, so they should be used sparingly when added to sauces or pickles. Chop and slice them, using the seeds as well as the flesh. With sweet peppers, it is the flesh one eats, either in salads or to give flavour to cooked dishes.

How to Prepare and Cook

If a recipe calls for cooked peppers, either red or green, the easiest method is to cook them in tinfoil. Cut off the stalks, slice or chop the peppers, removing the seeds, and place the pieces on half a long sheet of tinfoil. Season with salt and pepper, fold over the other half to make a loose envelope, seal the edges tightly, and cook under the grill for about 10 minutes. This method has the advantage of using no fat, and it gathers all the juices inside the foil envelope.

An even juicier way of cooking red peppers takes a little longer but produces superb results (also without cooking in fat). Place the whole pepper under a hot grill and cook each side until the skin turns black. Peel off the skin and then cut the pepper into slices and remove the pips. Red peppers cooked this way are wonderfully flavourful.

STUFFED GREEN PEPPERS

There are many ways of stuffing peppers, some more tasty than others. This one takes a little time because it requires a sauce as well as a stuffing, but don't save time by missing out on the sauce. It is the blending of the two tastes – the cheese sauce and the tomato and meat stuffing – that gives this recipe its rich flavour.

PEPPERS

4	large green sweet peppers	4
1 lb	ground beef	450 g
1	onion	1
½ lb	mushrooms	225 g
1½ cups	tomato sauce	375 mL
½ cup	red wine	125 mL
1 Tbsp	Bovril	15 mL
½ tsp	nutmeg	2 mL
¼ cup	tomato paste	62 mL
	salt and pepper	

SAUCE

1 Tbsp	butter	15 mL
2 Tbsp	flour	30 mL
1½ cups	milk	375 mL
1 Tbsp	grated parmesan cheese	15 mL
	salt	

Blanch the peppers by dropping them into boiling water and cooking for 4 minutes. Drain, cool, slice off the stem end, and remove the seeds.

Place the ground beef in a large frying pan and cook, stirring, until brown. Remove beef from pan. Drain off the fat. Peel and chop the onion and mushrooms, cook them gently in the frying pan and then combine them with the meat. Transfer the mixture into a saucepan, add the tomato sauce, wine, Bovril, and nutmeg, and simmer for 10 minutes. Then stir in the tomato paste and cook for a further 3 to 5 minutes. Season to taste with salt and pepper.

Tear off four lengths of tinfoil and shape each into a bowl to hold each pepper. Place the peppers in a baking dish and fill them with the hot meat stuffing. Cook in a pre-heated 350°F/180°C oven for 20 minutes. Meanwhile, make a white sauce (page 248) by melting the butter in a small saucepan and gradually adding the flour and milk. When smooth, stir in the cheese and add salt and pepper to taste.

To serve, remove the stuffed peppers from their tinfoil holders and spoon the sauce over them. The peppers should still be firm and juicy, rather than olive green and floppy. If the latter, they have been overcooked and will not taste so succulent. Serve them in a ring of boiled rice. *Makes 4 servings.*

RED PEPPER CREAM SAUCE

This sauce uses both sweet and hot peppers, but its taste is smooth and subtle rather than fiercely spicy. It makes a perfect accompaniment for skinless chicken breasts and also goes well with quenelles. Although the sauce takes time to make, it freezes well, so you can make enough at one time for two or three meals. To serve the sauce after freezing, simply thaw it in a saucepan with a little milk or cream.

3	large sweet red peppers	3
1	tomato	1
1	onion	1
2 Tbsp	butter	30 mL
¼ cup	flour	62 mL
1 cup	table cream	250 mL
2 cups	veal stock	500 mL
¼ tsp	hot red pepper, dried	1 mL
½ tsp	nutmeg	2 mL
3 Tbsp	brandy	45 mL

Cook the sweet red peppers in either of the ways described above. Skin (page 212), core, and chop the tomato. Peel and chop the onion.

Melt the butter in a saucepan over a low heat and cook the onion for 2 or 3 minutes. Sprinkle on the flour and stir in the cream and veal stock. Bring to a slow boil and then add the tomato, the hot pepper, chopped sweet pepper, and nutmeg. Simmer for 15 minutes, then blend in a blender until smooth. Return the sauce to the pan, stir in the brandy, and heat to boiling. *Makes 8 to 10 servings.*

 Storing and Freezing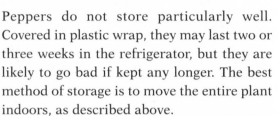

Peppers do not store particularly well. Covered in plastic wrap, they may last two or three weeks in the refrigerator, but they are likely to go bad if kept any longer. The best method of storage is to move the entire plant indoors, as described above.

Similarly, peppers are not really suitable for freezing: they go floppy and there is a distinct loss of quality. If you want to freeze them, wash and core the peppers, removing all seeds, blanch for 4 minutes, drain, cool, and pack in plastic bags, sucking out the air with a straw. To serve after freezing, remove from the bag and boil for 4 minutes.

Potatoes

Potatoes take up quite a bit of space in a garden, but they will grow in almost any soil and don't involve much work. They are grown by planting pieces of the potato itself, but you would be wise to buy special seed potatoes for this purpose rather than using those from a grocery counter, because the latter may have been treated with chemicals to discourage them from sprouting. Only if the potatoes in your kitchen push out shoots is it worth planting them.

How to Grow
Planting

As with all root vegetables, it is best to fertilize the soil the year before planting the crop. Spread some well-rotted manure over the entire bed in the fall and let it lie there over winter. Next spring, as soon as the ground can be worked, dig over the bed. Potatoes should be planted as early as possible.

All potatoes have "eyes" – small notches from which the sprouts grow. Cut your seed potatoes into two or three pieces so that each piece has one or more eyes. Then place them on a sunny windowsill for a few days to let the cut surfaces dry out and harden. To plant the potatoes, dig a trench about 10 centimetres (4 inches) deep and place the pieces about 30 centimetres (12 inches) apart with the eyes facing upwards. Cover over with earth and fill in the trench.

Ongoing Care

Two or three weeks after planting, the sprouts will push up through the soil. Cover them over with earth. As well as protecting the young shoots from frost, this starts the process known as "hilling." To hill the potatoes, you add more earth each time the sprouts become visible so that you gradually build a series of mounds of loose earth – or, better still, a continuous ridge – in which the potatoes can develop. Carry on adding earth up to a height of about 15 centimetres (6 inches). If you live in a very dry part of the country, a ridge is better than a mound, because you can hollow out a shallow trough along its top to collect rainwater, which will seep through to the roots below. However, this is not necessary where there is moderate rainfall.

Throughout the spring and early summer, as the bushy foliage grows above the soil, the potatoes will be developing inside the mounded earth. If any of them push out from the earth, cover them over immediately; potatoes turn green and develop a toxic substance when exposed to sunlight. Potato greens are poisonous and should never be eaten – not green leaves, not green skin, and not the shoots.

As the foliage increases, some of the leaves may develop black or brown spots. This fungus can spread quickly, so remove all infected leaves as soon as you notice the blight and either burn the leaves or put them in the garbage. If a plant is badly infected, remove all its greenery before it has a chance to infect neighbouring plants. This may not mean that you lose that plant's crop. If you dig into the earth, you will probably find a number of potatoes.

Small potatoes will already have developed by the time the plants come into flower, and you can harvest a few at this stage to eat as new potatoes. Gently push aside the earth at the base of the mound and pick off some of the potatoes. Then cover over the earth again, leaving the remainder to grow to full size.

The potatoes will be fully grown and ready for harvesting when the foliage withers and dies, but there is no need to dig them up at this stage. Unless the weather is unusually wet, they can be left in the ground for as long as a month; you can take them in as you need them during late summer and early fall. Dig up the remainder after the first light frosts. Potatoes come up most easily when dug with a fork, but be careful not to spear them.

They often lie deeper than you expect, so aim the fork well below soil level. If you are harvesting a large number, don't let them lie around in the sun. Place them straight into a covered bucket or bin so that they are protected from direct sunlight.

Leafhoppers and Colorado potato beetles are the main threat to the crop. Leafhoppers are agile and difficult to catch by hand, but it is easy to pick off Colorado beetles. The adult beetles have yellow and black stripes, and their grubs are an orange-red with rows of black dots. It is the grubs that cause the most damage. They can eat so much of the foliage that they halt the growth of the potatoes in the ground. If you can spare the time, you can destroy the grubs before they hatch by searching the leaves and crushing the eggs. The eggs are bright orange and are laid on the underside of the leaves.

There are two other ways of protecting the crop from insects. One is to plant marigolds among the potatoes. The other is to be sure to plant the potatoes very early. By the time leafhoppers and Colorado beetles are at their peak, the early crop is almost over, so the potatoes will already be large enough to harvest.

Pests

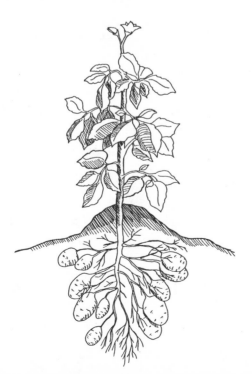

Potatoes are grown inside a hilled mound of soil. Make sure that they are always totally covered by the soil.

Potato Recipes

There may well be more ways of cooking potatoes than any other vegetable: boiled, mashed, roast, baked . . . scalloped, sautéed, deep-fried . . . potato chips, potato scones, potato pancakes, potato purée . . . and so on. Obviously, one cannot cover them all, but there is room to describe a few favourite methods, as well as giving a selection of recipes.

How to Prepare and Cook

NEW POTATOES To cook new potatoes, either scrape off the skin with a sharp knife or scrub them gently and leave the skin on. Bring a pan of salted water to the boil and add some sprigs of mint along with the potatoes. The cooking time will depend on the size, but don't make it too long or the potatoes will get soft and crumbly. About 10 minutes is usually enough for small new potatoes. Medium-sized take a bit longer. They are cooked when a knife can be inserted easily. After draining off the water, remove the mint and add butter and chopped parsley to the pan. Put the pan back on the heat for long enough to melt the butter and coat the potatoes with parsley. Serve immediately.

MASHED POTATOES Old potatoes are the most suitable ones to use for mashed potato. Peel and slice them and boil in salted water until soft. Drain thoroughly and mash until smooth, seasoning with more salt if desired and with white pepper. White pepper, rather than black, makes all the difference to mashed potatoes, and if you want them really delicious you must add butter and cream. Milk can be used instead, but they won't taste nearly so good. Mashed potatoes can either be served immediately or spooned into a casserole and placed in a moderate oven to make the top brown and crisp.

ROAST POTATOES Roast potatoes taste best when boiled first, just for 5 or 10 minutes so that they are only partially cooked. This produces a pleasantly crumbly roast potato that has a crisp but not hard crust. The potatoes will cook in just under an hour, so they should be added to the pan after the roast has gone into the oven. Roll them in fat from the roasting pan and stand them on a rack for the first 10 minutes of cooking. Then place them on the base of the pan and turn them at least once.

BAKED POTATOES For baked potatoes choose the largest ones you can find and scrub them thoroughly to remove all earth and blemishes from the skin. Pierce the top with a sharp knife to let the steam escape, and bake on a rack high in the oven at a temperature of 425°F/220°C for 60 to 70 minutes. This produces a potato that has a crisp skin and a moist and creamy interior. To serve, cut in half lengthwise, add butter, sour cream, or yogurt, and season with salt and black pepper. If you wish, you can scoop out the inside of the potato and mix it with various ingredients before piling it back into its skin. Or you can simply add a topping, such as sautéed mushrooms sprinkled with chives.

POTATO SOUP

This hearty soup is almost a meal in itself, especially when accompanied by various tidbits. I like to place three small bowls beside each setting, each containing a helping of croutons, crumbled bacon, and chopped green onions.

1 cup	chopped leeks	250 mL
1 Tbsp	butter	15 mL
2 lbs	potatoes	900 g
5 cups	chicken stock	1.25 L
3 cups	milk	750 mL
	nutmeg	
	salt and pepper	

In a large saucepan, sauté the leeks in butter. Meanwhile, peel and slice the potatoes. Add them to the saucepan together with the chicken stock and simmer for 30 minutes. Cool slightly, combine with the milk, pour into a blender, and blend until smooth. Return the soup to the pan and add nutmeg and salt to taste, as well as plenty of black pepper. A good potato soup needs to be very peppery. Heat to boiling, stirring to prevent the soup from sticking. *Makes 6 to 8 servings.*

POTATO SALAD

Almost everyone has a recipe for potato salad. I like this one because the dressing is light as well as pleasantly tangy.

3 cups	diced boiled potatoes	750 mL
1 cup	chopped celery	250 mL
½ cup	chopped green onions	125 mL
¼ cup	mayonnaise	62 mL
¼ cup	yogurt	62 mL
1 tsp	lemon juice	5 mL
	salt and pepper	

Combine the potatoes, celery, and green onions. In a separate bowl, mix the mayonnaise, yogurt, and lemon juice. Stir this dressing into the potato mixture, season with salt and pepper, and chill thoroughly. *Makes 4 servings.*

BUBBLE AND SQUEAK

Nobody could pretend that this traditional English supper dish is gourmet fare. It was invented, I suspect, to use up the potato and cabbage left over from lunch. Nevertheless, it is surprisingly appetizing, and children love it.

2 cups	boiled potatoes	500 mL
2 cups	boiled cabbage	500 mL
	salt and white pepper	
¼ cup	butter	62 mL

For this recipe, the cabbage should be very well cooked – boiled for at least 15 minutes – and the potatoes, too, should be boiled until soft. Mash the potatoes, drain and chop the cabbage, and mix together, adding salt and white pepper. Melt the butter in a frying pan, add the potato and cabbage mixture, and heat slowly, stirring and folding. When the mixture is thoroughly heated, flatten it in the pan to let the underside brown. To serve, invert onto a platter so that the crispy underside is facing up. *Makes 4 to 6 servings.*

Note: The traditional accompaniment to bubble and squeak is fried eggs or sausages, but it is also eaten without either.

 Storing

Potatoes should always be stored in absolute darkness to prevent them from greening and becoming inedible. They will keep for months in a cool moist environment, but first they should be placed somewhere warm for two or three weeks in order to heal any cuts or bruises that occurred during harvesting. A temperature of 60° to 70°F (about 15° to 20°C) is perfect for this first stage of storage. Then move them to a cool cellar or garage where the temperature is about 40°F (5°C).

Pumpkin and Squash

Pumpkins take up a lot of room, but they can be fun to grow, especially if you have children. Squash, too, requires lots of space, but most types don't dominate in the way pumpkins do and they can be fitted more easily into a small garden. Winter squashes such as acorn squash tend to be the most popular because they store so well, but there are many other varieties to choose from, including the novelty spaghetti squash.

Both pumpkin and squash like rich soil, and if you are aiming to grow an outsized pumpkin, the soil should be very rich indeed. Dig a large hole, about 38 centimetres (15 inches) deep, and fill it with sheep or cattle manure, enough to mound up slightly above the hole. Then add a thin layer of earth. After the weather has warmed up, and at least a week after all danger of frost is past, place two or three seeds on the mound, covering them over with earth so that they lie about 1 centimetre (⅓ inch) deep.

The procedure is the same for planting squashes, except that you don't need to be so heavy with the manure. A broad and shallow hole will do, about 60 centimetres (24 inches) wide and

How to Grow
Planting

15 centimetres (6 inches) deep. Heap up the manure into a slight mound and cover it with earth in the same way as for pumpkins, planting a few seeds in the earth on the mound.

Ongoing Care

Pumpkin and squash need plenty of water to grow well, but they don't like swampy soil. A thorough watering once or twice a week during hot weather works better than daily watering. If the plants seem slow in growing, add a side dressing of more manure, digging it in gently around the roots. If they are growing too fast – sending out vines throughout your vegetable plot – pinch off the ends of the vines with your fingers. As well as slowing the growth of the vines, this encourages the fruit to develop. For a really large pumpkin, allow the plant to grow only one, picking off the rest soon after they form.

You can harvest squash at any time, cutting it off with a knife; but if you are planning to store it over winter, leave it on the vine until the skin hardens. Pumpkins, too, should be left on the vine until they are fully ripe, which is usually around Thanksgiving. But take them in if there is a frost warning.

If flea beetles attack the young seedlings, zap them with a hand-held organic spray or dust. Do the same with any yellow and black cucumber beetles that come visiting. If you see brownish-black beetles on the plants, these are likely to be squash bugs. They are less nimble than cucumber beetles and are fairly easy to pick off by hand. They creep under stones and boards during the night, and you can trap them by putting one or two boards among the plants and catching them there next morning.

The squash vine borer requires a different approach. This brown-headed caterpillar gets inside the stems, causing the vine to wilt. If you inspect the vines carefully, you will be able to find the greenish-yellow castings it has pushed through a hole in the stem. Slit the stem there and remove the grub. Then mound the soil over the cut. It is also worth looking for the eggs so that you can destroy them before they hatch. They are reddish-brown and are found on the stem near the soil.

You will be less likely to have problems with these insects next year if you clean up the bed as soon as the crop has been harvested. Remove all the vines and put them in the garbage.

Pumpkin and Squash Recipes

Pumpkin is more of a tradition than a food, for it has very little taste in itself and relies on spices for its flavour. Some squashes are similarly insipid, but others have a pleasantly delicate flavour that needs little adornment.

 ## How to Prepare and Cook

With a sharp knife, cut the pumpkin or squash into quarters, peel it, remove the seeds, and cut the flesh into cubes. Cook slowly in butter until soft, or steam until soft. Then mash, drain, and add flavouring such as ginger and sugar, or pepper and salt.

Cubes of butternut squash make a pleasant accompaniment to a roast and can be cooked in the roasting pan. Roll them in juices from the pan, sprinkle with salt and pepper, and bake alongside the roast for about 30 minutes, turning once or twice.

PUMPKIN PIE

This is by far the most popular way of eating pumpkin, though it takes a great many pies to use up one pumpkin. The pie is equally good hot or cold, and although it can be eaten without cream, it is far better with it; the cream adds a subtle new dimension to the taste.

	PASTRY	
½ lb	flour	225 g
¼ lb	fat	112 g
½ tsp	salt	2 mL
⅓ cup	water	83 mL

	FILLING	
1 cup	mashed cooked pumpkin	250 mL
1 Tbsp	melted butter	15 mL
¾ cup	brown sugar	187 mL
1 Tbsp	cinnamon	15 mL
½ tsp	ginger	2 mL
¼ tsp	nutmeg	1 mL
¼ tsp	ground cloves	1 mL

½ tsp	salt	2 mL
1 Tbsp	lemon juice	15 mL
2	eggs	2
1 cup	milk	250 mL

Make the pastry (page 251) and line a 23-centimetre (9-inch) pie dish (or thaw a ready-made pie shell). Bake the pastry shell in a 425°F/220°C oven for 10 to 12 minutes.

In a large bowl, combine the pumpkin, butter, sugar, spices, salt, and lemon juice. Lightly beat the eggs and add them to the mixture, then stir in the milk. Pour into the pie shell and bake in a preheated 450°F/230°C oven for 10 minutes. Turn down the heat to 325°F/160°C and bake for a further 45 minutes or until a knife inserted into the centre comes out clean. Serve with whipped cream. *Makes 6 to 8 servings.*

BAKED ACORN SQUASH

There are various theories on "the perfect way" of cooking acorn squash, and most have one thing in common – that the flesh does not get dry and stringy while the squash is baking. I find the following method as good as any.

2	acorn squash	2
1 Tbsp	butter	15 mL
	salt and pepper	
4 Tbsp	brown sugar	60 mL

Cut the squash in half crosswise, remove the seeds, and cut the tip off the pointed ends so that all four pieces will be able to sit upright on a plate.

Place the pieces cut side down in a baking dish, add about 2 centimetres (¾ inch) of boiling water, and bake in a preheated 375°F/190°C oven for 40 minutes. Turn the squash cut side up, spread butter on the cut surfaces, and sprinkle them with salt and pepper. Place a tablespoon (15 mL) of brown sugar in each cavity and bake for a further 15 minutes. *Makes 4 servings.*

This is the basic recipe, but anything that has a cavity offers the inventive cook all sorts of opportunities for fillings. Try chopped prunes and crumbled bacon or raisins and nuts. Or make a spicy rice filling and pile it in after the squash has cooked.

Storing and Freezing

Pumpkins will keep for several months if handled carefully, and winter squashes will keep all winter, as their name implies. When cutting them from the vine, make sure that some of the stem remains on and store them in a warm environment. Unlike most vegetables, pumpkin and squash store best at a temperature of about 55°F/13°C.

If you have cut into a pumpkin or large squash and can't eat all the flesh at one time, it can be cooked and frozen for later use. Steam or boil the peeled flesh until soft, then mash it and pack in freezer bags, sucking out the air with a straw. To serve after freezing, remove from the bag and thaw in a saucepan with a little water.

Radishes

Everyone has room for a few radishes, since they mature in less than a month and can be planted among slow-growing crops without using extra space. They can also be planted as markers to show where you have sown carrots or other seeds that take several weeks to germinate. If you want to spark a child's interest in gardening, radishes make a good start, because they pop up so quickly – and, of course, make a tasty snack.

How to Grow
Planting

Radish seeds can be sown as soon as the ground can be worked in spring, and this is a good time to make the first sowing because they do best in cool conditions. Radishes will grow in almost any soil but prefer one that is light and fertile, though there is no need to add manure unless your soil is very poor. Black earth or other rich topsoil will usually give the radishes enough nutrients. Spread it in a layer over the bed and place the radish seeds about 2.5 centimetres (1 inch) apart, covering them over with a light dusting of earth. The seeds are quite large, so are easy to place by hand. After planting, water gently, just enough to moisten the earth.

You can make several sowings while the weather is cool, but in most parts of Canada you will not have much luck with radishes in full summer. Wait until about five weeks before the first frost and then make a fall sowing.

The most succulent and tender radishes are those that grow quickly and steadily. This means preventing them from getting hot and dry. Keep the bed well watered, especially if the weather turns hot, and pick them as soon as they are ready. Radishes turn coarse and stringy when left in the ground too long. If they begin to split, this is a sign that they are getting too old.

Ongoing Care

Flea beetles are the most likely pests. These tiny black insects love radish leaves so much that some gardeners grow radishes simply to keep flea beetles off other crops. Fortunately, they are easy to control. Simply squirt them with a hand-held organic dust or spray, or use a homemade repellant (page 238). You may have trouble from root maggots too, but they usually only attack radishes that have been in the ground a long time.

Pests

Radish Recipes

The best way to eat succulent homegrown radishes is plain. Simply brush off the earth, run them under a tap (leaves and all), and bite off the juicy red root. Or wash them and heap them on a plate to accompany lunchtime sandwiches. Served this way, there is no need to cut off the green stems, but these should be removed before adding radishes to a salad.

RADISH COCKTAIL PLATE

You can make a decorative cocktail plate by preparing radishes in three different forms: as radish roses, as buttered radishes, and as radish crackers. When set on a bed of dark green watercress, they look very attractive.

1 lb	radishes	450 g
2 Tbsp	butter	30 mL
	salt	
12	crackers	12
3 oz	cream cheese	85 g
	dill	
4 oz	watercress	112 g

To make radish roses, cut off the stalk end of the radish to give it a flat base to stand on, and snip off any trailing root ends at the tip.

Make six cuts from the tip to within about 6 millimetres (¼ inch) of the base. Then slide a sharp knife under the skin to make six petals. Place the radishes in a bowl of water. This will cause the cut segments to curl outwards, giving you six red petals around a white centre. Drain and dry before serving.

To make buttered radishes, cut off the stalk end to provide a firm base. Then cut a thin wedge from the tip and fill the space with butter. Dip the buttered end in salt and stand the radish upright on its base.

To make radish crackers, chop off both ends of the radish and slice it thinly. Spread the crackers with cream cheese and top with radish slices and a little dill. Sprinkle lightly with salt if desired.

To serve, wash the watercress and arrange it on a large platter or serving tray so that it makes a green bed for the radishes. Add the radish crackers, interspersing them with radish roses and buttered radishes. *Makes about 12 servings.*

RADISHES AND SMOKED MACKEREL

Packages of smoked peppered mackerel are available in many supermarkets, and they can be made into a tasty low-fat paté. Usually, smoked mackerel and smoked trout are served with horseradish sauce, but this recipe uses the common red radish blended with cottage cheese and therefore avoids the sharpness of horseradish.

10	radishes	10
¼ cup	cottage cheese	62 mL
3 Tbsp	lemon juice	45 mL
3	smoked mackerel fillets	175 g
½ tsp	mustard powder	2 mL
	salt	

Peel five large radishes, slice the white flesh and place it in a blender with the cottage cheese and lemon juice. Blend to a smooth paste. Remove the skin from the mackerel fillets, chop them very finely, and combine them with the paste. Add the mustard powder and add salt to taste. If the mackerel fillets were not already peppered, grind in some black pepper. Spoon the mackerel paté onto a serving dish, shaping it into an oblong. Slice the remaining five radishes and use them as decoration, placing them around and on top of the paté. Serve with toast. *Makes 4 servings.*

 **Storing**

Radishes can be stored in the refrigerator in plastic bags for several weeks. Remove all greenery before packaging.

Raspberries

For many people, raspberries are more than a favourite summer fruit. They are a golden memory of childhood – standing among grandma's shoulder-high bushes with raspberry-stained hands and that delectable taste on your tongue. Or maybe the memory is of a birthday party or school treat. Whatever the case, almost everyone seems to have a wistful nostalgia about raspberries in a way that is not true of strawberries, probably because strawberries are far more obtainable.

Because the fruit can be hard to come by, I place raspberry plants high on my list for home gardeners. They need no specialized treatment. The high prices charged in the stores are not because raspberries are hard to grow but because they are difficult to transport and store without losing quality. In fact, raspberries are exceptionally easy to grow and will give an abundance of fruit, especially the everbearing varieties that continue to produce right through until frost – and sometimes afterwards, too. We have been known to eat the last of our garden raspberries in November.

How to Grow
Planting

Spring is the best time to plant raspberry canes, since they may not survive if planted in the fall. They are sold at most garden centres and nurseries, and usually look rather uninspiring – leafless canes with a few roots on the end. The roots are the important part, because they will spread underground to give you a new crop of canes, so choose those that have the most healthy looking roots, and keep the plants in the shade and the roots moist if there is any delay between purchase and planting.

When buying the canes, make sure you get the type you want. There are two types of raspberries: summer bearing and ever-bearing. The former will give only one crop each year (usually in July) whereas everbearing will give a small crop in late July and then a fall crop that starts in late summer and continues until frost. In my experience, summer-bearing raspberries are more invasive than everbearing; they send out particularly strong underground runners, which can be hard to control.

In any case, it is wise to plant raspberries where their runners can easily be dug up if they spread too far. You can grow straw-berries or vegetables nearby, but you don't want to plant raspber-ries right next to currant bushes or anything permanent, in case the roots get intertwined. If possible, leave at least 90 centimetres (36 inches) between raspberries and other fruit bushes. Like most fruit, raspberries do best in full sun, but they will grow in a bed that gets shade for part of the day.

Dig plenty of well-rotted manure into the bed before you plant the canes. If your soil is heavy clay, also add peat moss and a little sand. The plants should be spaced at least 60 centimetres (24 inches) apart. Mark where you plan to have each cane and then scoop out a shallow hole about 8 centimetres (3 inches) deep and broad enough to receive the roots. Water thoroughly to make the earth nice and muddy, then stand the cane in the hole, spreading out the roots in the direction you want them to go. Cover over with earth and firm down the soil with your feet so that the canes stand upright. Immediately after planting, cut off the top of each cane about 30 centimetres (12 inches) above ground level.

Ongoing Care

Do not expect much fruit the first year, but keep the bed well watered and add some more manure in the fall. When the roots push up new shoots, just let them grow.

By the following spring you will have quite a number of canes. There will be the tall brittle ones that grew last year and the new green shoots pushing up this year. Since your July crop will come from last year's growth, do not cut those canes down, even though they look ragged and dead. Give them time to produce leaves so that you can distinguish the living from the dead. Then remove all dead canes, cutting them off at ground level. You can also remove the thinnest live canes in order to encourage the plants to concentrate their energy on producing a good crop of berries on the thicker canes.

Summer-bearing raspberries

Summer-bearing raspberries will have produced their only crop by the end of July. As soon as you have picked the berries from a cane, cut that cane off at ground level and either burn it or put it out with the garbage. Do not let cut canes lie around near the raspberry patch, since this is a way of spreading disease. Leaving dead canes uncut also can spread disease. Sometimes it can be hard to find all the fruited canes, because a forest of new shoots will have grown up among the old. These are the canes that will give you next year's crop, so let most of them remain; remove only the thinnest and most crowded.

Everbearing raspberries

With everbearing raspberries, you can get a summer crop from the canes that grew late last year and also a fall crop from the canes that appear during spring and early summer. Some people choose to forfeit the July crop in order to get a heavier fall crop. If you want to do this, cut back all the canes in late autumn. Personally, I never bother. I simply shorten the canes in late autumn, after the first frost, cutting off the section at the top where the fruit grew. Then, in spring, I prune everbearing raspberries just like summer-bearing ones, cutting out all dead canes and those that are thin or overcrowded. This system works beautifully. I get a light summer crop around the end of July and a magnificent fall crop that starts in late summer and carries on until frost.

Both summer-bearing and everbearing raspberries may need some form of support to help them stay upright when they grow tall. You can set up a permanent arrangement by running parallel wires about 120 centimetres (48 inches) high on either side of the raspberries, securing them at each end with posts. However, this is rather ugly and not necessary for a small patch. For home gardens, it is just as easy to hammer in a few poles to support any canes that fall over. Most of the canes usually serve as their own support, holding one another upright.

Although all this may sound like hard work, it takes hardly any time, and in fact a raspberry patch needs very little attention for most of the year. The most arduous job is probably the harvesting, especially with everbearing raspberries, which can produce such an abundance that they need picking every day or two in the fall. But this is likely to be a pleasure rather than a chore.

The other major task occurs in the spring, just after the new shoots have appeared and the old shoots have come into leaf. As well as cutting away the dead canes, pull up any shoots and roots that are spreading where you don't want them. Raspberries are easy to keep under control if you take this vigorous action. At the same time, give the bed a little manure and a thorough weeding. This will be the main weeding of the year, because you should weed as little as possible during the summer, otherwise you may disturb the roots, which lie near the surface.

Water the bed well in hot dry weather and also when the fruit is forming, since this helps the plants produce large juicy berries. If the weather is very hot and humid, you may get powdery mildew on the leaves – a white fungus. There are organic fungicides that will cope with this disease, and they are available in hand-held sprays.

Pests

In all the years I have grown raspberries, I have only twice had to spray to get rid of an infestation of insects. Fortunately, most insects can be controlled without resorting to a chemical spray. This includes the raspberry cane borer, which cuts two rings around the stem near the tip, causing the leaves above the rings to wither and dry up. If you notice a cane with a wilted tip, cut the stem off well below the wilted part. If you do this promptly, you will prevent the larvae from boring down to the root and killing the entire cane.

You may or may not have trouble from cane borers, but you are almost certain to be plagued by sap beetles. They are about 6 millimetres (¼ inch) long, and they love ripe raspberries and strawberries. If you want to kill them, it is easy enough to do so by setting a bait nearby – a half-open can with something sweet inside it, such as mashed bananas or melon (see page 238). When the beetles have gathered in the can, immerse it in soapy water. Or set a liquid bait made of cider vinegar and a few drops of detergent – a deadly mixture in which the beetles drown.

If you prefer a more friendly course, you can pick the raspberries before they are fully ripe, leaving just a few overripe berries for the sap beetles to feed on. This also works for wasps, which sometimes descend on the raspberries en masse during very dry spells – I think because they are thirsty. You can leave a few berries for the wasps and sap beetles, and pick all the rest when they are still quite firm, dark pink rather than deep red. Bring the berries indoors and place them in a sunny window if you want to eat them that evening or place them on the counter if you want to eat them the next day. In warm weather, the raspberries will ripen very fast and without any loss of flavour. The same strategy works well if birds feast on your raspberries. Blue jays can be infuriating, dive bombing the bushes and knocking the canes flat. But they don't like unripe fruit and will stay away if you keep picking the berries just before they ripen.

On the prairies, where the summers are very dry, you may have trouble from spider mites. Keep an eye out for their delicate webs; they can infest a raspberry patch very quickly during dry spells. If you see any sign of them, take immediate action. There are now organic hand-held sprays that can be used on spider mites.

Raspberry Recipes

By far the best way to eat raspberries is raw, with sugar and cream or with vanilla ice cream. But both can be fattening if the raspberry season lasts for a month or more. After revelling in a few raspberry-and-cream meals at the beginning of the season, we usually cut back to raspberries with milk only, a pleasant compromise that in no way lessens the flavour of the berries. Raspberries are also good with plain yogurt or added to fruit salad, and of course they make excellent jam. By the second year, you are likely to have such a large crop that you will be looking for other ways to serve the fruit. Here is your chance to have fun trying raspberries in meat dishes as well as in desserts.

RASPBERRY AND CHICKEN BREAST SALAD

This is one of those recipes that seem impressively exotic and yet are very easy to prepare; and the result is delicious – lightly flavoured chicken breasts on a bed of lettuce, served with a delicate raspberry vinaigrette. The chicken breasts should be served warm, and the vinaigrette too is more flavourful when served warm. And do use leaf lettuce, not iceberg.

	SALAD	
4	chicken breasts	4
¼ cup	white wine	62 mL
1 Tbsp	lemon juice	15 mL
2	rosemary sprigs	2
1	Boston lettuce	1

	DRESSING	
1 cup	raspberries	250 mL
2 Tbsp	sugar	30 mL
2 Tbsp	wine vinegar	30 mL
1 Tbsp	canola or corn oil	15 mL
½ tsp	Dijon mustard	2 mL

First, make the raspberry dressing. Place the raspberries in a saucepan without any water. Heat slowly, crushing to produce juice, then add sugar and simmer for 5 minutes. Strain through a sieve to separate the pulp from the juice. Discard the pulp and combine the juice with the vinegar, oil, and mustard.

Skin and bone the chicken breasts, and place them in a small bowl with the wine, lemon juice, and rosemary. Leave to marinate for half an hour or longer. To cook, lay a length of foil on a baking tray, place the chicken breasts on half the foil, and fold over the rest, sealing the edges to form an envelope. Cook under the grill for 18 minutes.

While the chicken is cooking, wash the lettuce and divide it among four serving plates. Warm the raspberry vinaigrette. To serve, cut the cooked chicken breasts into two or three pieces and arrange them on the lettuce. Give the raspberry dressing a quick whisk with a fork and drizzle it over the chicken. *Makes 4 servings.*

Note: Keep any liquid that is left over from the marinade or the cooking envelope. It can be added to a chicken stock to give extra flavour.

RASPBERRY AND MERINGUE SUPREME

This spectacular dessert is great for serving to guests, because it can be prepared in advance and assembled at the last moment. It consists of raspberries and whipped cream sandwiched between meringues and topped with more cream and raspberries. Very rich – but oh so delicious!

	MERINGUES	
3	egg whites	3
¼ tsp	cream of tartar (optional)	1 mL
6 oz	fine sugar or instant dissolving sugar	170 g

	FILLING	
3 cups	raspberries	750 mL
2 Tbsp	sugar	30 mL
1 Tbsp	water	15 mL
1 cup	whipping cream	250 mL

The meringues can be made in advance. You should have no difficulty with them provided you take the following precautions. First, separate the egg whites the previous day and let them stand outside the refrigerator for 24 hours unless the weather is so hot that the eggs might go bad. In that case, keep the separated whites in the refrigerator for 24 hours, but let them warm to room temperature before you beat them. Second, use very fine sugar; the meringues may "weep" if you use

coarse granulated sugar. Third, beat the eggs in a wide bowl, adding the sugar very gradually, especially at the beginning. Making meringues is rather like making mayonnaise in that you should add very little at a time and beat it in thoroughly before adding more.

To make the meringues, whisk the whites until they are stiff and then beat in the cream of tartar. Continue to beat the whites while gradually adding the sugar. Place a large piece of tinfoil on a baking dish and lightly oil it. Add dollops of the meringue mixture. You will need eight in all, four small dollops to serve as the tops of the "sandwiches" and four large dollops, smoothed flat with a knife, to serve as the bases. Place at the bottom of a preheated 150°F/70°C for 30 minutes. Then turn the heat down to 100°F/38°C and leave for

another 1½ hours. The meringues should dry out rather than actually cooking. If they are not totally dry after 2 hours, leave them another hour, turning the oven even lower.

To make the filling, place 1 cup (250 mL) of the raspberries in a saucepan, together with 2 tablespoons (30 mL) of sugar and 1 tablespoon (15 mL) of water. Heat gently for a few minutes to make a raspberry sauce. Cool and set aside. Meanwhile, beat the cream until stiff.

Do not assemble the dessert until just before serving. Then place the four meringue bases on a large plate. On top of them pile half of the whipped cream and all the raspberry sauce, and cap with the meringue tops. Add the remaining cream on top of this, decorated with one or two fresh raspberries. Pour the remaining raspberries around the meringues. *Makes 4 servings*.

🍅 Freezing

Raspberries freeze better than almost any other fruit – they retain their shape and flavour so well that it can seem as if they have come straight from the garden rather than straight from the freezer. At the height of the season, I always put down a large quantity for winter, because there is nothing like the taste of fresh raspberries to cheer up a bleak January day.

To freeze raspberries, simply wash and dry the berries, then stand them singly on a metal baking sheet not quite touching one another. Place in the freezer until hard, then package immediately in plastic bags, sucking out the air with a straw.

The raspberries will remain separate in the bags, so you can remove a few whenever you need some to decorate a dessert. They can also be eaten like fresh raspberries with sugar and cream. In this case, pour the frozen berries onto a large plate so that all will thaw evenly. If you serve them while they are still cold and not totally thawed out, they will taste just like fresh raspberries.

Rhubarb

Rhubarb is one of the easiest plants to care for, and it will live for years, but it needs plenty of space because its huge leaves shade anything growing nearby. To prevent the plant crowding out the vegetable plot, you can give it a bed of its own, and this need not be in some hidden spot, because rhubarb is quite decorative. I've seen it grown as a rockery. You can have it in the back or front garden – anywhere will do, provided it gets sun for at least half the day.

How to Grow
Planting

Rhubarb is planted as "crowns" or cuttings, which are available at garden centres and nurseries. The crowns are roots with buds on; the cuttings come in the form of small plants.

The best time to plant rhubarb is early spring, and it should be started with plenty of fertilizer because it is going to live a long time. Dig a hole about 30 centimetres (12 inches) deep and fill it three-quarters full of sheep or cattle manure covered with a thin layer of earth. Flood the hole with water twice, letting it soak in each time, and then set the rhubarb in the hole so that the buds at the top of the crown are about 5 centimetres (2 inches) below soil level. If planting a cutting, set that too so that its root is well below soil level. Add earth as necessary to cover the hole and to hold the rhubarb firm. If you are growing more than one plant, space them at least 1 metre (3 feet) apart.

✐ Ongoing Care

Like asparagus, rhubarb needs to develop its root system before being picked, so leave it alone for the first year and don't pick any stalks until the following spring.

Rhubarb is one of the first plants to poke up through the soil in spring, and this is the time you should give it its annual feeding. Spread some fertilizer around the plant, digging it in carefully with a small hand fork to avoid disturbing the roots. As soon as the stalks begin to grow, you can "force" them by placing a box over the plant. This will give you an early crop that is extra pink and tender. Cut both ends off a box that is about 50 centimetres (20 inches) high and place it over the plant to make the stalks reach up towards the light. The stalks can be picked as soon as they are a reasonable length; rhubarb is at its best when young. To pick the stalks, hold them near their base and twist as you pull. You can go on harvesting rhubarb throughout early summer, as long as new stalks continue to appear, but be sure to

leave plenty of leaves growing in late summer so that the plant can build up its strength for next year's crop.

Each year, soon after the first stalks are full length, the rhubarb will grow seedheads. Cut these off immediately; you will get fewer stalks from a plant that is allowed to flower.

After six or seven years, your rhubarb plant will have grown so big that it needs dividing. Dig it up in spring as soon as the first buds push through the soil, wash the root under a hose so that you can see what's what, and cut it into several parts, making sure that there is at least one bud on each part. Then start the cycle over again, planting these crowns with plenty of fertilizer.

Rhubarb rarely suffers from insect pests. Sometimes earwigs will invade a plant, but they seem to do it little harm.

Pests

Rhubarb Recipes

The deliciously tart taste of rhubarb is a sign of approaching summer in our house. It marks the beginning of the fruit season, the first of our homegrown fruit. Before long, the red currants will ripen and then the black, and by that time the strawberries will be ready for picking. But first of all there is rhubarb, to be stewed or baked, or made into mousse or ice cream or pie, or served as a filling in pancakes or patty shells. Hardly ever is there any left over to make jam.

How to Prepare and Cook

The most important thing to know about cooking rhubarb is that you must not eat the leaves. They contain oxalic acid, which is poisonous to humans, so cut off the leaves when you pick the rhubarb and put them straight in the garbage. Then wash the stalks, trim off both ends, and cut the rhubarb into pieces about 2.5 centimetres (1 inch) long. Young rhubarb does not need peeling, but you will need to strip older stalks if they don't cut through easily.

When cooking rhubarb, allow about ¼ cup (62 mL) of sugar to 1 cup (250 mL) of rhubarb. You can add more sugar if this proves too tart, but tartness is part of the character of rhubarb; it should be sharply sweet, not cloyingly sweet. Rhubarb is more successful baked than stewed, since it tends to disintegrate when stewed. Of course, this does not matter if you are using the rhubarb for a filling – and it makes a great filling for crêpes, served with a dollop of sour cream. The main advantage of stewing rhubarb is that it is quick; it takes only 15 to 20 minutes to cook. Place the rhubarb in a pan with the sugar and a few spoonfuls of water, and simmer gently until soft. To bake rhubarb, you need add no water. Simply roll the rhubarb pieces in the sugar, place them in a covered casserole, and cook in a preheated 350°F/180°C oven. They will take between 40 and 45 minutes.

RHUBARB FOOL

Rhubarb makes an excellent base for various types of mousse, but I have chosen rhubarb fool to give here, since it has less cholesterol than mousses, which require eggs as well as cream. If you want to cut out the cream too, simply substitute plain yogurt. You will get a notably different flavour but one that is equally good.

2 cups	chopped rhubarb	500 mL
½ cup	white sugar	125 mL
½ cup	whipping cream	125 mL

Place the rhubarb and sugar in a saucepan with about 3 tablespoons (45 mL) of water and stew gently. The rhubarb will produce juice as it cooks, but add another spoonful of water if it looks as if it will dry out before it is soft. It will take about 15 minutes to cook thoroughly. Then press it through a strainer or pass it through a moulin (food mill). Cool the rhubarb. Meanwhile, whip the cream until thick. Fold the cream into the rhubarb, spoon into four glasses or small bowls, and chill thoroughly before serving. *Makes 4 servings.*

RHUBARB CRUMBLE

Also known as Rhubarb Betty, this is an old favourite and far easier than a pie because there is no pastry to be made. Rhubarb Crumble can be baked only once, rather than in two steps as suggested here, but that method is less successful because the rhubarb sinks during the baking.

4 cups	chopped rhubarb	1 L
1 cup	white sugar	250 mL
2 Tbsp	grated lemon peel	30 mL
1 cup	flour	250 mL
4 Tbsp	butter	60 mL

Toss the rhubarb in the sugar and lemon peel, and place in an 18-centimetre (7-inch) casserole or soufflé dish. The rhubarb should fill the dish to the brim. Cover tightly and bake in a preheated 350°F/180°C oven for 40 minutes. Meanwhile, sift the flour into a mixing bowl, chop in the butter, and rub the two together with your fingers until the mixture is evenly crumbled. As soon as the rhubarb is cooked, pile flour and butter mixture on top of it and place the casserole uncovered in the oven for a further 15 minutes. Serve with cream or with plain yogurt. *Makes 4 servings.*

RHUBARB AND YOGURT ICE CREAM

Yogurt combines well with most fruit to make light ice cream, and it is particularly good with rhubarb. If you have no jelly available, the rhubarb can be stewed in sugar, but it has a far richer flavour when cooked in crabapple or red currant jelly.

1 lb	rhubarb	450 g
1 cup	crabapple jelly	250 mL
2 cups	plain yogurt	500 mL

Cut the rhubarb into short lengths, discarding any peel that is tough and stringy. Melt the crabapple jelly in a saucepan, add the rhubarb, and simmer for 15 minutes, stirring with a wooden spoon to prevent sticking. Cool, then blend with the yogurt in a blender. Pour the mixture into a plastic bowl and place in the freezer compartment of the refrigerator. After an hour, stir and mash with a fork to prevent the ice cream from freezing solid. Return it to the freezer for another hour, and then mash and stir again. If the mixture is still fairly liquid, give it another half hour or more in the freezer and mash again before serving. The consistency should be creamy and solid but not hard. *Makes 4 servings.*

 **Freezing**

Rhubarb can be frozen raw. Simply wash the stalks, cut them into convenient lengths, and package them in freezer bags, sucking out the air with a straw. To thaw after freezing, remove from the bag, tip into a saucepan, add a few tablespoons of water, and cook with sugar as for stewed rhubarb. Another method is to stew or bake the rhubarb before freezing. This way, too, it can be thawed by heating gently in a saucepan with a little water.

Spinach and Swiss Chard

S pinach is easiest to grow in spring and fall because it quickly goes to seed in full summer, but Swiss chard can withstand very hot weather and it tastes almost as good. The nice thing about growing spinach is that you can pick just a few leaves whenever you want them, rather than having to get a whole bunch. I like to add spinach leaves to salads; young crisp leaves straight from the garden have a pleasantly strong flavour, and their dark green contrasts attractively with the pale green of the lettuce.

How to Grow
Planting

Spinach and Swiss chard can be planted as soon as the ground can be worked in spring. They do best in a light but rich soil, so dig in plenty of well-rotted manure or compost, and add a light topsoil such as black earth if your soil is heavy clay. The seeds are large enough to be placed individually. Drop them about 8 centimetres (3 inches) apart and then press them in with a finger or cover them over with earth so that they are about 1 centimetre (⅓ inch) deep.

Spinach does best when it is not planted in one long row. If possible, sow the crop in short rows or in a group, because this will help provide the roots with shade and make the plants less likely to bolt and go to seed. For the same reason, spinach does best in a bed that gets shade for part of the day. Swiss chard, on the other hand, can be grown in full sun and it will do just as well in a row as in a group.

To get a continual crop of spinach greens, you can make a series of plantings: one or two sowings of spinach early in spring, then a sowing of Swiss chard a few weeks later, and more sowings of spinach in late summer for harvesting during the fall.

Ongoing Care

Swiss chard really needs no care except picking. In early summer you can thin the row by pulling up entire plants as you need them, leaving just a few to grow to full size. These remaining plants can be harvested throughout the summer by cutting off the outer leaves at their base. More leaves will continue to develop in the centre, so you can go on picking from the same plants right until frost.

Swiss chard withstands heat better than spinach and can be planted to succeed a spring sowing of spinach.

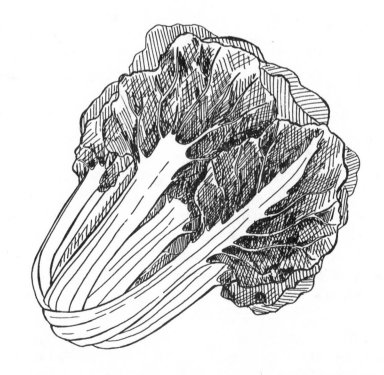

Spinach, too, can be harvested leaf by leaf or by pulling up the entire plant. Some varieties are more heat-resistant than others, but even the most resistant are likely to bolt to seed in sudden heat. This can sometimes be prevented by keeping the earth very moist, but a heatwave generally means that the spinach grows long stalks and begins to form flower heads. When this happens, there is no point in leaving it to go to seed. Pull up the plant and take it in.

Spinach and chards usually have very little trouble from insects, though leafminers may be a nuisance, causing blister-like blotches on the leaves. A few are not worth worrying about, but if they become a serious problem and you don't want to use insecticide, try growing New Zealand spinach, which does not get attacked by leafminers.

Pests

Spinach Recipes

Like many other green vegetables, spinach can be either delicious or disgusting. It all depends on the cooking. I hated it as a child because it was usually a bitter green mush, but nowadays it is one of my favourite vegetables. Raw, it has a pleasantly musky flavour that goes well in salads. Cooked, it can form the basis of all sorts of tasty dishes, especially when combined with a mild cheese.

Swiss chard is cooked the same way as spinach and can be used in all the following recipes. Chard can also be added to salads – but sparingly, because it tastes rather strong when raw.

How to Prepare and Cook

Spinach needs to be washed very thoroughly because it is so easy for grit to collect in the crinkly leaves. To be sure of removing all grit, wash the spinach twice, once in a sinkful of water and once under a running tap. Then shake off the water, break off and discard the very large stems, and pile the leaves into a roomy saucepan. Add nothing to the saucepan – no liquid and no seasoning. Cook over a moderate heat, turning the leaves until all are wilted and dark green. This will take only a few minutes, during which the leaves will give off their liquid. Drain well (keeping the liquid for spinach soup), chop roughly, and add salt and pepper, a touch of nutmeg if desired, and a pat of butter.

SPINACH SOUP

This soup tastes equally good whether made with spinach or Swiss chard, and the stalks can be used as well as the leaves. If there is any liquid left over from cooking other spinach, that too can be used by incorporating it in the chicken stock.

½ lb	spinach	225 g
1	onion	1
1 Tbsp	butter	15 mL
3 Tbsp	flour	45 mL
3 cups	milk	750 mL
2 cups	chicken stock	500 mL
	nutmeg	
	salt and pepper	

Set aside a few spinach leaves to add later. Wash and chop the rest of the spinach, and peel and chop the onion. In a large saucepan, gently cook the onion in butter, then sprinkle on the flour and gradually add the milk, stirring until the liquid thickens. Add the chopped spinach and the chicken stock and simmer for 20 minutes. Blend the soup in a blender until smooth and return it to the pan. Thinly slice the remaining leaves and add them to the soup. Season to taste with nutmeg, pepper, and salt. *Makes 4 to 6 servings.*

Note: For a richer soup, ½ cup (125 mL) of cream can be added. Pour it into a bowl and slowly stir in the soup. Return the soup to the saucepan and heat through but do not boil.

SPINACH CUSTARDS

Individual spinach custards, made in small custard molds, are an attractive way of serving spinach – in flavour as well as appearance. I find them handy for dinner parties, because there is nothing to do at the last minute except unmold them; or they can be served in their molds.

½ lb	spinach	225 g
2 Tbsp	butter	30 mL
2	eggs	2
1 cup	milk	250 mL
	nutmeg	
	salt and white pepper	

Place the well-washed spinach in a saucepan and cook briefly as described above. Drain and chop the spinach and return it to the pan with 1½ tablespoons (23 mL) of butter. Cook over a moderate heat, stirring with a fork, for about 3 minutes. Remove from heat. Break the eggs into a bowl, whisk lightly, and continue to whisk while adding the milk. Season with a little nutmeg, salt, and pepper.

Use the remaining ½ tablespoon (7 mL) of butter to grease four individual custard molds. Combine the spinach with the custard mixture and divide it among the molds. Line the bottom of a small roasting pan with wax paper. Cut a cross in the centre of the paper and place a mold on each of the four segments. Then pour water into the pan so that it comes about halfway up the sides of the molds. Bake in a preheated 350°F/180°C oven for 30 to 40 minutes, until the custards are set. To unmold them, slip a knife around each mold and invert the custard onto a plate. *Makes 4 servings.*

SPINACH AND CHEESE FILLING

Every few months I make a large batch of crêpes to store in packages in the freezer so that I can always produce a quick meal just by making a filling. This cheese and spinach combination is one of my favourite fillings. Simply add a dollop to each crêpe, roll it up, and then add another small dollop on top.

½ lb	spinach	225 g
3 Tbsp	butter	45 mL
4 Tbsp	flour	60 mL
2½ cups	milk	625 mL
1 cup	grated Swiss cheese	250 mL
	nutmeg	
	salt and pepper	

Place the washed spinach leaves in a saucepan without any water and cook just long enough to wilt the leaves. Drain and chop finely. In a separate saucepan, melt the butter and gradually add the flour and milk to make a white sauce (page 248). Add the grated cheese and season to taste with salt, pepper, and nutmeg. Stir in the spinach. The filling is now ready. If you have no crêpes handy, you can spoon it into pastry shells. It is also a great filling for filo pastry (which can be bought frozen at most supermarkets). *Makes 4 to 6 servings.*

SPINACH AND SALMON PIE

This quick and easy pie is a result of my efforts to make kachaphuri – *that delicious melange of fresh salmon, Jarlsberg cheese, cream, and spinach, all baked inside a round loaf of bread. It took a whole afternoon the first time I made it, but each time after that I simplified a little until I ended up with this labour-saving recipe that uses canned pink salmon, ready-made puff pastry, and super-market Swiss cheese. It is not* kachaphuri, *but it tastes remarkably good.*

1 lb	spinach	450 g
	nutmeg	
	salt and pepper	
22½ oz	pink (or red) salmon, (3 cans)	650 g
¼	lemon	¼
2 cups	grated Swiss cheese	500 mL
6 oz	puff pastry	175 g

Wash the spinach thoroughly and wilt it in a large saucepan. Drain and chop finely, flavouring with nutmeg, salt, and pepper. Remove the skin from the canned salmon, mash the salmon flesh in its juice, and flavour with lemon juice and salt and pepper to taste. Spread the salmon over the bottom of a 23-centimetre (9-inch) pie dish. Cover with the spinach and then with a layer of grated cheese. Roll out the puff pastry and lay it on top, sealing down the edges. (This can be done by moistening the lip of the dish with water so that the pastry will stick firmly to it.) Bake in a preheated 400°F/200°C oven for 30 to 40 minutes until the pastry is cooked and the pie is heated through. *Makes 4 servings.*

Freezing

Spinach and Swiss chard both freeze superbly. Wash the leaves thoroughly, place them in a large saucepan, and heat slowly. After the leaves have turned dark green and given out their liquid, simmer gently for 2 minutes. Pour into plastic sandwich boxes, dividing the liquid equally, and allow to cool. Freeze the spinach solid, then pop out the frozen blocks and package them in freezer bags, sucking out the air with a straw. To serve after freezing, remove from the bag and heat slowly in a saucepan. Boil for 1 minute, then drain and chop.

Strawberries

Backyard gardeners love to grow strawberries, and with good reason. Homegrown berries have far more taste than any sold in the stores. Also, picking your own strawberries can give a wonderful sense of satisfaction. This has nothing to do with the taste. It's simply the idea of being able to wander out back and gather the fruit from your very own strawberry patch – a romantic idyll, especially for first-time gardeners.

Like raspberries, there are two types of strawberries: one-crop and everbearing. The one-crop varieties bear fruit in June, whereas the everbearing give a June crop, then take a brief rest, and then start up again and continue until frost.

How to Grow
Planting

The best time to plant strawberries is in spring. Having decided whether you want one-crop or everbearing (or both), you will find that you have a further choice within each group, because a large number of strawberry varieties have been developed. Some are firmer than others, and some are sweeter or more juicy. The salespeople at your garden centre will be able to explain the characteristics of those they carry.

Like raspberries, strawberries do best in full sun but can also be grown in a bed that gets shade for part of the day. Before planting, dig over the bed and add plenty of well-rotted manure. If the soil is heavy clay, also add peat moss.

The plants should be set at least 30 centimetres (12 inches) apart, and it is best to allow at least 90 centimetres (36 inches) between rows if you plant more than one row. Dig a shallow hole to receive each plant and build up a small mound of earth at its centre. Water the mound and drape the strawberry plant over it, spreading out its roots. Then fill in the hole with earth, firming down the soil so that the crown of the strawberry plant is level with the surface. The crown is the junction between the plant and the roots, and you should make sure that it is not buried under the soil, since this can cause the plant to rot.

Set the crown at soil level

Ongoing Care

Since strawberry roots lie near the surface, they dry out quickly in hot weather, so you need to keep the bed well watered, especially when the plants are producing fruit. If you can bear to, do not let them develop fruit the spring you plant them. Pick off any flowers that form. This will encourage the plants to put out long runners.

A number of small plants will develop along each runner, and it is these young plants that will give you your next generation of strawberries. Try to arrange the runners so that the daughter plants grow well apart from the mothers. You will need to know which are which, because next spring you should dig up the mothers after they have borne fruit, and by that time the mothers and daughters can both look much the same.

An easy way to distinguish the two is to plant the mothers in one single line down the centre of the bed. You then direct the runners outwards so that the daughters grow well apart from the mothers. If some of the daughters are too near, you can move them any time after they have established roots. Simply cut the connecting runner and replant the daughter where you want it to grow (following the planting procedure described above). Your aim should be to get three clearly separate rows: the mother row in the centre and a daughter row on either side.

The following year, the daughters will become mothers. In June, you will get a triple crop – one from the first-generation mothers and one each from the second-generation mothers. As

Year 1

Arrange the runners so that the daughter plants form two rows on either side of the mothers.

Their daughters

1st-generation mothers

Their daughters

soon as the fruit has been picked, dig up and discard the first-generation plants. This will leave space in the middle of the bed so that you can direct all this year's runners inwards to form a new central row.

By this system, you can move the plantings back and forth year after year, always keeping track of what is what. The method works for both types of strawberries, even though the everbearing ones will give their first fruit the same year they develop. If you sometimes miss a few mother plants and leave them in by mistake, it doesn't matter. They will still bear fruit, but it will get smaller each year. Your best fruit will come from the younger plants. Some years, you may have far too many young plants. If so, simply pull up the smaller ones or give some away to friends. You will enjoy your strawberry patch more if you can keep it

Year 2

2nd-generation mothers	Their daughters	2nd-generation mothers

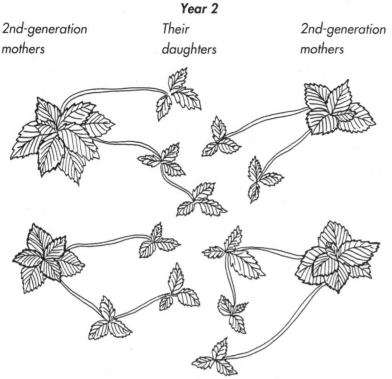

Never be afraid to thin strawberries. Some of these daughter plants should be removed in the fall.

under control and prevent it getting clogged with plants. (Nor should you let it get clogged with weeds!)

Apart from directing the runners and keeping the bed weeded, there is not much to do for most of the year. If a frost hits the flowers in early spring, turning their centres black, pick off the spoiled ones. You can also pick off any small flowers on very thin stems so that the plants can concentrate on developing large juicy fruit on the thicker stems.

As soon as the fruit begins to form, it should be kept off the ground. The easiest method is to place clean straw around each plant. This has a double benefit because it prevents weeds growing and also keeps the roots moist. If you can't obtain straw, use short sticks to prop up the stems. When the soil is dry, the fruit may not suffer from touching the ground, but usually the berries get soft and go rotten when in contact with the earth.

In the milder parts of Canada, strawberries don't need special winter protection, but where temperatures drop to –30°C/–22°F or more, it is best to give them some covering, such as straw or peat moss.

🐞 Pests

Almost everything likes eating strawberries, including slugs, insects, birds, and squirrels. Slugs are not much problem if the plants are bedded in straw, since this makes the berries hard for them to get at. Straw also seems to deter sap beetles, though it does not stop them from gorging on very ripe fruit. To outwit sap beetles, either pick the fruit as soon as it is ripe or lay a bait to trap the insects. A good homemade bait can be made from over-ripe strawberries and mashed banana or melon (see Strawberry Sap Beetle Bait, page 238). Place the mash in a can, and plunge the can into soapy water when it has attracted a crowd of beetles. Or fill a saucer with vinegar and a few drops of detergent. This concoction drowns the beetles.

Unfortunately, most insects cannot be dealt with so easily. Some feed on strawberry leaves, some on the fruit, and some on the blossoms. One of the most destructive is the tiny strawberry weevil, which cuts the stems, causing the flower buds to drop off. Since this means that you will get no strawberries, you cannot afford to ignore them. You can try zapping the weevils with a squirt from an organic spray bottle, but this is not likely to get rid of them altogether. The most effective course is to do a blanket spray of the whole bed with a non-organic insecticide. I find I have to do this about every three years because of weevils or other insects.

Sometimes, birds and squirrels can be more of a nuisance than insects. You can keep birds off by covering the bed with fruit netting. This often works for squirrels too, though squirrels can show great ingenuity when barred from something they very much want to eat. If the netting is held up by posts, they may take a flying leap so that they flatten it and thus reach the straw-berries. I have also known squirrels to chew holes in the netting. If your squirrels prove as determined as mine, you will have to use blood meal as well as fruit netting. Sprinkle it all round the edge of the bed. The squirrels won't cross it; the smell scares them off.

Strawberries Recipes

O ne of my favourite treats as a child was a strawberry picnic under the big oak tree in the
garden. Somehow, the strawberries tasted extra
good when eaten outdoors. They were, of course, served
with sugar and cream. It is hard to avoid cream when
eating strawberries. Every type of cream works well –
clotted cream, sour cream, cream cheese, ice cream –
and inevitably cream is an ingredient in most strawberry recipes. Strawberry shortcake needs lashings of it
and so do strawberry pies. Worse still are soufflés and
mousses, which call for eggs as well as cream – all very
high in cholesterol. This is one of the problems of
growing a large crop of strawberries. Over the years, I
have therefore experimented with other ways of serving
the berries, aiming for less fat content but just as much
tastiness. Three of my favourites are given here.

STRAWBERRY YOGURT

*Nearly all fruit combines well with yogurt, but
strawberries seem to work best of the lot. In
its own way, this dessert is as delicious as
strawberries and cream.*

1 cup	strawberries	250 mL
4 Tbsp	sugar	60 mL
2 cups	plain yogurt	500 mL
16	small strawberries for garnish	16

Wash, hull, and chop the strawberries. Place
them in a saucepan with the sugar and heat
slowly. Cook, stirring, for about 5 minutes to
make a sauce. When the sauce has cooled,
mix it thoroughly with the yogurt. Pour into
serving dishes, dot with a garnish of whole
strawberries, and leave to set in the refrigerator for at least 4 hours. *Makes 4 servings.*

STRAWBERRY AND CHOCOLATE FLAN

Decorative, delicious, and drudgery-free – these "three d's" are well represented in this dessert. It looks exquisitely ornate, like an offering on a sweet trolley at an expensive restaurant, yet it is deceptively easy to make, especially if you use a ready-made pie crust.

PASTRY

½ lb	flour	225 g
¼ lb	fat	112 g
½ tsp	salt	2 mL
⅓ cup	water	83 mL

FILLING

6 oz	chocolate pudding and pie filling (1 pkt)	170 g
3 cups	milk	750 mL
1 Tbsp	sherry or rum (optional)	15 mL
2 cups	strawberries	500 mL
¼ cup	red currant or crabapple jelly	62 mL

If you are not using a ready-made pie crust, make the pastry (page 251) and roll it out to line a 23-centimetre (9-inch) pie plate. In either case, cook as follows. Lay a length of tinfoil over the pastry, weighting it down with dried beans to prevent it rising during cooking. Place in a preheated 425°F/220°C oven for 15 minutes. Then remove the foil, lower the heat to 300°F/150°C, and cook for a further 7 to 10 minutes, pressing down the pastry with a spoon if it bubbles or rises. Remove from the oven and leave to cool.

Pour the chocolate-pudding powder into a saucepan, mix with the milk, and heat to boiling while stirring constantly. Add the sherry or rum and continue to cook until the pudding is thick. Pour into the pie shell and cover with plastic wrap to prevent a skin forming on the chocolate.

When the pudding has cooled, remove the plastic wrap, wash and hull the strawberries, cut them in half, and lay them dome-side up on top of the chocolate. Then add the finishing touch – the glaze – by melting the red currant jelly in a saucepan and brushing it over the surface. Return to the refrigerator to set. *Makes 6 to 8 servings.*

STRAWBERRY ICED DRINK

This refreshing drink is made entirely in the blender. However many strawberries you grow, you will never have enough if you make a habit of serving this fruit cup, which tastes far richer than it in fact is. It is also good when made with raspberries.

1 cup	1% milk	250 mL
10	ice cubes	10
3 cups	strawberries	750 mL
2 Tbsp	lemon juice	30 mL
2 Tbsp	sugar	30 mL

Pour the milk and ice cubes into a blender and blend for about a minute, starting at a low speed and moving up to high. Then add 2 cups (500 mL) of the strawberries, together with the lemon juice and sugar, and blend until smooth. Chop the remaining strawberries, stir them in, and serve immediately. *Makes 4 servings.*

 **Freezing**

Strawberries lose most of their taste and shape when frozen raw, so it is better to make them into a sauce and freeze that. Wash, hull, and chop the berries and heat slowly in a pan without water. For every cup (250 mL) of strawberries, add 3 tablespoons (45 mL) of sugar. This may be less sweet than you like, but you can always add more, according to taste, when you later serve the fruit. Boil the fruit gently for 5 minutes, then cool and pour into sandwich boxes. When the contents are frozen solid, pop them out and package in plastic bags, sucking out the air with a straw. To serve after freezing, thaw in the bag or empty into a saucepan and heat slowly.

Tomatoes

Tomatoes are surely the most popular home-grown vegetable, raised not only in backyard gardens but on city balconies and patios. The pungent smell of a tomato vine ripening in the sun is one of the pleasures of summer, second only to eating tomatoes straight from the vine. To me, the first true taste of summer comes with the first mouthful from one of our own tomatoes. Sometimes this happens as early as June, because I like to start a few of the plants in February so that they are in flower before I move them into the garden. The aim, of course, is to spread the tomato season over as many months as possible.

How to Grow

If you have a window that gets plenty of sun, it is well worth starting some tomato plants indoors (pages 229–33). Starting tomatoes from seed has a double benefit, since you not only lengthen the tomato season but you have a far greater choice of the type of tomato you grow. The seed catalogues offer a mouth-watering range of every size and shape, from Giant Beefmaster to Tiny Tim. I like to grow three or four different varieties, some large enough to stuff, others bred for their juice, and still others suitable for salads. One of my favourites is a cherry tomato called Sweetie. It grows like a vine, climbing the side of our deck and branching over the railings, spreading at least two metres high and sometimes even more in width and – here is the greatest delight – growing so many clusters of tiny sweet tomatoes that we can pick them by the bowlful almost every day.

Planting

Whether or not you started the tomatoes indoors, the procedure is the same. First, wait until the weather is really hot. Don't be tricked into thinking that the May 24 weekend is safe. Tomatoes like a lot of heat, and if subjected to a cold wind and cool temperatures they can take some time to recover. They won't actually die, but they will stop growing, some of their leaves may fall off, and they will bear fruit later than if you had waited another week or two before putting them out.

The bed where you plant them should of course get full sun, but try and avoid planting them during the heat of a sunny day. The tomatoes will suffer less shock if you wait until the cool of the evening or when the sky is overcast. This is not so important if you have grown the plants in Jiffy-7s and they can be moved without disturbing the roots, but if you have bought the plants in flats, they are likely to suffer from the move and may look very wilted for several days after transplanting. This, of course, slows down their growth.

If you have the space, allow at least 45 centimetres (18 inches) between the plants. Mark where you plan to grow them and then dig the holes about 15 centimetres (6 inches) deep. In each hole place a generous handful of well-rotted manure, and add an equal amount of peat moss if your soil is heavy clay. Fill the holes with water twice, each time letting it soak right in. Then gently press in the tomato plants, setting them deeper than they were growing in their pots and pinching off the bottom pair of leaves. Fill up the holes with earth, press in firmly, and give each plant a stake to lean against. Tie the stake and tomato stem together with string, but not too tightly; the stem will widen as it grows. The best method is to wind the string in a figure of eight around stake and stem, allowing a little flexibility.

✍ Ongoing Care

If, despite your precautions, the weather turns unseasonably cool, cover the plants with large plastic bags overnight and give them some daytime protection too, such as a garden chair shielding them from the wind.

In the case of a heatwave, garden chairs can again come in useful, placed over the newly transplanted tomatoes to give shade if they show signs of wilting. This should be necessary only for a couple of days after planting. Meanwhile, keep the bed well watered; the roots should never be allowed to dry out completely.

Given plenty of sun and water, the tomato plants will thrive with very little attention on your part. As they grow and gather strength, they will produce small suckers in the junctions of the leaves. Cut these off as soon as they form, otherwise they will grow to become new branches, and the plant will be putting so much energy into producing greenery that it will be slow to produce fruit.

As the plants grow, they may need more support. I find that tomato cages work best, set in place a few weeks after planting. These wire frames are available at hardware and garden stores, and they make an excellent support for branches that are heavy with ripening tomatoes. If you paint the frames green, they are barely visible among the foliage and are therefore not the eyesore they may seem in the stores.

Around midsummer, when the tomatoes are getting very leafy, some of the first leaves will wither and die off. Remove them immediately. Also remove any leaves that get dark spots on them. The spots are caused by a fungus that spreads rapidly in damp weather, but you should be able to keep it under control if you cut off the infected leaves and put them straight in the garbage. An alternative is to spray with an organic fungicide.

Another possible problem is blossom-end rot – a hard, dark patch that appears on the bottom of tomatoes. Pick off any affected tomatoes and make a point of watering the plants regularly. Blossom-end rot is caused by a combination of factors, but the underlying one is lack of water during a dry spell.

Hot and humid weather is what tomatoes love most, and if you have this type of summer you may get an enormous crop that will carry right through to fall. There are usually far too many tomatoes still on the vine when the first frost is threatened, but there is no need to lose them; they can be ripened indoors. Pick all you can find, regardless of how green they are, and place them in bowls in the kitchen or in any other warm place. There is no need to wrap them in newspaper or keep them in the dark or do anything special. Just keep them on the kitchen counter if that is most convenient. A sunny window is equally good. Over the next few weeks and months, they will gradually turn red. It is usually late in November that we eat the last of our fresh tomatoes.

Remove any suckers that form in the junctions of the leaves.

Pests

The best protection against insects is to grow marigolds among your tomatoes. Marigolds are effective against nematodes in the soil as well as against whitefly, which otherwise may hatch in great numbers on the underside of tomato leaves. Since growing marigolds between my tomato plants, I have never had any trouble from insects. Moreover, the bushy marigolds help hold up tomato branches that are heavy with ripening fruit.

Tomato Recipes

I t seems inconceivable that anyone should ever have too many tomatoes. There are so many ways to prepare them, both raw and cooked, and any surplus can always be made into soup and stored in the freezer. Also, one often wants to eat tomatoes just as they are. Cherry tomatoes are exquisite eaten like candy – popped into the mouth and savoured individually. But they are also delicious cooked, as are all tomatoes.

How to Prepare and Cook

Tomatoes quickly disintegrate when boiled, but they are perfect for broiling and baking. To broil, slice the tomatoes in half, season with pepper and salt, and grill dome-side down for about 5 minutes. To bake, slice in half, season with pepper and salt, and cook dome-side down in a preheated 350°F/180°C oven for 20 minutes. In both cases, a pat of butter can be added if desired, or the tomatoes can be sprinkled with various toppings, such as cheese or herbs or finely chopped onions; or, for a change, try seasoning the tomatoes with sugar instead of salt.

Some recipes require that the tomatoes be peeled. In this case, immerse them in boiling water for about 30 seconds and then plunge them into cold water. The skins can then be slipped off easily.

CREAM OF TOMATO SOUP

Tomatoes make superb soups – cold gazpacho, hot bouillon, spicy minestrone – but my favourite of all is this thick soup, which includes basil and celery leaves for additional flavouring.

4.4 lbs	12 large tomatoes	2 kg
2 Tbsp	butter	30 mL
1	onion	1
1	potato	1
4	young celery ribs, with leaves	4
10	large basil leaves (or 1 Tbsp/15 mL dried basil)	10
2	bay leaves	2
1 Tbsp	sugar	15 mL
1 cup	milk	250 mL
1 tsp	salt	5 mL
	black pepper	
	chopped chives or parsley for garnish	

Wash and chop the tomatoes and place in a large pan together with the butter. Stew gently to allow the juice to appear. Meanwhile, peel and chop the onion and potato. Add them to the pan, along with all other ingredients and simmer for 45 minutes. To extract the seeds and skin, pass the soup through a moulin (food mill) or through a sieve. Discard the seeds and skin, return the soup to the saucepan, reheat, and serve with a garnish of chopped chives or parsley. *Makes about 8 servings.*

For an extra-rich soup, and one that is even more delicious, a cup of cream can be added, though this must be done carefully to avoid curdling. Cool the soup a little, pour the cream into a bowl and then add the soup very gradually, stirring constantly. Return the soup to the saucepan and reheat but do not allow to boil. Serve immediately with a garnish as above.

COLD STUFFED TOMATOES

One could write a whole cookbook on stuffed tomatoes, both oven-baked and raw, for they have inspired a rich assortment of mouth-watering recipes. Here I simply offer a couple of ideas for a quick light lunch.

Scoop out the insides of the tomatoes and insert chopped hard-boiled egg and mayonnaise combined with the tomato flesh; or placed the scooped-out tomato flesh on small lettuce leaves and fill the tomatoes with cottage cheese flavoured with salt, black pepper, and chopped chives.

TOMATO AND BASIL SALAD

So simple to make and so exquisitely flavourful, this salad tastes as if it has a subtly complex dressing, yet it has no dressing at all. The tomatoes themselves make the juice, and the wonderful flavour comes from the fresh herbs, especially the basil leaves. Incidentally, the herbs must be fresh; dried herbs will not give the required flavour.

4	tomatoes	4
2 Tbsp	chopped basil leaves	30 mL
2 Tbsp	chopped parsley	30 mL
2 Tbsp	chopped green onions	30 mL
1 Tbsp	finely sliced green or red pepper (optional)	15 mL
	salt and black pepper	

Slice the tomatoes and lay them in layers in a dish, sprinkling each layer with the herbs and seasonings. Cover with plastic wrap and leave to marinate in the refrigerator for 15 minutes before serving. *Makes 4 servings.*

TOMATO PIE

A hearty dish, rich with flavour, this is rather like a pizza except that it is made in a pie shell.

	PASTRY	
½ lb	flour	225 g
¼ lb	fat	112 g
½ tsp	salt	2 mL
⅓ cup	water	83 mL

	FILLING	
1 lb	about 4 tomatoes	450 g
2	garlic cloves	2
1 Tbsp	oil	15 mL
2 Tbsp	oregano, fresh (or dried, 1 tsp/5 mL)	30 mL
2 Tbsp	basil, fresh (or dried, 1 tsp/5 mL)	30 mL
⅔ cup	1 can tomato paste	156 mL
	salt and pepper	
10	olives	10

1	small green pepper	1
1 cup	grated mozzarella cheese	250 mL

Make the pastry (page 251), roll it out to line a 23-centimetre (9-inch) pie plate, and bake the pie shell in a 425°F/220°C oven for 10 to 12 minutes.

To peel the tomatoes, plunge them into boiling water for 30 seconds, then into cold water, and then slip off their skins. Core, chop, and place in a strainer to drain off surplus liquid. Peel the garlic, cut it into thin slices, and gently fry it in oil in a small saucepan until soft. (Be careful not to burn it!) Add the chopped tomatoes, oregano, and basil. Simmer covered for 15 minutes. Then stir in the tomato paste and season with salt and pepper.

Halve the olives, finely chop the green pepper, and spread both on the pie shell. Cover with the tomato sauce and top with grated mozzarella. Bake in a preheated 350°F/180°C oven for about 35 minutes until the top is crisp and lightly brown. *Makes 4 to 6 servings.*

 Freezing

Tomatoes can be frozen uncooked. Simply skin them by dropping them into boiling water and then cold water so that the skins come off easily; pack them in freezer bags, sucking out the air with a straw. To serve after freezing, remove from the bag, tip into a saucepan, heat gently, and cook through;

or drop them whole into a soup or stew.

Although tomatoes keep their shape when frozen raw, I find that they lose much of their taste. I prefer to freeze them as a purée, which in some ways is even simpler than freezing them raw. Chop the tomatoes in quarters and heat them in a large saucepan with a little sugar, salt, and pepper. Simmer gently for 15 minutes and then either sieve them or pass them through a moulin (food mill) to remove the skin and seeds. Pour into sandwiches boxes, popping them out after they have frozen solid, and package them in airtight plastic bags. To serve after freezing, remove from the bag and heat slowly in a saucepan with a little water.

Watercress

Y ou don't need a garden pond in order to grow watercress, nor do you need a stream running through your lot. These tasty green leaves will grow almost anywhere, even in a windowbox, provided they are watered regularly and never allowed to dry out.

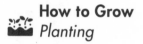

How to Grow
Planting

Buy a bunch of watercress at the supermarket and place the healthiest sprigs in a glass of water. Over the next week or two they will grow long roots.

If you are lucky enough to have a stream or pond on your property, plant the watercress along the mud on the bank. The plants should be near enough for the roots to grow down to the water but should not be permanently immersed. In any case, if you plant them on the edge, they will spread to where they grow best.

If, like most of us, you have no pond or stream available, dig a small trench in a corner of the garden that gets partial shade. Fill the bottom with well-fertilized soil and add enough water to make a mud pie. Press the watercress into the mud at intervals of about 15 centimetres (6 inches), and keep the trench well watered so that the soil is always moist. From time to time, a heavy rain may fill the trench, but this is all to the good. Just let it soak in at its own pace, even if this takes a day or more.

Given suitably moist conditions, the watercress will spread rapidly, so there is little danger of overpicking. You can pick it at any time, but break or cut off the stems; do not pull up the roots.

Also, be sure to leave some roots in over winter; watercress can survive surprisingly low temperatures, so yours may still be alive in spring.

Watercress Recipes

Watercress is a greatly overlooked green, used principally as a garnish with roast duck and other dishes. This is too bad, because it makes a superb salad – just on its own with a vinaigrette dressing. It is also adaptable to a wide range of recipes, as well as making an excellent soup.

WATERCRESS SOUP

Watercress soup can be served either hot or cold, and it is hard to know which is the tastier. Even when made with an instant chicken stock of chicken powder and water, this soup has a very savoury quality.

3 Tbsp	butter	45 mL
1 cup	chopped leeks	250 mL
3 cups	chopped watercress stalks and leaves	750 mL
3 Tbsp	flour	45 mL
1 cup	milk	250 mL
4 cups	chicken stock	1 L
½ cup	whipping cream salt and pepper	125 mL
¼ cup	watercress leaves for garnish	62 mL

Melt the butter in a saucepan, add the leeks and sauté until soft. Then stir in the watercress and cook a further 5 minutes. Sprinkle the flour over the watercress mixture and stir. Add the milk and 1 cup (250 mL) of stock, stirring until the soup thickens. Then add the remaining stock and simmer for 15 minutes. Blend in a blender until smooth.

If serving hot, pour the cream into the saucepan and gradually stir in the soup. Heat slowly but do not allow the soup to boil, since this will make it curdle. If desired, season with a little pepper and salt. Serve with a garnish of watercress leaves.

To serve cold, beat the cream until thick and add it after the soup has cooled. Add pepper and salt to taste. Place in the freezer for about 10 minutes before serving, then add the watercress leaves as garnish. *Makes 4 servings.*

WATERCRESS AND SHRIMP

This dish is expensive because of the shrimp, but it is just the thing for a small dinner party when you want to impress – or just want to enjoy showing off! It looks original as well as attractive, it tastes delicious, and all except the final four minutes of cooking can be done in advance.

1½ lbs	tiger shrimp	675 g
	(6 to 8 per person)	
½	lemon	½
1	bay leaf	1
4	peppercorns	4
½ lb	watercress	225 g
½ cup	fresh chopped parsley	125 mL
1	garlic clove	1
1 Tbsp	oil	15 mL
1 Tbsp	butter	15 mL
	salt	
	DRESSING	
2 Tbsp	canola or corn oil	30 mL
1 Tbsp	wine vinegar	15 mL
	salt	

First, mix the dressing and set it aside. The next step is to cook the shrimps. Add the lemon, bay leaf, and peppercorns to a saucepan half-filled with water. Bring it to a rolling boil, then drop in the shrimps. (If using frozen shrimps, do not thaw them first.) Let the water return to the boil and then cook the shrimps for 1 minute only. They should be barely cooked – still moist in the middle. Drain and shell them, and make a shallow cut down the back in order to remove the vein.

Wash the watercress and place it in a wide bowl. Chop the parsley, peel and mince the garlic, and place both in a frying pan along with the butter and cooking oil. You are now ready for your guests and can devote your entire attention to them until mealtime.

When ready to eat, heat the frying pan and lightly cook the parsley and garlic. Add the shrimps and heat them in this mixture for about 4 minutes, seasoning with salt if desired. Give the salad dressing a final whisk and pour it over the watercress. Toss lightly, then add the shrimps and toss again. The warmth of the shrimps will wilt the watercress slightly, blending all the flavours together. Thinly sliced brown bread makes the perfect accompaniment to this meal – plus, of course, chilled white wine. *Makes 4 servings.*

Zucchini

Zucchini is one of Canada's most popular backyard crops. It is easy to grow, needs no special care, and is usually very prolific, producing far more than you can cope with. I suspect that many a suburban family first became acquainted with the neighbours by being offered a zucchini over the fence.

How to Grow
Planting

Zucchini seeds germinate best at a temperature of 21° to 24°C (70° to 75°F), so wait until the soil is warm and the summer truly underway. The plants do best in full sun, though they will grow in partial shade. They should be spaced about 50 centimetres (20 inches) apart, because they take up a lot of room when mature, but you won't need many of them. Three or four plants provide enough for the average family.

Zucchini is like cucumber in that it needs plenty of water but will wilt if its roots stand in water. The common way of avoiding this is to plant it on small mounds of earth, but I find it works better to give the plants a porous underlayer. For each zucchini, dig a hole about 15 centimetres (6 inches) deep. Fill the bottom 10 centimetres (4 inches) of the hole with peat moss, cover this with well-rotted manure, and top with a thin layer of black earth. Then place three zucchini seeds on the earth, covering them over so that they are about 1 centimetre (⅓ inch) deep. Water the soil lightly.

Ongoing Care

The purpose of planting three seeds in each spot is to allow for wastage. If all three germinate, let them grow for a week or two and then remove the two smallest. Water very sparingly while the plants are small, but don't let the soil dry out.

As the plants grow larger, you can water more generously, especially when the fruit begins to form. Since the leaves are susceptible to mildew, the best way to water is by hand, holding the head of a hose or a watering can under the leaves so that the earth around the roots gets plenty of moisture and the leaves do not. This is far better – and more economical with water – than soaking the whole bed; and if you have provided good drainage underneath the plant, you can water quite heavily without flooding the roots.

Once the fruit begins to form, it will increase in size very quickly. Some of the small ones may wither, rather than developing, in which case cut them off with a sharp knife. The others can be cut for the table at any time and whatever their size. Even if you allow some to grow to full size and then leave them on the vine for several weeks, they will still be edible, though their skins will get hard and brittle.

Zucchini does not as a rule suffer from insect pests, though it is susceptible to the same creatures that attack cucumbers, melons, and squash. The brown squash bug can be picked off by hand, but the yellow and black cucumber beetle is more agile. If there are only a few cucumber beetles and you can see no obvious damage, you can leave them alone. Otherwise, squirt them with an organic dust or spray from a hand-held dispenser.

Pests

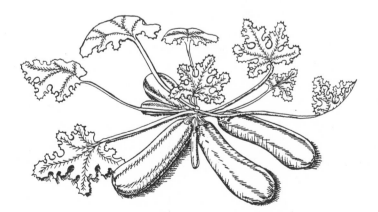

Zucchini Recipes

There comes a time each summer when it seems that everyone in the neighbourhood is trying to give away zucchini. You get a spell of hot weather and suddenly there's more than anyone can handle. That small protuberance on the plant today will be twice the size by the end of the week, and there are still all those larger ones that were ready last week. None of this need be a problem if you make zucchini soup. This is far more sensible than making zucchini bread (which doesn't even use that much zucchini) because the soup freezes superbly and can be made in large quantities and then stored for later consumption. Since any size of zucchini can be used in soup, this leaves you free to pick from your crop only as you need, choosing those that are just the right size for your recipes.

How to Prepare and Cook

Zucchini can be eaten at any stage of growth, even when it is no longer than the length of your finger. When zucchini is that young, it needs no cooking. Cut it off the plant, wash it, trim off the stalk end, and slice the zucchini lengthwise to accompany a dip, or cut it crosswise like a cucumber to add to a salad.

Zucchini can be treated the same way when it is about 15 centimetres (6 inches) long and 4 centimetres (1½ inch) wide, though this is also a perfect size for cooking. Slice the zucchini into widths of about 1 centimetre (⅓ inch), plunge them into boiling salted water, and cook for 3 to 4 minutes. Drain immediately and serve plain, or toss in butter with a sprinkling of thyme and black pepper. Zucchini slices boiled this briefly retain a pleasant crispness. If cooked for much longer, they quickly become limp and soggy.

Zucchini is also tasty grilled. Slice it in half lengthwise and place it cut side down on a baking sheet. Cook for 4 minutes, then turn, spread the cut surfaces with butter, sprinkle with salt and pepper, and grill for a further 4 minutes; or you can omit the butter and spread a slice of cheese on the zucchini.

ZUCCHINI SOUP

When I first heard of zucchini soup, my reaction was "Yuck!" I couldn't believe it would taste even passable. But it is not merely passable, it is delicious, especially when served with a dollop of yogurt in each bowl. Any size of zucchini can be used, but the very large and old ones will need to have the seeds and peel removed before cooking. If you can prick the skin with a thumbnail, the zucchini is tender enough, however large, for all of it to go into the soup.

3 lbs	zucchini	1.35 kg
3 cups	chicken stock	750 mL
1 Tbsp	fresh basil	15 mL
	(or 1 tsp/5 mL dried)	
1 Tbsp	fresh thyme	15 mL
	(or 1 tsp/5 mL dried)	
1 Tbsp	fresh marjoram	15 mL
	(or 1 tsp/5 mL dried)	

2 cups	milk	500 mL
	salt and pepper	

Chop the zucchini (removing skin and seeds if they are coarse and brittle) and place in a large saucepan with the chicken stock and herbs. Simmer for 30 minutes, then blend in a blender until smooth. Pour the milk into the saucepan, stir in the zucchini stock, season with salt and pepper to taste, and heat to boiling. *Makes 6 to 8 servings.*

ZUCCHINI PANCAKES

Here is a light lunchtime dish that is quick and easy to prepare. Do not skin the zucchini before grating it. Simply wash it and cut off the stalk.

2 cups	grated zucchini	500 mL
2	eggs	2
3 Tbsp	flour	45 mL
2 Tbsp	grated parmesan cheese	30 mL
1 Tbsp	chopped chives	15 mL
½	small clove garlic, minced	½
	salt and pepper	
	cooking oil	

Place the grated zucchini in a strainer and drain it well. Whisk the eggs with a fork, then stir in the zucchini, flour, cheese, chives, and garlic. Season with salt and pepper. Lightly grease a thick-bottomed frying pan and heat until hot. Ladle spoonfuls of the zucchini batter onto the pan, two or three at a time, and cook like pancakes, turning to brown each side. *Makes 4 servings.*

CRAB IN ZUCCHINI BOATS

Zucchini and seafood can make a tasty combination when served in a light sauce. This recipe takes the easy route by using canned crabmeat, but it is also very good with fresh shrimp and scallops. Serve it in individual baking dishes.

1	large zucchini	1
8½ oz	crabmeat (2 cans)	240 g
2 Tbsp	butter	30 mL
3½ Tbsp	flour	52 mL
1½ cups	milk	375 mL
¼ cup	white wine	62 mL
3 Tbsp	grated parmesan cheese	45 mL
	salt and pepper	

Peel the zucchini, cut off both ends and chop them into cubes. From the centre portion of the zucchini, make four boats by cutting four lengthwise slices from the edges and scooping out their soft inner flesh. Place the boats and the cubes on half a large sheet of tinfoil and season with salt and pepper. Fold over the remaining half of the tinfoil to make an envelope and seal the edges tightly. Lay on a baking sheet and cook under a hot grill for 6 minutes. Open the envelope immediately to prevent the zucchini from continuing to cook. It should still be quite firm at this stage.

Drain the liquid from the cans of crabmeat and mix it with the wine. Melt the butter in a saucepan and gradually add the flour, the crab-wine liquid, and the milk to make a white sauce (page 248). Season with pepper and salt, and stir in the cheese. Cook gently for 2 or 3 minutes, stirring constantly.

Place a zucchini boat on each individual baking dish, top with the crabmeat and zucchini cubes, and cover with sauce. Sprinkle a little parmesan on each serving and place under a hot grill for a few minutes until brown and bubbling. *Makes 4 servings.*

 **Freezing**

Zucchini can be blanched and frozen, but it is hardly worth the effort because it becomes very floppy. If you have a surplus of zucchini, you will do far better to make it into soup and freeze that. Freeze it in sandwich boxes, then pop out the frozen cubes and package them in freezer bags. The soup will keep for at least a year.

Gardening Tips

How to Plan Your Garden

The most common design for a vegetable garden is a large square or rectangle in which all the plants are set in rows, the tallest at the back. Although this works well for many gardeners, I prefer an arrangement of several small beds. One advantage is that you can reach the plants without getting muddy feet – not that muddy shoes matter if you are spending a whole afternoon gardening, but they can be annoying if you have just popped out to pick some tomatoes for supper.

Even more to the point is the difficulty of making this type of garden look at all nice. It may seem appealing on paper, with everything neatly in its place, but nature tends to be untidy, and inevitably a vegetable plot takes on a ragged, gap-toothed appearance as the various crops are harvested. If you live in the country and have space to hide the vegetable garden behind a hedge, appearance doesn't matter, but most Canadian houses are built on relatively small lots, and you don't want to create an eyesore that will spoil the view for your neighbours as well as yourself.

Gardens should be pretty, and even vegetable gardens can be made attractive when given a little thought. For instance, if one of the beds is in full view of the house, plant it with a crop that will look good all year, such as rhubarb or peppers, and consider adding a border of bushy flowers – yellow daisies, perhaps, or golden marigolds. If you decide on one large bed, you can make it more attractive and easier to work by running some paths through it. Grass paths are the prettiest, and they are not much trouble to keep neat with a small hand mower.

The first step, however, is to decide what you want to grow. This is particularly important if you have a small lot where space is limited, because the beds should be dug to suit your needs, rather than digging a large bed and then wondering what to put in it. Start by listing, in order of preference, the fruit and vegetables you like best or use most, and then let your imagination roam round the garden, thinking how and where you might be able to fit them in. There may be space for a narrow bed behind the garage where you could grow leeks, onions, lettuce,

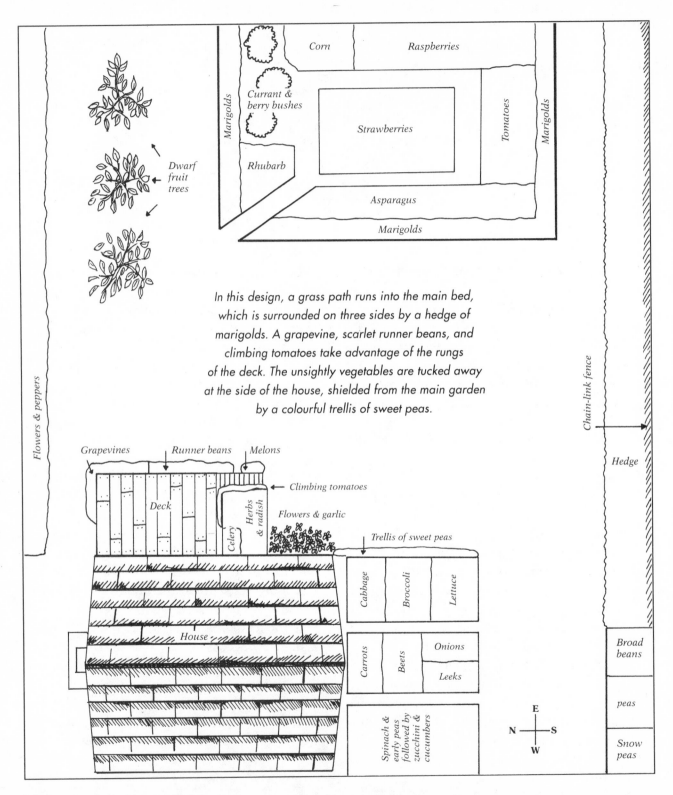

Corn

Raspberries

Marigolds

Currant &
berry bushes

Tomatoes

Marigolds

Strawberries

Rhubarb

Asparagus

Marigolds

Dwarf
fruit
trees

Flowers & peppers

Chain-link fence

In this design, a grass path runs into the main bed,
which is surrounded on three sides by a hedge of
marigolds. A grapevine, scarlet runner beans, and
climbing tomatoes take advantage of the rungs
of the deck. The unsightly vegetables are tucked away
at the side of the house, shielded from the main garden
by a colourful trellis of sweet peas.

Grapevines   Runner beans   Melons

Climbing tomatoes

Deck

Herbs
& radish

Celery

Flowers & garlic

Trellis of sweet peas

Hedge

Cabbage

Broccoli

Lettuce

House

Carrots

Beets

Onions

Leeks

Broad
beans

peas

Spinach &
early peas
followed by
zucchini &
cucumbers

E

N   S

W

Snow
peas

and other vegetables that would make the main garden appear unsightly. Or maybe some "unsightly" beds could be fitted at the side of the house.

When planning these hideaway beds, make sure that they will get sufficient sunlight. Most vegetables will grow well even if shaded for half a day, but tomatoes, cucurbits (cucumbers, squash, etc.), and several others need full sun. The south side of a house or garage is therefore an excellent site for a bed; west and east are good for most crops, and north is dubious for almost everything.

If there is a fence bordering your property, it can be put to use as a support for climbing plants. A chain-link fence in full sun is a gardener's delight. As well as making an excellent trellis for beans and peas, it can help hold up tomato plants or sunflowers. The rungs of a deck can be put to similar use – as a climbing frame for attractive scarlet runner beans or as support for a grapevine. Cherry tomatoes can be trained to climb up the handrail of the deck, intertwined with nasturtiums for maximum effect; and alongside the steps you might plant a couple of melons or cucumbers, to be directed up the steps as they grow, thus saving space in the bed itself.

When trying to grow as much as possible in a limited space, remember that early and late crops can take turns in the same bed. A first sowing of peas, spring onions, and radishes can all be grown in a bed that will later be used for zucchini, cucumbers, or anything that is not planted out until late May or early June. Similarly, a late sowing of spinach can fill the gap where lettuce grew earlier in the year.

Another point to bear in mind is that there is no law saying that flowers and vegetables may not be grown in the same bed, and by no means all vegetables are unsightly. Pepper plants look elegant in a flower bed; garlic is appropriate because it keeps the bugs off roses and other flowers; and some herbs blend in well, though you may prefer to grow herbs in pots on a patio or in a bed of their own near the kitchen door.

Large plants such as rhubarb can always be given a bed of their own if they take up too much space in the main plot. I have seen rhubarb holding pride of place in a rockery on the front lawn. It looked magnificent. In much the same way, asparagus, fruit bushes, and raspberries can form part of the design of a small backyard, acting as a hedge or screen.

Planning a garden can be almost as much fun as working one. Things never turn out exactly as planned, but that is half the fun; and there's always the possibility of working to a slightly different plan next year.

How to Dig and Prepare the Beds

When digging a new bed, you will need to make it suitable for the plants to grow in. First, cut away the turf, then dig over the earth to a depth of about 20 centimetres (8 inches), removing any stones and breaking up large lumps. The digging can be done with a spade or fork (whichever you find easier), or a rototiller can be used. The aim is to make the soil loose and crumbly so that the roots of the plants can penetrate easily. If the soil is heavy clay and difficult to work, add peat moss or sawdust as you dig. This will help lighten the earth and improve its texture.

The next step is to enrich the soil so that the plants will have plenty of nourishment. I find that the best fertilizer is manure – for instance, sheep or cow manure. Compost is an excellent fertilizer too, but most home gardeners are unlikely to have any available, whereas bags of manure can be bought at supermarkets as well as garden centres. The manure can be spread on top of the soil and then worked in with a spade or fork until it is well mixed with the earth, or it can be added systematically, as follows.

At one end of the bed, dig a trench about 20 centimetres (8 inches) deep and 60 centimetres (2 feet) wide, and pile the earth from it at the other end of the bed. Place a layer of manure at the bottom of the trench. Then dig a similar strip next to the trench, and pile the earth from it on top of the manure in the first trench. This will fill trench number 1. Add manure to trench number 2, then dig trench number 3, piling its earth into trench number 2. Carry on digging and filling trenches in this manner until you reach the end of the bed, where you fill the final trench with the earth from trench number 1.

Needless to say, if all this seems like too much hard work, you can hire someone to do the digging. In both spring and fall there are plenty of people advertising in the gardening columns of local newspapers, and they are usually knowledgeable as well as cheerful and inexpensive.

Ideally, new beds should be dug in the fall, because the freezing and thawing during winter helps to break up the soil, and the manure has time to mix in and become part of the earth. Similarly, fall is the best time to add manure to established beds. Since plants feed on the nutrients in the earth, more nutrients need to be added from time to time, and it is easiest to do this overall fertilizing when the beds are clear of plants.

If you don't have time to add manure in the fall, be sure to dig some in early in spring – though not where you will be growing root crops such as carrots and beets, because strong fresh manure can cause them to become knobbly and hairy. Whether you add the manure in spring or in fall, the earth should be dug over and weeded each spring and then raked smooth so that it is in perfect condition to receive the seedlings.

How to Know Your Climate

With the beds well prepared, the next step is to plant the crop, and this brings up the tricky question of climate. One of the most common gardening instructions is "Plant when all danger of frost is past" – but how, during a Canadian spring, can you be sure that there won't be another frost?

The table of first and last frosts (pages 243–44) can serve as a general guide, but the weather varies so much from year to year that you will need to pay particular attention to the forecasts as well as using a bit of common sense. A heatwave in April may cause you to feel as if summer has arrived, but every

Canadian knows how quickly the temperature can drop, bringing a return of winter in May.

There is never any harm in sowing seed a little earlier than is wise, because you can always make a second sowing if frost destroys the first sowing. On the other hand, it is not a good idea to put out tender plants while there is still the likelihood of frost. Although you can protect the seedlings by covering them at night (and in the daytime too, if need be), the cold will slow their growth. The weekend of 24 May is the traditional planting-out time in most parts of Canada, but this can be a little early for tomatoes and cucumbers. Unless you live on the West Coast, you would be wise to wait another week or two before putting out these hot-weather plants.

Because the climate varies so much within provinces as well as between provinces, Agriculture Canada has published a map of growing zones. The zones are numbered 0 to 9, the higher numbers representing the warmer regions. Most vegetables can be grown in all zones (except, of course, in the parts of the Arctic that are permanently frozen), but some fruit bushes and trees such as peaches are suitable only for the warmer zones. The zoning numbers are particularly useful when buying from a mail-order catalogue. If you are buying locally, they need not concern you, since your garden centre will be unlikely to carry anything that doesn't do well in your area.

Knowing what will survive the winter is partly a matter of trial and error. If your garden is very exposed, it may be colder than the average in your zone. If it is sheltered, it may be warmer. One way of judging what can be grown is by looking around your neighbourhood. If you see a grapevine just down the road, it is well worth planting one too, even if you live in a zone that is said to be a little too cold for grapes.

For vegetable gardeners, the main problem is not the coldness of the winter; it is the short length of the summer. Canadian seed houses (page 238) have developed a wonderful variety of seeds to cope with this problem. If you want to grow melons in Alberta, for instance, you can order a variety that will mature in 70 days or less – and the melons may ripen even more quickly if you live in the northern part of the province. Although summers tend to be shorter in the north, the days are longer, so the plants get more light and therefore develop more quickly.

The best way to lengthen the summer is to start seed indoors early in the year. This not only lengthens the growing season; it increases the time you can take pleasure from gardening. When the snow is knee-deep outside, it can be great fun to potter with seed packets and soil – an act of faith, a promise that summer isn't all that far away.

How to Start Seed Indoors

Indoor gardening can range from growing a few tomato plants in a sunny window to running a full-scale operation in the basement, complete with "gro-lamps" and other gadgets. It is the former that I shall deal with here, since most backyard or balcony

Canada's Plant Hardiness Map

Miles
0   75   150

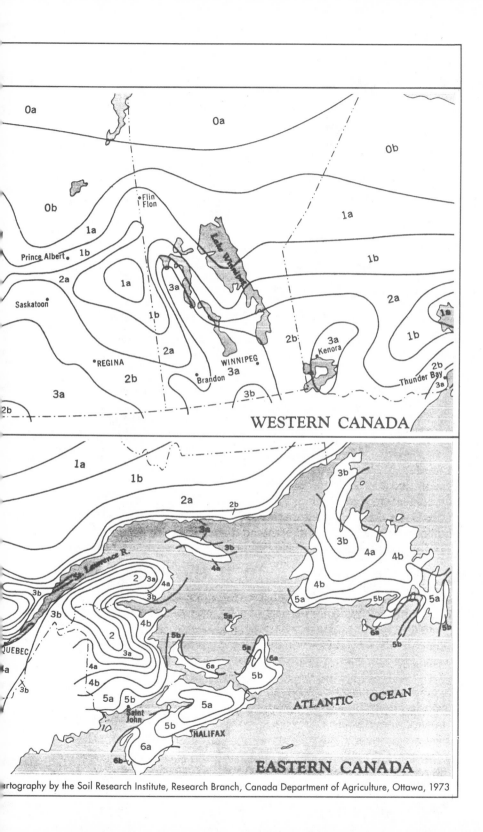

WESTERN CANADA

EASTERN CANADA

rtography by the Soil Research Institute, Research Branch, Canada Department of Agriculture, Ottawa, 1973

How to Sow Seed indoors

1 Sow only as much as you need. One packet can last several years.

2 Jiffy-7s are sold as dried peat pellets.

3 The pellets expand when soaked in water.

4 When moving or thinning young seedlings, hold them by the leaves to avoid breaking the delicate stems.

5 Place the seedling deep in the Jiffy-7 so that most of its stalk is covered.

6 The roots grow into the Jiffy-7, which remains attached to the plant when it is set in the garden.

gardeners have neither the time nor the equipment for growing plants under lights, but many like to get a jump on the season by starting a few vegetables indoors. Tomatoes come high on the list, and cucumbers are worth raising too if you want an early crop. Melons definitely need to be started early, and so do other long-season crops, though it is often more convenient to buy these as small plants. How much you grow indoors will depend on your window space and whether or not you have a greenhouse or solarium.

Before you begin, always read the seed packet carefully, since it will give directions on planting and will say how far in advance you should sow the seed. Tomatoes, for instance, need to be started at least two months before the weather is warm enough for them to be planted outside. On the other

hand, if you start cucumbers that early, you will have vines crawling all over the windowsill long before the plants can safely be moved outdoors.

To give the seed a good chance of success, do not use earth from the garden. Buy a bag of sterile potting soil. Place two or three spoonfuls of the soil in a small, clean flowerpot or in any container that has holes for the water to escape. Various pots and propagating trays are made for this purpose, but an ordinary tinfoil pie pan works just as well if you prick holes in the bottom. Dampen the earth with a little water and sprinkle on a few seeds. Sow just enough seeds to allow for some wastage. For instance, if you are planning on six beefsteak tomato plants, you won't need to sow more than about eight seeds. Cover the top of the container with plastic wrap to hold in the moisture, and place it on a saucer or plant tray. Be sure to label each container, and continue to label everything at each stage.

Seeds don't need light in order to germinate, but they do need warmth, so put the pots in the cosiest place in the house. If you have a warm laundry room or furnace room, that will do nicely. Check after a few days to see if anything is happening, and as soon as the first shoots appear, move the pots to a windowsill or somewhere with plenty of light.

About one week later, when the shoots are large enough to handle, they will need to be moved out of their pots into more spacious holders. Jiffy-7 peat pellets are the best bet, especially for cucumbers, melons, and other plants that suffer if their roots are disturbed. Jiffy-7s are disc-like pellets that expand to become compact cubes of nutrient-rich soil when soaked in water. They provide a contained and undisturbed environment for the roots to grow in, and consequently the plant suffers no shock when it is set in the garden.

Soak the pellets in water for ten minutes or more until they are thoroughly damp all through as well as fully expanded. Then spear the top of each with a toothpick to make a narrow hole to receive the roots of the seedling. Young seedlings are very delicate and their stems break easily, so be careful how you handle them. The best way is to pull them from their containers very gently, holding them by the top leaves rather than by the stem. Then lower the roots and the bottom part of the stem into the hole you have made in the pellet, and gently squeeze

the hole shut so that the stem is held firmly.

Place the pellets in a plant tray in a sunny window, and water them as often as is necessary to keep them moist but not soggy. A little water poured into the tray each morning is generally sufficient. Too much water may cause them to suffer from damping off – a fungus disease that weakens the stems and can kill young seedlings. If you see a mould growing on the surface of the pellets, sprinkle them with a little dry peat moss and cut down on the watering.

Plants started early will outgrow their Jiffy-7s after six or seven weeks. The most likely to do so are tomatoes, which will need larger containers when they reach a height of about 18 centimetres (7 inches). As soon as they begin to look "leggy," move them to flowerpots, setting them low in the pot and nestling the Jiffy-7 in a mix of earth and manure. Pull off the lower pair of leaves when potting the tomatoes, and place the plants deep enough in the flowerpot for the earth to cover much of the stalk. This will help strengthen the stalk and encourage root growth.

Cucumbers and melons do better with a different approach because they need plenty of feeding but not too much watering. As soon as they begin to branch and grow strong, fill the tray they are standing in with well-rotted manure and place the Jiffy-7s on top of it. If you water the manure regularly so that it is constantly damp, the roots of the plants will extend out of the Jiffy pellets and into the manure, regulating their own intake of water and nutrients. By the time you set them in the garden, the roots will have attached themselves to the manure, but this doesn't matter; the basic root structure inside the Jiffy-7s will remain compact and undisturbed, so the plants will suffer no shock when they are transplanted into the garden.

How to Transplant into the Garden

If your plants have had plenty of sun on the windowsill, they will not need much hardening off before being planted in the garden. Hardening off is the process of toughening the plants to accustom them to the wind and temperature changes that they will get outdoors. This can be done by placing them outside in the daytime, giving them just a few hours the first day and gradually increasing their time outside.

When transplanting anything, whether it is a small vegetable or a large bush, never put it into dry earth. Dig a hole larger than the size of the roots, place some manure at the bottom, plus some peat moss if your soil is heavy clay, and then fill the hole with water. If you are planting something large, fill the hole with water twice, letting it soak in each time. This gives the plant a reservoir of water where it is needed – around the roots – and is far more effective than watering the surface of the soil after you have set the plant in the bed.

Having made the hole suitably moist and muddy, you then gently tap the plant out of its pot while holding the pot upside down. Often the plant will come out in one piece, and of course Jiffy pellets will remain undisturbed too. Set the plant in the hole so that it stands a little lower than it was in its pot. Then fill in the hole with earth and press down firmly.

Transplanting is best done on a cloudy day or in the evening, because cool conditions are less likely to be stressful to the plants. Even so, some plants may go limp and droopy if the following day is very hot. The droopiness usually lasts only a day or two, and you can alleviate it to some extent by keeping the plants under a mist of water from a soaker hose or by giving them protective shade. The easiest way to shade small plants is to stand a garden chair over them. This allows them plenty of air as well as keeping off the sun.

How to Water Your Garden

How often should you water your garden and how much? The first point to bear in mind is that a light sprinkling with the hose on a hot day can do more harm than good. Light watering wets only the top of the soil, attracting the roots to the surface, where they quickly dry out. Whenever you water, you should do so long enough to give the soil a thorough soaking. If using a sprinkler, keep it on for about half an hour. To check whether the water has penetrated thoroughly, poke a stick into the earth. If there is still dry soil underneath the top layer, continue watering.

In very hot, windy weather the soil may dry out so quickly and so completely that you will need to water once a day. In less extreme conditions, a thorough watering once or twice a week should be sufficient, provided you keep an eye on the garden to make sure that nothing is drying out. In a wet summer, the sky will do the watering for you most of the time.

There are several different ways of watering – sprinkler, soaker hose (mister), hand-held hose, and so on – and I find that different approaches suit different plants. A sprinkler works well for a bed of mixed vegetables such as spinach, lettuce, cabbage, potatoes, and beans. Strawberries, too, are best watered by sprinkler. For seedlings, a soaker hose works best, because it can be kept on for an hour or more without using an unnecessary amount of water and making the bed sodden. As mentioned above, a light misting gives seedlings protection from the sun on a hot day.

My preferred method for many plants, especially during heatwaves, is to flood the soil around the roots by taking the nozzle off the hose and letting the water flow gently over the bed. The hose can be moved around the garden, lying five minutes or more in each position. This system uses water more efficiently than a sprinkler does, and it is particularly suited to raspberries, currants, peas, and tomatoes, all of which need a thorough watering but are susceptible to mildew on the leaves. Cucumbers, zucchini, and melons can be treated the same way, except that they will get enough water in a matter of seconds. Water them by hand rather than leaving the hose lying on the bed.

As a general rule, watering should be done either early in the morning or in the evening, because too much moisture is lost through evaporation during the heat of the day. The best time is the evening, especially in very hot weather, because the plants are thirsty after a day under the burning sun, and they will have all night to drink in the water and gather strength to face the next day's heat.

How to Deal with Slugs and Snails

Slugs and snails are every gardener's bane. They seem unaffected by insecticides, nor do they turn over and die when squirted with organic soaps and dusts. The only sure way to kill them is to stamp on them, but they sensibly keep out of sight during the daytime. You may be able to find a few snails, but slugs are usually well hidden.

There are various ways of keeping slugs and snails off your vegetables even if you can't find where they are hiding. You can surround leafy lettuce and spinach with sandpaper or with anything prickly enough to prevent the slugs gliding over it. Beans, cabbages, and anything that grows up from a stalk can be protected by wrapping tinfoil or newspaper around the stem to prevent slugs climbing up it. But such measures protect only individual plants; if there are slugs around, they will have to find something else to eat, either in your vegetable patch or in the flower bed.

In any case, defensive measures on their own are little use as a long-term policy, since the slug population can multiply at an alarming rate if you don't mount an attack on the creatures. In my early days of gardening, I decided to be altruistic and "live with the slugs" – and I found myself doing just that. They took over the whole garden. Within three years, there were so many that not a single vegetable escaped. They even climbed the tomato stalks and got inside each tomato. Fortunately, we had to move to another province at the height of this slugfest, so I was able to flee the problem rather than dealing with it. But my motto when starting my next garden was "Death to All Slugs!"

And this brings us back to the problem itself: How do you get rid of slugs? It is said that if you put out a saucer of stale beer in the evening, the slugs will crawl into it, get drunk and then drown. This trick has never worked for me. All I've succeeded in drowning are a few drunken spiders. Slug bait is a sure killer, but it kills worms too, and unless you hide the pellets under a heavy brick or plank, you run the risk of poisoning birds and your own pets as well. Also, I don't like the idea of placing poisonous pellets on soil that grows vegetables. Recently, a less poisonous type of bait has come on the market, a crystalline powder that is said to be harmless to birds and animals. But anything that is laid down indiscriminately can kill indiscriminately too, and this means worms and spiders and others that do no harm to your crop.

The best bet, in my view, is a totally harmless bait such as an overripe piece of melon tucked under a cabbage leaf. The melon attracts the slugs, and the cabbage leaf provides the dark and moist conditions they feel safe in, so they are likely to stay there in the daytime. Lift up the leaf next morning, and you may find five or six slugs, which you can dispatch forthwith by stepping on them or squashing them with a trowel.

It is also worth going on a slug hunt very early in the morning when the plants are still wet with dew and the slugs are still feeding. If you get up just before sunrise and search the underside of the leaves, you may catch as many as a hundred, even in a comparatively slug-free garden. Two or three morning hunts are usually enough, and make them in early summer when the slugs are still very small and have not yet reproduced. Granted, this is not a pleasant way to begin a fine summer's day, but it is by far the best method of slug control, and at least the slugs die instantly, rather than suffering a slow and lingering death as they do after eating slug bait.

Another method, which can also be very effective, is to encourage toads to live in your garden. They eat slugs and will hunt them down in their hiding places. If you come across a toad on the lawn or in a nearby ravine, put on your gardening gloves, pick up the toad, and place it where you have the greatest slug problem. If it finds enough to eat, it will settle in there. Moreover, toads multiply quickly if given half a chance, and it doesn't take long to build up quite a large tribe of them.

How to Deter Squirrels and Other Rodents

The simplest way of keeping squirrels, rabbits, groundhogs, and other rodents from eating your vegetables is by laying a tangle of netting around the bed and a sprinkling of blood meal. Tangled netting on the ground is more effective than an enclosure of taut netting, because the animals cannot easily find their way over it, and they tend to panic when their feet get caught in the threads. I have known squirrels gnaw through carefully erected fences of garden netting, and rabbits and groundhogs can burrow under a wire fence, but it doesn't occur to them to burrow under strands of netting that are lying on the ground.

If you accompany the netting with blood meal, you should have no trouble. The smell of blood meal scares rodents so much that they will not cross it. Blood meal is fairly expensive, but one bag is usually enough to last the whole summer. Sprinkle it sparingly around the edge of the bed or on the leaves of the most tempting vegetables. Light watering will not wash it away, but you will need to put on a new application after a heavy rainstorm. This is all to the good, because heavy rain washes the blood meal into the soil, and blood meal is a wonderfully rich fertilizer. So as well as guarding your crop from rodents, it helps you grow magnificently large and healthy vegetables. Incidentally, do not confuse blood meal with bone meal. Both make good fertilizers, but bone meal is not nearly so effective as a repellant.

How to Make Organic Repellants and Insecticides

The following concoctions are all non-toxic. They are easy to make and use ingredients that can be bought at any supermarket if they are not already on hand in your kitchen.

PEPPERY RODENT REPELLANT

a few shots	Tabasco	a few shots
1 tsp	chili powder	5 mL
2 cups	water	500 mL
½ tsp	dishwashing soap	2.5 mL

Mix the ingredients together and pour into a clean spray bottle. Spray on the leaves of plants that are clearly being eaten. This repellant is effective against squirrels, groundhogs, rabbits, and other rodents. The peppery taste of the "sauce" on the leaves can prove so unpleasant that the animals may leave your garden alone and look elsewhere for their food. The repellant also discourages insects. Respray after heavy rain.

APPLE MAGGOT AND WASP TRAP

4 Tbsp	jam	60 mL
1 Tbsp	water	15 mL

Mix the jam and water together and pour it into the bottom of a slender jam or pickle jar. The perfect sized jar is about 12 centimetres (5 inches) tall, with an opening of about 5 centimetres (2 inches) wide. The insects will be attracted into the jar and down into the jam solution, where they will drown. Hang two bottles on each apple tree in June and July when the fly of the apple maggot is active. Later in the year, when fruit is ripening, the bottles can be hung on peach, plum, and pear trees to catch wasps.

DOG REPELLANT

10	garlic cloves	10
1	medium onion	1
4 cups	water	1 L
1 tsp	Tabasco	5 mL

Peel and chop the garlic and onion. Combine with the water and Tabasco, and blend in a blender. Strain, pour into a clean spray bottle, and spray on and around plants where dogs are being a nuisance.

APHID SPRAY

| 10 | garlic cloves | 10 |
| 4 cups | water | 1 L |

Peel the garlic, chop it finely, and soak in water overnight. Strain, and pour the liquid into a clean spray bottle. Spray on infested plants. This spray is effective against flea beetles and other small insects as well as aphids. It works chiefly by keeping the insects off the plants rather than killing them, though they may die if hit by the spray.

STRAWBERRY SAP BEETLE BAIT

| 4 | overripe strawberries | 4 |
| ½ cup | mashed banana or melon | 125 mL |

Mash the strawberries, combine with the banana/melon mash, and place in a can. Set the can in the strawberry bed. Check from time to time, and as soon as the bait has attracted a number of sap beetles, plunge the can into soapy water.

Where to Get Seed Catalogues

Occasionally, a seed catalogue may arrive by mail without being ordered, but most need to be specifically requested. Even if you are only growing a few tomatoes, it is worth ordering them from a catalogue, because this gives you a far greater choice than you can get from your local garden centre or supermarket. Dominion Seed House, for instance, offers more than forty different varieties of tomato, along with a mouth-watering selection of other vegetables. Other large companies have a similarly good selection. There are also smaller concerns that concentrate on specialties such as herbs or organic products.

The following list gives a cross section of some of the leading Canadian seed companies. All those listed send their catalogues free.

Alberta Nurseries & Seeds Ltd.
Box 20, Bowden, Alberta
T0M 0K0

Dominion Seed House
115 Guelph Street
Georgetown, Ontario
L7G 4A2

Early's Farm & Garden Centre Inc.
2615 Lorne Avenue, Box 3024
Saskatoon, Saskatchewan
S7K 359

Halifax Seed Co. Inc.
Box 8026
Halifax, Nova Scotia
B3K 5L8

Island Seed Co. Ltd.
Box 4278, Station A
Victoria, British Columbia
V8X 3X8

Lindenberg Seeds Ltd.
803 Princess Avenue
Brandon, Manitoba
R7A 0P5

McFayden Seed Co. Ltd.
Box 1800
Brandon, Manitoba
R7A 6N4

Ontario Seed Co. Ltd.
Box 144
330 Philip Street
Waterloo, Ontario
N2J 3Z9

Rawlinson Garden Seed
269 College Road
Truro, Nova Scotia
B2N 2P6

Stokes Seeds Inc.
6009 Stokes Building
39 James Street, Box 10
St. Catharines, Ontario
L2R 6R6

Territorial Seed Co.
Box 46225, Station G
Vancouver, British Columbia
V6R 4G4

Vesey's Seeds Ltd.
Box 900
Charlottetown, Prince Edward Island
C0A 1P0

Where to Ask for Help

In most large towns throughout the country there is an office of the provincial department of agriculture, and the staff are usually very helpful in answering gardening questions. They will also be able to tell you whether their department (or a local horticultural society or university) operates a gardening hotline during the summer. Some provinces employ home garden specialists for this purpose.

Most agricultural departments, including that in the Yukon, issue publications for home gardeners which are given out free on request, and it is worth dropping in at your local office to see what is available. Alternatively, you can write to the following:

Yukon
Department of Renewable Resources
Agriculture Branch
Box 2703
Whitehorse, Yukon
Y1A 2C6

British Columbia
No longer issues home gardening publications, nor will the department give gardening advice.

Alberta
Alberta Department of Agriculture
Publications Office
Main Floor, 7000 – 113 Street
Edmonton, Alberta
T6H 5T6

Saskatchewan
Saskatchewan Department of Agriculture
and Food
Communications Branch
Walter Scott Building
333-3085 Albert Street
Regina, Saskatchewan
S4S 0B1

Manitoba
No longer issues home gardening publications, nor will the department give gardening advice, but in some years the University of Manitoba operates a gardening hotline.

Ontario
Ministry of Agriculture and Food
Consumer Information Centre
801 Bay Street, 1st Floor
Toronto, Ontario
M7A 1A3

Québec
Ministère de l'Agriculture, des Pêcheries et de l'Alimentation
Gouvernement du Québec
Boite 1693
Québec, Québec
G1K 7J8

New Brunswick
New Brunswick Department of Agriculture
Box 6000
Fredericton, New Brunswick
E3B 5H1

Nova Scotia
Nova Scotia Department of Agriculture
and Marketing
Box 550
Truro, Nova Scotia
B2N 5E3

Prince Edward Island
Prince Edward Island Department
of Agriculture
Box 1600, Crops Section
Charlottetown, Prince Edward Island
C1A 7N8

Newfoundland
Newfoundland Department of Forestry
and Agriculture
Provincial Agricultural Building
Box 8700, Brookfield Road
St. John's, Newfoundland
A1B 4J6

Glossary of Gardening Terms

ANNUAL a plant that completes its life cycle within one year (in contrast to a perennial, which carries on from year to year).

BLACK EARTH a light topsoil consisting of peat loam.

BLOOD MEAL dried animal blood, used both as a high-nitrogen organic fertilizer and as an organic repellant to deter squirrels and other rodents.

BOLTING a term that refers to plants such as lettuce and spinach when they form a seed-stalk and go to seed.

BONE MEAL dried animal bones, used as a slow-release organic fertilizer.

CHEMICAL FERTILIZER a synthetic fertilizer which generally comes in powder or granule form and is diluted with water (or watered after application).

COMPOST a mixture of decaying organic substances, such as dead leaves and manure, which break down to form a rich fertilizer.

CROWN the part of a plant where the root joins the stem.

DAMPING OFF a fungus disease that causes seeds to rot and seedlings to weaken and die; it is carried in the soil and is most likely to occur when seedlings are grown in unsterilized soil.

FERTILIZER a substance that enriches soil and aids plant growth; organic fertilizer is composed of natural substances, while chemical fertilizer is synthetic.

GERMINATION the sprouting of a seed.

HARDENING OFF the process of helping plants started indoors adapt to an outdoor environment.

HARDY PLANTS are those that can survive a spring frost (in contrast to tender plants, which are killed by frost).

JIFFY-7 a peat pellet which, when soaked in water, expands to become a nutrient-rich environment for growing seedlings; since the Jiffy-7 remains in place when the seedling is transplanted, it is suitable as a starter for cucumbers and other plants that suffer from having their roots disturbed

LONG-SEASON CROP a plant that requires a long period of frost-free days in order to grow to maturity and produce a satisfactory crop.

MULCHING covering the surface of the soil with material such as straw or black plastic sheeting in order to conserve moisture and control weeds.

ORGANIC FERTILIZER a natural fertilizer such as manure, compost, worm castings, blood meal, bone meal, kelp meal, and fish emulsion.

PEAT MOSS a form of sphagnum moss that absorbs water and assists drainage, lightening heavy soil.

PERENNIAL a plant that lives for several years (in contrast to an annual, which lives only one year).

POTTING SOIL a mix of sterilized soil, organic fertilizer, and drainage materials such as peat moss or vermiculite; it is a suitable medium in which to start seeds and grow seedlings.

SEEDLING a young plant.

STERILE SOIL earth that is free of bacteria and weeds. To sterilize soil, place it in a large baking dish, such as a turkey roaster, moisten the earth enough to make it muddy but not sodden, and bake in a preheated 275°F/140°C oven for 1½ hours.

TENDER PLANTS are those that cannot survive a light frost.

THINNING removing crowded seedlings or young plants to allow enough space for the remaining plants to grow to full size.

TOPSOIL the fertile upper part of the soil.

VERMICULITE a sterile material that holds water well and is mixed with earth and organic fertilizer to make a light potting soil.

First and Last Frost Dates

	Average Last Spring Frost	Average First Fall Frost
British Columbia		
Fort Nelson	25 May	9 September
Penticton	8 May	4 October
Prince George	6 June	31 August
Prince Rupert	11 May	15 October
Vancouver	31 March	3 November
Victoria	16 April	4 November
Alberta		
Banff	4 June	2 September
Calgary	25 May	15 September
Edmonton	25 May	8 September
Fort McMurray	7 June	31 August
Grande Prairie	18 May	12 September
Medicine Hat	15 May	22 September
Peace River	31 May	2 September
Saskatchewan		
Prince Albert	1 June	5 September
Regina	24 May	11 September
Saskatoon	21 May	16 September
Swift Current	23 May	19 September
Manitoba		
Churchill	24 June	9 September
Flin Flon	22 May	19 September
The Pas	27 May	17 September
Winnipeg	23 May	22 September
Ontario		
Kitchener	10 May	9 October
London	10 May	5 October
Moosonee	19 June	29 August
Ottawa	7 May	2 October
St. Catharines	28 May	18 October
Sudbury	18 May	24 September
Thunder Bay	30 May	12 September
Timmins	4 June	4 September
Toronto	8 May	5 October
Windsor	26 April	21 October

First and Last Frost Dates

	Average Last Spring Frost	Average First Fall Frost
Quebec		
Bagotville	24 May	19 September
Chicoutimi	17 May	30 September
Gaspé	5 June	19 September
Montreal	3 May	8 October
Quebec	13 May	28 September
Schefferville	17 June	3 September
Sept Îles	27 May	19 September
Sherbrooke	2 June	10 September
New Brunswick		
Chatham	19 May	23 September
Fredericton	19 May	23 September
Moncton	22 May	24 September
Saint John	16 May	3 October
Nova Scotia		
Halifax	12 May	15 October
Sydney	23 May	14 October
Yarmouth	2 May	21 October
Prince Edward Island		
Charlottetown	16 May	15 October
Newfoundland		
Corner Brook	21 May	8 October
Gander	3 June	7 October
St. John's	5 June	8 October
Northwest Territories		
Yellowknife	27 May	16 September
Yukon		
Dawson	13 June	17 August
Whitehorse	8 June	30 August

Source: Environment Canada

SPRING PLANTING CHART
Annual Vegetables

AFP = After all danger of frost is past
SGW = As soon as the ground can be worked in spring
LSC = Long-season crop, easier to buy as seedlings than to sow outdoors

Vegetable	Germination Time	Outdoor Sowing	Depth of Seed	Indoor Sowing Before Planting Out AFP	Space Between Plants	Space Between Rows
Beans, broad	4–10 days	SGW	2.5 cm/1 in		5 cm/2 in	Plant as clumps
Beans, bush	4–10 days	AFP warm soil	2.5 cm/1 in		8 cm/3 in	40 cm/16 in
Beans, climbing	4–10 days	AFP warm soil	2.5 cm/1 in		5 cm/2 in	
Beets	7–14 days	SGW	1 cm/⅓ in		Scatter seed; first thinning to 5 cm/2 in; then 8 cm/3 in	15 cm/6 in
Belgian endive	5–14 days	SGW	1 cm/⅓ in		Scatter seed; thin to 5 cm/2 in	15 cm/6 in
Broccoli	6–10 days	LSC	1 cm/⅓ in	6–7 weeks	45 cm/18 in	60 cm/24 in
Brussels sprouts	6–10 days	LSC	1 cm/⅓ in	5–6 weeks	45 cm/18 in	60 cm/24 in
Cabbage	6–10 days	LSC	1 cm/⅓ in	4–6 weeks	30 cm/12 in	60 cm/24 in
Carrots	2–3 weeks	SGW	6 mm/¼ in		Scatter seed; thin to 2.5 cm/1 in	45 cm/18 in
Cauliflower	6–10 days	LSC	1 cm/⅓ in	6–7 weeks	45 cm/18 in	60 cm/24 in

SPRING PLANTING CHART
Annual Vegetables

AFP = After all danger of frost is past
SGW = As soon as the ground can be worked in spring
LSC = Long-season crop, easier to buy as seedlings than to sow outdoors

Vegetable	Germination Time	Outdoor Sowing	Depth of Seed	Indoor Sowing Before Planting Out AFP	Space Between Plants	Space Between Rows
Celeriac	10–20 days	LSC	3 mm / ⅛ in	10–12 weeks	15 cm/6 in	45 cm/18 in
Celery	10–20 days	LSC	3 mm / ⅛ in	10–12 weeks	15 cm/6 in	25 cm/10 in
Corn	5–10 days	AFP warm soil	2.5 cm/1 in		20 cm/8 in	Plant as clumps
Cucumber	7–10 days	AFP warm soil	1 cm/⅓ in	4 weeks	20 cm/8 in	60 cm/24 in
Eggplant	6–14 days	LSC	1 cm/⅓ in	6–8 weeks	40 cm/16 in	60 cm/24 in
Kohlrabi	6–9 days	AFP	1 cm/⅓ in		15 cm/6 in	40 cm/16 in
Leeks	10–20 days	SGW	6 mm/¼ in		Scatter seed; thin to 10 cm/4 in	30 cm/12 in
Lettuce	4–12 days	SGW	6 mm/¼ in		Scatter seed; first thinning to 5 cm/2 in	40 cm/16 in
Onions	6–12 days	SGW	6 mm/¼ in		Scatter seed; thin to 10 cm/4 in	30 cm/12 in
Parsnips	3–4 weeks	SGW	6 mm/¼ in		Scatter seed; thin to 4 cm/1½ in	15 cm/6 in

AFP = After all danger of frost is past
SGW = As soon as the ground can be worked in spring
LSC = Long-season crop, easier to buy as seedlings than to sow outdoors

Vegetable	Germination Time	Outdoor Sowing	Depth of Seed	Indoor Sowing Before Planting Out AFP	Space Between Plants	Space Between Rows
Peas	6–15 days	SGW	5 cm/2 in		5 cm/2 in	25 cm/10 in
Peppers	1–2 weeks	LSC	1 cm/⅓ in	6–8 weeks	30 cm/12 in	40 cm/16 in
Potatoes	"eyes"	SGW	10 cm/4 in		30 cm/12 in	60 cm/24 in
Pumpkins	7–12 days	AFP warm soil	1 cm/⅓ in	3–4 weeks	2–3 seeds at 30 cm/12 in	2 m/7 ft
Radishes	3–5 days	SGW	1 cm/⅓ in		2.5 cm/1 in	10 cm/4 in
Rutabaga	1–2 weeks	SGW	1 cm/⅓ in		Scatter seed; thin to 13 cm/5 in	30 cm/12 in
Spinach	7–12 days	SGW	1 cm/⅓ in		8 cm/3 in	Plant as clumps
Squash	6–12 days	AFP warm soil	1 cm/⅓ in		15 cm/6 in	50 cm/20 in
Swiss chard	7–12 days	SGW	1 cm/⅓ in		8 cm/3 in	20 cm/8 in
Tomatoes	6–14 days	AFP warm soil	3 mm/⅛ in	8 weeks	45 cm/18 in	45 cm/18 in
Turnips	3–10 days	SGW	1 cm/⅓ in		8 cm/3 in	40 cm/16 in
Zucchini	6–12 days	AFP warm soil	1 cm/⅓ in		50 cm/20 in	50 cm/20 in

Basic Recipes

WHITE SAUCE

When I was ten, my grandmother told me that knowing how to make a white sauce was the first step in cookery. I had thought the first step was boiling an egg, but she tossed that aside with a derisive, "When you are older, dear, you will know the difference between egg boilers and cooks." She then proceeded to show me how to make the sauce, and a beautifully smooth one it was too. Inevitably, when I first tried, the result was horribly lumpy. The trick in getting the sauce smooth is to add the flour and milk very gradually. There are various ways this can be done, but my grandmother's is one of the easiest, so I pass it on to you here. It is different from the usual method in that some of the milk is added before the flour. This recipe is for a medium-thick sauce. For a thinner sauce, add less flour; for a thicker one, add more.

1 Tbsp	butter	15 mL
2 cups	milk	500 mL
3½ Tbsp	flour	52 mL
	pinch of salt	

Three things will help you get the sauce smooth: instant blending flour, a small saucepan with a thick base, and a plastic or wooden spoon. Melt the butter in the saucepan and then add ¼ cup (62 mL) of milk. Warm the milk but do not bring it to a boil. Remove the pan from the heat and with your left hand sprinkle the first tablespoon of flour on the milk while stirring with your right hand. Take time over this, sprinkling a little at a time rather than dumping the flour in all at once. After the first tablespoon is well stirred in, do the same with the second and then the third.

Return the saucepan to the burner over a low heat and stir constantly. As soon as the sauce begins to thicken, add a little more milk and continue to add milk, bit by bit, until all is in the saucepan.

If, in the early stages, the sauce becomes solidly thick, remove the pan from the heat and stir vigorously to gather the mixture into a smooth ball of paste. Then add about a tablespoon of milk and stir it in, then a little more milk and a little more, until the paste is diluted to a thick liquid. Return the pan to the burner and gradually stir in the remaining milk.

As soon as the sauce is smooth and creamy, season it to taste with salt. Bring the mixture to a gentle boil, still stirring, and boil it for 3 or 4 minutes to complete the cooking of the starch in the flour.

If, despite all these efforts, you end up with a lumpy sauce, use a blender to make it smooth. This is an advantage that modern cooks have over my grandmother. But her main premise still holds – that a white sauce is the first step in cookery. It is the basis of many of the classic sauces. Velouté, mornay, and countless others with high-sounding names are no more than ordinary white sauces with variations.

CHICKEN STOCK AND OTHER MEAT BROTHS

A well-flavoured stock is like a white sauce in that it is a basic element from which you can make other things – in this case, soups. I rank stock-making as a cook's second most important skill, though it should probably come first because it is so easy. Making fresh stock simply involves boiling up bones and scraps of meat with a few vegetables and herbs.

Chicken, beef, and veal are the most common stock bases. There is ham stock too, of course, but it is usually included as part of the soup-making process rather than as the base of a separately made stock. Any bones and any bits of meat are suitable, either cooked or uncooked. For chicken stock, use the leftovers of a roast chicken (stuffing and all) or the parts you don't normally eat, such as giblets and neck; or use the uncooked bones cut from chicken breasts. For veal stock, the best bargain is to buy veal shoulder chops, cut away the lean part to flatten and cook as veal escalope, and use all the rest for making stock. Similarly, beef shanks are a good base for beef stock, though leftovers from the Sunday roast will do equally well.

The other ingredients will depend partly on what you have on hand. A little wine helps enrich the flavour, especially when balanced by herbs. Leftover vegetables can always go in, for they add to the nutritiousness as well as the taste. However, each stock needs a few basic flavours, derived from certain herbs and vegetables, and these are listed below.

CHICKEN STOCK

	chicken bones, giblets, and meat	
1	onion	1
2	celery sticks with leaves	2
1	carrot	1
1	garlic clove	1
2	bay leaves	2
1 Tbsp	thyme	15 mL
2	chicken cubes	2
1	beef cube	1
½ cup	red wine	125 mL
6 or more cups	water	1.5 L or more

BEEF STOCK

	beef bones, gristle, and meat	
1	leek (or onion)	1
1	carrot	1
1	celery stick with leaves	1
1	turnip	1
1	garlic clove	1
2	bay leaves	2
1 Tbsp	thyme	15 mL
3 or 4	parsley sprigs	3 or 4
3	beef cubes	3
10	peppercorns	10
1 cup	red wine	250 mL
6 or more cups	water	1.5 L or more

VEAL STOCK

	veal bones, gristle, and meat	
1	onion	1
1	carrot	1
3	celery sticks with leaves	3
3 or 4	parsley sprigs	3 or 4
2	bay leaves	2
1 Tbsp	thyme	15 mL
3	chicken cubes	3
½ tsp	nutmeg	2 mL
¼	lime, squeezed	¼
1 cup	white wine	250 mL
6 or more cups	water	1.5 L or more

To make the stock, divide the bones and meat into manageable pieces, and peel and chop the vegetables. Heat a cauldron of water and add all the ingredients. There should be enough liquid to cover them by about 4 centimetres (1½ inches). Bring to a rolling boil, skim off any scum that forms, then reduce the heat and simmer for about 3 hours. Top up with more water during the cooking if the level gets too low.

Towards the end of the cooking time, taste the stock so that you can make adjustments in flavouring. If it is too strong, add more water. If it is too bland, either boil it hard to reduce the amount of liquid or add more herbs and more chicken or beef cubes. Adjust the flavour to your liking, strain the stock, and discard everything except the liquid. Cool the liquid, store it overnight in the refrigerator, and skim off the hardened fat next morning. The stock is now ready to use as a basis for soups or to decant into containers and store in the freezer.

SOUPS FOR THE FREEZER

As well as storing stocks in the freezer, it is worth putting away soups too. Almost all vegetables can be made into soup, and even a small garden can provide enough to last most of the winter. This is by far the simplest way of dealing with a surplus of garden vegetables, since soup takes little time to make and it is as easy to cook up a large amount as a little. And not only do the various soups freeze extremely well, but some actually gain in flavour as a result of being frozen. They last at least a year.

Whether you are freezing a soup or a stock,

it should be cooled first. Then pour it into plastic sandwich boxes – small boxes for a family of two, larger boxes for a family of four or more. Ideally, each box should contain enough to provide a helping of soup for the whole family. Fill the boxes no more than three-quarters full, otherwise the contents will be difficult to remove after freezing. Place the boxes in the freezer until the soup or stock is solid and then pop out each block like an ice cube and package in plastic bags, sucking out the air with a straw.

To serve after freezing, remove the plastic bag and place the solid block in a saucepan with a little milk or water. Use only water for stocks and meat-based soups; use a mixture of milk and water, or milk only, in soups that already have milk as one of their ingredients. Heat slowly, stirring to prevent sticking, and bring to a gentle boil. Since the soup has been diluted by the additional liquid, it may need more seasoning at this stage. Salt and pepper will do in many cases, but any soup with a chicken base gains a richer flavour if you add chicken powder rather than salt.

If any soup is left over, it can be eaten the following day, provided it is boiled thoroughly before serving. All thick soups, whether previously frozen or not, should always be boiled for 10 minutes if they are more than a day old. Thick soup is a perfect breeding ground for bacteria. Although a soup kept overnight in the refrigerator will be unlikely to give you stomach trouble, it is wise to make a habit of boiling up soup that is a day or more old. For the same reason, frozen soups that are to be served cold are best boiled up first. Treat them the same as hot soups, bringing them to a boil and adjusting the seasoning before cooling them and adding cream or garnish.

PASTRY

There are a great many myths about pastry making – that it is time-consuming and difficult, that it is a talent rather than an art and that only people born with exceptionally cold hands can make really light pastry.

In fact, it is easy to make pastry that is light and crumbly if you follow two simple guidelines. First, use ice-cold water. Second, let in as much air as possible at every stage. You do this by sieving the flour through a strainer at the beginning and, later, by lifting handfuls of the mixture and letting it sift through your fingers. There is no great difficulty about that.

Pastry does take a certain amount of time to make, but you can save time overall by preparing it in large batches. If you need pastry for a pie shell, make enough for three or four and store the extra pie shells in the freezer for later use. This is far more economical than buying ready-made frozen pie shells. Pastry keeps well in the freezer for at least six months.

The general rule for pastry is to use twice as much flour as fat and as little water as possible. The fat can be a combination of butter, margarine, or shortening, or one of them alone. My preference is half soft margarine and half shortening. The amounts given here will make a 23-centimetre (9-inch) pie shell.

⅓ cup	water	83 mL
½ lb	flour	225 g
½ tsp	salt	2 mL
¼ lb	fat	112 g

First, measure the water, pour it into a container that has a sprinkler top, and place it in the refrigerator. Sift the flour through a strainer into a small bowl and weigh it to the right amount. Then sift it again, this time into a larger mixing bowl. Add the salt, then add the fat, cutting it into lumps and covering them with flour. Now lightly rub in the fat with your fingertips until you get an evenly crumbled mixture with no large lumps. To incorporate air, put both hands into the mixture and lift up as much of it as possible, letting it dribble back between your fingers. Do this whenever you feel like a pause in the rubbing, and do it two or three times at the end, before adding the water.

Sprinkle the water over the surface of the flour while mixing it in with a round-ended knife. Continue to stir with the knife (using a slightly upward movement in order to incorporate more air) until large lumps begin to form. Then draw the mixture together with your hands and knead it lightly so that it becomes a malleable ball of dough. Wrap it in wax paper or plastic wrap and leave it to settle for about 10 minutes.

Lightly flour a pastry board and roll the dough flat with a rolling pin, using short, sharp, forward strokes. Keep the dough the same side up; never turn it over once you have started to flatten it. When you have got it to about ½ centimetre (¼ inch) thick, cut it to the shape you need and drape it around the rolling pin so that you can easily move it onto the pie plate. Trim the edges so that the pastry just overlaps the pie plate. Then press down with a knife or with your thumbs, working your way round the pastry to give it a scalloped edge.

Leave the pastry to settle for at least 10 minutes before putting it in the oven, and keep it cool during this period. You will get a lighter pastry if it never gets warm enough to melt the fat before the cooking begins.

To cook a pie shell without any filling, place a sheet of tinfoil or a foil pie case on top of it, weighting it down with bread crusts or dried beans, Cook in a preheated 425°F/220°C oven for 10 to 12 minutes. Remove the tinfoil and turn off the oven, but leave the pastry in the oven for a few minutes longer to allow the centre to dry. If the pastry bubbles up, prick the bubbles with a fork or press them down with a spoon.

The pie shells will now be partially cooked and just right for quiches and pies that need more cooking after a filling has been added. Cool them before adding the filling, then return them to the oven and cook according to the recipe.

If the pie is to have a cold filling, cook the pastry for a further 10 to 15 minutes at a temperature of 350°F/180°C, pricking any bubbles that form. Let the pastry cool before adding the filling.

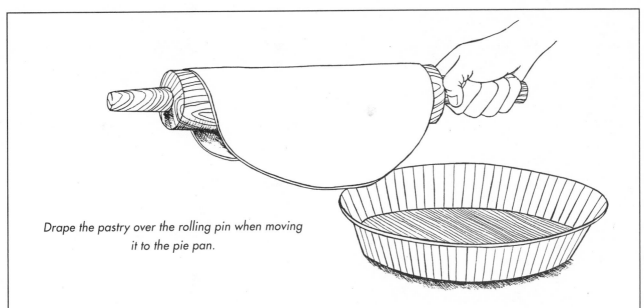

Drape the pastry over the rolling pin when moving it to the pie pan.

BREADCRUMBS

It may seem odd to include breadcrumbs among basic recipes, but many a meal has been ruined by a cook's using store-bought rather than homemade breadcrumbs. Store-bought crumbs nearly always have an unpleasantly stale taste that can be remarkably pervasive, and it seems a shame to risk this when it is so easy to make the breadcrumbs yourself.

Simply cut the crusts from the leftover end of a white loaf – or, even better, from fresh bread – crumble or cut the bread into pieces, and place on a baking tray. Set the tray on the lowest rack of a preheated 200°F/100°C oven and leave for between 30 minutes and one hour, depending on the freshness of the bread.

Remove the tray from the oven when the bread is crisp and thoroughly dry. Roll with a rolling pin to form fine crumbs. Use immediately or store in an airtight container. The crumbs will retain their freshness for two or three weeks if kept in dry and airtight conditions.

Bon appétit!

Index